D0204707

HUSSERL'S PHENOMENOLOGY

and the

FOUNDATIONS OF NATURAL SCIENCE

Husserl's Phenomenology

and the
Foundations of Natural Science

By Charles W. Harvey

Ohio University Press
Athens

© Copyright 1989 by Charles W. Harvey.
Printed in the United States of America.
All rights reserved.

Ohio University Press books are printed on acid-free paper. ∞

LIBRARY OF CONGRESS CATALOGING-IN-PUBLICATION DATA

Harvey, Charles W., 1954-
    Husserl's phenomenology and the foundations of natural science /
by Charles W. Harvey.
        p.   cm. — (Series in continental thought ; v. 15)
    Bibliography: p.
    Includes index.
    ISBN 0-8214-0939-5
    1. Husserl, Edmund, 1859-1938. 2. Phenomenology. 3. Science-
Philosophy — History. I. Title. II. Series: Series in continental
thought ; 15.
B3279.H94H37   1989   89-15943
193 — dc20   CIP

TABLE OF CONTENTS

To Jeanne, Whitney, and Tristan,
whom I love.

LIST OF FIGURES

ABBREVIATIONS

The following abbreviations indicate references internal to the text. Only Husserl's works have been internally documented. All other references are indicated in endnotes. Where not too cumbersome I have included the section number (marked by "§") just prior to the page numbers in order to facilitate cross-referencing with the German editions.

CM   *Cartesian Meditations*. Trans. by Dorion Cairns. Nijhoff, The Hague, 1977. (*Cartesianische Meditationen und Pariser Vorträge*. Ed. by S. Strasser [*Husserliana I*]. Nijhoff, The Hague, 1973.)

C   *The Crisis of European Sciences and Transcendental Phenomenology*. Trans. by David Carr. Northwestern University Press, Evanston, IL, 1970. (*Die Krisis der europäischen Wissenschaften und die transzendentale Phänomenologie*. Ed. by Walter Biemel [*Husserliana VI*]. Nijhoff, The Hague, 1954.)

EJ   *Experience and Judgment*. Trans. by James S. Churchill and Karl Ameriks. Northwestern University Press, Evanston, IL, 1973. (*Erfahrung und Urteil*. Ed. by Ludwig Landgrebe. Claassen, Hamburg, 1964. Originally published in 1939.)

EP I   *Erste Philosophie*, Erster Teil, "Kritische Ideengeschichte." Ed. by Rudolf Boehm. Nijhoff, The Hague, 1956. (*Husserliana VII*.)

EP II   *Erste Philosophie*, Zweiter Teil, "Theorie der Phänomenologischen Reduktion." Ed. by Rudolf Boehm. Nijhoff, The Hague, 1959. (*Husserliana VIII*.)

FTL   *Formal and Transcendental Logic*. Trans. by Dorion Cairns. Nijhoff, The Hague, 1969. (*Formale und transzendentale Logik*. Niemeyer, Halle, 1929.)

I   *Ideas: General Introduction to Pure Phenomenology*. Trans. by Boyce Gibson. Collier Books, New York, 1975. (*Ideen zu einer reinen Phänomenologie und phänomenologischen Philosophie*. Erstes Buch. Ed. by Walter Biemel [*Husserliana III*]. Nijhoff, The Hague, 1950. Originally published in 1913.)

I II   *Ideen zu einer reinen Phänomenologie und phänomenologischen Philosophie*, Zweites Buch, "Phänomenologische Untersuchungen zur Konstitution." Ed. by Marly Biemel. Nijhoff, The Hague, 1952. (*Husserliana IV.*)

I III   *Ideas Pertaining to a Pure Phenomenology and to a Phenomenological Philosophy*, Third Book, "Phenomenology and the Foundations of the Sciences." Trans. by Ted E. Klein and William E. Pohl. Nijhoff, The Hague, 1980. (*Ideen zu einer reinen Phänomenologie und phänomenologischen Philosophie*. Drittes Buch. Ed. by Marly Biemel [*Husserliana V*]. Nijhoff, The Hague, 1952.)

IP   *The Idea of Phenomenology*. Trans. by William P. Alston and George Nakhnikian. Nijhoff, The Hague, 1964. (*Die Idee der Phänomenologie. Fünf Vorlesungen*. Ed. by Walter Biemel [*Husserliana II*]. Nijhoff, The Hague, 1950.)

LI   *Logical Investigations*. Trans. by J. N. Findlay. Prolegomena and Investigations I-VI in 2 vols. Humanities Press, New York, 1970. (*Logische Untersuchungen*. Vols. 1 and 2. 2nd ed. Halle: Max Niemeyer, 1913.)

OG   *The Origin of Geometry*. Appendix VI in *C*.

P   *Phenomenology*. Trans. by Richard E. Palmer. Contained in *SW*. Originally published in *Encyclopedia Britannica*, 14th ed., 1929.

PA   *Philosophie der Arithmetik*. Ed. by Lothar Eley (Husserliana XII). Nijhoff, The Hague, 1970.

PP   *Phenomenological Psychology*. Trans. by John Scanlon. Nijhoff, The Hague, 1977. (*Phänomenologische Psychologie*. Ed. by Walter Biemel [*Husserliana IX*]. Nijhoff, The Hague, 1962.)

PRS   *Philosophy as Rigorous Science*. Trans. by Quentin Lauer. Contained in *Phenomenology and the Crisis of Philosophy*. Harper Torchbooks, New York, 1965.

SW   *Shorter Works*. Edited by Peter McCormick and Frederick A. Elliston. University of Notre Dame Press and Harvester Press, South Bend, IN, 1981.

Time   *Phenomenology of Internal Time-Consciousness*. Trans. by J. S. Churchill. Indiana University Press, Bloomington, IN, 1964. (*Vorlesungen zur Phänomenologie des inneren Zeitbewusstseins*. Ed. by Martin Heidegger. Niemeyer, Halle, 1928.)

WLP   *The World of the Living Present and the Constitution of the Surrounding World External to the Organism*. Trans. by Frederick A. Elliston and Lenore Langsdorf in *SW*.

Acknowledgements

By way of thanks I would like to mention Eugene Kaelin, who, for better or worse, let me write freely — something, so I've learned, many dissertation directors do not do. I thank him for being teacher and friend and especially for being teacher *as* friend. I thank Jaakko Hintikka for his contagious enthusiasm about "writing ideas" and for a brainstorming seminar on Husserl which brought a number of these ideas to fruition. And I thank Vern Denning, without whom I would not have started. Among graduate chums, I thank James Garrison for the dialectic which lasted seven years, Ed Jones for innumerable after-hours discussions, and Dane Depp for teaching me a small amount of speculative restraint. I thank the University of Central Arkansas for a research grant which made completion of this work possible. I thank Jim Shelton and Margaret Morgan who read the manuscript and Donna Peterson for being so helpful in so many ways. And Jeanne, who typed the manuscript and who is always there.

PREFACE

It is probably easiest to say what this book is about by first saying what it is not. The title can be our guide. It is not, in any straightforward sense, a book that develops Husserl's philosophy of science. It would be more accurate to say it is propaedeutic to such a work. The "and" in the title makes this point, though perhaps too unobtrusively. The title *Husserl's Phenomenology* and *the Foundations of Natural Science* indicates that the book focuses upon Husserl's phenomenology in so far as *it* can be understood in relationship to the "foundations" of the natural sciences. The "foundations" spoken of here are both the classical metaphysical foundations and the alternative phenomenological foundations proposed by Husserl. In short, the book offers a reading of Husserl's philosophy in terms of its critical and constructive dimensions that developed as a reaction to foundational problems in the sciences.

Parallel to this procedure is a consideration of Husserl's phenomenology in relationship to the history of modern philosophy — from Kepler and Galileo to Descartes, and then from Locke through Berkeley to Hume and Kant. The history of modern philosophy is inextricably tied to the attempt to provide foundations for the achievements of natural science, and, hence, any consideration of one demands consideration of the other. Husserl realized this and thereby correlated the "two" movements in his considerations of them.

By considering Husserl's phenomenology in relation to these historical developments, we will try to clarify the meaning of Husserl's important prefatory statement to early versions of the *Crisis*. Namely, that the work "makes the attempt, by way of a teleological-historical reflection upon the origins of our critical scientific situation, to establish the unavoidable necessity of a transcendental-phenomenological reorientation of philosophy" (§1, p.3). We will argue that Husserl's work can be understood in terms of the historical philosophical traditions upon which he reflects in the *Crisis* and that the whole of his philosophy can be best understood in light of these traditions. In short, we will attempt to show how the early attempts to provide foundations to the achievements of natural science, and the ensuing problems of early modern philosophy, promote "the unavoidable necessity of a transcendental-phenomenological reorientation of philosophy."

A broad view of this work can be given in more particular form by reference to Eugen Fink's famous distinction between "operative" and "thematic" concepts. By "operative" concepts Fink meant concepts *used* by philosophers to *carry out* their philosophical activities, while by "thematic" concepts he meant concepts made *the object of* philosophical scrutiny perhaps *by way of operative concepts*.[1] Every philosophy, Fink argued, has its operative and its thematic concepts. Some operative concepts will persist no matter what and will be the inevitable "dark spots" at the heart of any philosophy. In Husserl's thought, Fink went on to suggest, these concepts that were doomed to the penumbra of the very light that they cast were the concepts of "epoche," "reduction," and "constitution." This book is largely a reading of these operative concepts in terms of Husserl's reconstructive critique of the foundations of natural science. The background belief that motivates the text is that problems concerning the foundations of natural science and the operative concepts of Husserl's thought are essentially connected.

In this vein the book attempts to do two related things: First, to understand the methodological device of epoche and the event of reduction as steps in the critical phase of Husserl's analyses of the foundations of natural science while understanding his procedure of constitutional description as the reconstructive facet of his understanding of those foundations. Second, it attempts to cast light upon these foundations via Husserl's analyses. To the extent that Husserl's philosophy of science is developed here, it is developed under the constraint of these broader goals.

By way of forewarning, two points about content can now be made. First, the reading of epoche and reduction developed here is admittedly only a partial reading of these notions. It is partial in the sense that it deals with these phenomenological devices only insofar as they relate to sensory appearances and their object-referentiality, that is, insofar as epoche and reduction permit a new orientation towards objects. But the work is not an attempt to explain Husserl's theory of intentionality in terms of objects; rather, it attempts to *describe how intentionality works as reflected from its objects as those objects appear at various levels of reduced experience*. It does not, then, concern itself with the abstract notion of "sense." Reasons for this are given explicit consideration in section 4.7(a), but the actual (procedural) significance of this restriction is shown in sections 4.4(a)-(b) and throughout Chapter 5.

The second point to be mentioned concerns the somewhat idiosyncratic reading of the reduced "immanent domain" as that domain is explicated in sections 4.4(a)-(b). It will seem to those familiar with *Ideas* that the descriptions of the immanent domain contained herein do not precisely match the descriptions that Husserl provided in his work of 1913. That is so. There is something like a suppression of the immanent going on even in the early sections of this work that is not fully accounted for until later sections, especially section 5.1(b). This occurrence is partially the result of the chronologically reversed reading of Husserl's philosophy developed here. We hope that given Husserl's constant revaluations of his own earlier thinking (at any point beyond that "earlier" thinking), this feature of the work will be seen to have its own justification.

---

1. Eugen Fink, "Operative Concepts in Husserl's Phenomenology," trans. by William McKenna in *A Priori and World: European Contributions to Husserlian Phenomenology*, ed. by W. McKenna, R. M. Harlan, and L. E. Winters (The Hague: Martinus Nijhoff, 1981), p. 59.

Analytical Table of Contents

HUSSERL'S PHENOMENOLOGY

and the

FOUNDATIONS OF NATURAL SCIENCE

1
Introduction: Husserl, History, and the Natural Sciences

In the penultimate paragraph of his recent work *Husserl's "Introductions to Phenomenology"* William McKenna writes:

> . . . originally, and I believe always, for Husserl, the thesis that consciousness constitutes the world is a response to "foundational problems" in the sciences. What really were these problems? Are they still problems? Or, if not, are there still similar problems? How do these problems motivate a *transcendental* phenomenology? These questions . . . would have to be considered in any new "introduction to phenomenology."[1]

It would be difficult to list more precisely the questions to which this book attempts to offer a response. We concur with Professor McKenna's initial statement concerning the motivation for transcendental phenomenology and the following essay attempts to demonstrate how this motivation occurred. It will attempt to explain *what* these problems were and show *that* they still persist. In performing these tasks the following work can be thought to function as a new introduction to Husserlian phenomenology.

From another perspective this work is an attempt to give an answer, via example, to the question, "What is Husserl's epoche supposed to accomplish?" Although the epoche and, correlatively, the phenomenological reductions were meant by Husserl to be used in a vast array of phenomenological investigations, we will attempt to clarify the general philosophical value of these methodological devices by applying them to one problem area in twentieth-century philosophy. The problem area that will be focused on has been called by E. A. Burtt *The Metaphysical Foundations of Modern Physical Science*.[2] It is these not-so-well-founded foundations that will supply the content area for our exposition and application of Husserl's methods.

As is well known, Husserl had a penchant for spicing his general methodological expositions with particular, but brief and incomplete, phenomenological analyses. This tendency often has the effect of whetting one's philosophical appetite in relation to some particular problem, only to leave that appetite unsated by a rapid veer back into pure methodological pronouncements. By attempting consistently to apply Husserl's phenomenological devices to one particular philosophical problem—albeit one with its tentacles extending everywhere—we hope to provide a concrete instance of phenomenology as applied philosophy. That is, phenomenology is here understood as a philosophy that, when applied, is meant to dissolve traditional philosophical problems by showing how they should never have gotten off the ground. At the same time it would provide more secure foundations for the sciences and natural knowledge generally.

As a self-proclaimed perpetual beginner Husserl was a more revealing beginner in his later works. In these works, the way into phenomenology is sometimes achieved in relation to the history of philosophy and, in large part, as a reaction to it. Since the "what" and "why" of Husserlian phenomenology is still sometimes an issue in itself, an explication of its aims in relation to the history of philosophy provides the most direct means for understanding its sense—at least for the professional philosopher familiar with his or her historical inheritance. In the many attempts to explicate the sense of Husserl's work, this historical perspective on his phenomenology has not always received the attention it deserves. There are many reasons to develop this perspective, however. In the "Author's Preface to the English Edition" of *Ideas*, Husserl had written that "the whole course of philosophical development since

Descartes has been preparing the way for" transcendental phenomenology (*I*, p. 5). And later, in the same work, he makes the seemingly ostentatious claim that "phenomenology is . . . the secret nostalgia of all modern philosophy" (*I* §62, p. 142). In volume I of the 1923/24 lecture series entitled *Erste Philosophie*, Husserl devoted 412 pages to a "critique of the history of ideas" ("Kritische Ideengeschichte"), which led, quite naturally, to volume II of *Erste Philosophie*, "Theorie der Phänomenologischen Reduktion." Finally, Husserl went so far as to preface the first publication of the *Crisis* by describing the text as making the attempt "by way of a teleological historical reflection . . . to establish the unavoidable necessity of a transcendental-phenomenological reorientation in philosophy" (*C* §1, p. 3, n. 1). An attempt will be made in what follows to unpack these claims concerning the relation between the history of philosophy and phenomenology, and we will attempt to show how both are intrinsically tied to foundational problems in the natural sciences. We hope to show how all of this, in turn, promoted the "unavoidable necessity" of the phenomenological reductions as well as Husserl's program for constitutional descriptions.

The reading of Husserl's project developed here will be motivated by the final work Husserl published in his own lifetime, *The Crisis of European Sciences and Transcendental Phenomenology*, subtitled, significantly, *An Introduction to Phenomenology*. The problems developed in the historical part of this work reveal that Husserl's concerns with some particular philosophical problem areas stand in close relationship to the concerns of other philosophers of his day, e.g., E. A. Burtt, Alexander Koyré,[3] and Ernst Cassirer, while his positive response to these problems provides us with the sense and method of Husserlian phenomenology. Like Burtt, Koyré, and Cassirer, Husserl provides a critique of the metaphysical foundations of modern natural science,[4] while, somewhat more than the first two, he provides an alternative explanatory basis — a descriptive phenomenological basis rather than a metaphysical one — for the possibility of natural scientific knowledge.

But Husserl was not only the "philosopher of infinite tasks," as Maurice Natanson calls him[5]; he was also a philosopher of innumerable incomplete tasks, and *The Crisis of European Sciences and Transcendental Phenomenology* is probably the most renowned of these incomplete tasks. Since its publication much speculation has arisen over the implications of this work for the Husserlian corpus as a whole and over the direction Husserl would have taken in this work had he completed it or the direction he would have taken after this work had he lived past it. It is sometimes suspected that Husserl's concern in the *Crisis* with such issues as history, the "life-world" (*Lebenswelt*), and the loss of meaning for life depict a final remorseful shift from pure phenomenology to an acceptance of the existential implications battering upon it from all sides — political, social, and philosophical. In the essay that follows we will attempt to work through the implications of the *Crisis* for Husserl's corpus generally and, in doing this, attempt to show that the phenomenological investigations made in the *Crisis* are compatible with Husserl's lifelong project. In fact, it will be argued that the appeals to phenomenology made in the "crisis approach" reveal, more than any previously suggested method, the general sense of Husserl's lifelong project for phenomenology, and indeed nowhere indicate a radical transfer of allegiance on Husserl's part.

Another reason for using the *Crisis* as the *terminus a quo* and the *terminus ad quem* for an understanding of Husserl's project is that throughout his career Husserl's greatest discoveries almost always appeared in deed, years before they were explicitly recognized in word. This was the case (as has been shown by both Theodore De Boer[6] and Philip Bossert[7]) with the method of phenomenological epoche and reduction that was implicitly used in the *Logical Investigations* (1900-1), though first recognized and announced as a methodological procedure only in *The Idea of Phenomenology* (1907) and *Ideas* (1913). Likewise, Husserl's analyses of temporality in *The Phenomenology of Internal Time Consciousness* (1905) and temporalized intersubjectivity, dating from that same time through the *Cartesian Meditations* (1929), evolved into the recognition of the need for historical investigations in phenomenology. These investigations appeared in *Erste Philosophie* (1923-24) and later in the *Crisis* (1934-37). (This point has been made by David Carr in his work *Phenomenology and the Problem of History*.[8]) This continual process of making explicit on Husserl's part indicates his relentless attempt to expose all presuppositions, including those inherent to phenomenology itself.

Since Husserl's tendency to extract continually the hidden implications of his own previous work is fairly well established, it can be argued that with the *Crisis* we have Husserl's last deed, though probably not what would have been his last word about this deed or about the strategies employed therein. In part, we hope to provide a bit of this reflective "afterword" that Husserl was unable to. Although David Carr has already developed the set of *problems* that the historical analyses of the *Crisis* bring to pure phenomenology, we will use the historical analyses of the *Crisis* in another way by showing how the historical *facts* noted in the *Crisis* reveal the deep *raison d'être* of Husserl's phenomenology.[9]

Besides substantiating the general claim made by De Boer—that in Husserl's work the deed often appears before the word—our investigations will also provide one more instance in which Husserl applied phenomenological reflection to phenomenology itself. In the *Crisis* this occurred by clarifying the *raison d'être for* phenomenology by revealing the metaphysical problems that grew from and plagued the philosophical progenitors *of* phenomenology. By reading Husserl backwards, so to speak, we will see that within Husserl's own thought there is what he would later call, in relation to the history of philosophy, a historical-teleological development, that is, a temporal development in which only the end of a project fully reveals the inherently rational sense of the beginning (*C* §15).

It should also be noted that numerous essays have appeared concerning the relation of Husserl's phenomenology to natural science and the philosophy of science. Until recently, most of these have been rather general, and usually, though not always, programmatic for future studies on Husserl and natural science. So, in what follows, we will interpret the methodological devices of Husserl's phenomenology *precisely as* a manner of procedural approach to the resolution of the historical problems of "natural philosophy." It is our contention that until this is done the aims and methods of Husserl's work must, in large part, remain enigmatic. Hence, in what follows we attempt to develop a systematic reading of Husserl's guiding operative concepts ("epoch," "reduction," and "constitution") by reading his philosophy as a response to problems in the philosophy of science and, in particular, to problems in the philosophy of the natural sciences.

Indeed, as early as the *Logical Investigations* Husserl had referred to phenomenology as the "science of science" whose task it was to develop a "theory of science" (*Wissenschaftslehre*) (*LI* 60), which would be supplemented by "particular [phenomenological] investigations concerning the theory and method of the separate sciences . . ." (*LI* 68). Husserl had also noted in the *Logical Investigations* that the separate sciences, especially the sciences of "actual reality" (that is, sciences of the physical), require theoretical completion by metaphysics and epistemology (*LI* 59). And, as early as this, Husserl intimates that metaphysics alone is not fit to achieve this task; in fact, "first philosophy" must itself be grounded in phenomenological-epistemic investigations of the sciences. As this essay proceeds, we shall see that the entire development of Husserl's thought can be read as an attempt to achieve this theoretical understanding of natural science and its objectivistic achievements.

A general outline of the argument developed in this book can now be given. To aid us, an epochal distinction from Aron Gurwitsch on the "phases in the modern theory of science" can be applied.

Gurwitsch distinguishes three phases in the historical development of the theory of natural science: (1) the period of validation, (2) the period of acceptance of science as fact, and (3) the period of science as a problem.[10] He dates the period of validation "from the middle of the seventeenth to the middle of the eighteenth century." A representative instance of this phase is Descartes' attempt in the *Meditations* to "provide a foundation for, and a validation of, the new [objectivistic] science." The period of "acceptance of science as fact" Gurwitsch posits as beginning approximately around 1748 when Leonard Euler argued, in his *Reflexions sur l'espace et le temps*, that the natural sciences themselves must be the final judges as to whether the concepts of science be admitted as valid. Philosophy's role was here conceived as having to "accept this decision and accommodate its constructions accordingly."[11] Kant, of course, accepted this idea of "science as fact" no less than did the logical positivists of more recent times. Under the category of "acceptance" philosophy of science was and has actually been the *apologetics of science*. Finally, Gurwitsch dates the period of science as a problem as having its birth in Husserl's "Galileo analysis," first published in *Philosophia* in 1936. Here, rather than a fact, science is seen as a problem. But the problem Husserl recognizes does not concern the techniques or results of natural science; rather, it concerns the objectivistic *interpretation* of the possibility for the success and validity of these techniques and results.

For introductory purposes we need not further consider Gurwitsch's essay. His epochal distinction will suffice to provide a general insight into the argument to be presented in this text. Recall the essential aspects of the periods demarcated: (1) validation, (2) acceptance, and (3) problematics. We will show in the following essay how Husserl's phenomenology can be read as starting with the idea of (3) science as problematic, which demands a suspension of judgment about (2) science as fact (acceptance), which in turn makes (1), validation, problematic once more. Finally, we will show how, through constitutional analyses, validation can be reachieved, but without appeal to a fictional world of reified metaphysical entities.

What has preceded is, of course, a very broad scheme. It now remains to be developed. Chapter 2 will be devoted to revealing the roots of Husserl's problem in the period of validation. Chapter 3 will update and articulate the problems that grew out of this objectivistic mode of validation. Chapter 4 will interpret Husserl's phenomenological devices of epoche and reduction as the first steps in his response to these problems. Chapter 5 will consider the constitutional analyses that must follow epoche and reduction by redescribing the foundations for natural science, and Chapter 6 will summarize Husserl's achievements and then consider these achievements in relation to Husserl's critics and successors.

NOTES

1. William McKenna, *Husserl's "Introductions to Phenomenology"* (The Hague: Martinus Nijhoff, 1982), p. 228.

2. E. A. Burtt, *The Metaphysical Foundations of Modern Physical Science* (Garden City, NY: Doubleday Anchor Books, 1954).

3. Koyré, of course, was a one-time student of Husserl's and purportedly visited Husserl during the period that Husserl was working on the historical sections of what would later be the *Crisis*. David Carr speculates that Koyré's visit may have influenced Husserl to compose the "Galileo section" (§9) of the *Crisis*. See Carr's introduction to the *Crisis*, p. xix, n. 7.

4. For Koyré, see *Etudes Galiléennes* (Paris: Herman, 1966). For Cassirer, see *Substance and Function* (La Salle, IL: Open Court Pub. Co., 1923). *Das Erkenntnisproblem in der Philosophie und Wissenschaft der neueren Zeit*, 3 volumes (Berlin, 1906-20), and *The Philosophy of Symbolic Forms* (New Haven and London: Yale University Press, 1957), v. 3.

5. Maurice Natanson, *Edmund Husserl: Philosopher of Infinite Tasks* (Evanston IL: Northwestern University Press, 1973). Natanson's description of Husserl probably stems from Husserl's description of philosophy. See *C* 291.

6. Theodore De Boer, *The Development of Husserl's Thought* (Hague: Martinus Nijhoff, 1978), pp. 46-50, 178-79, 195-202, 305-22, 397-425.

7. Philip Bossert (unpublished dissertation), *The Origins and Early Development of Edmund Husserl's Method of Phenomenological Reduction* (St. Louis: Washington University, 1973).

8. David Carr, *Phenomenology and the Problem of History* (Evanston, IL: Northwestern University Press, 1974), see esp. Ch. 3-4. For an abbreviated version of the argument in this text see Carr, "Husserl's *Crisis* and the Problem of History," *Journal of*

Southwestern Philosophy (Fall 1974): 127-48. Hereafter referred to as "Husserl's *Crisis*." For a brief exposition of these works see below §4.5.

9. For a comparison of Carr's approach to the historical analyses of the *Crisis* and the approach taken in this work, see below §4.5. The thesis concerning the long-term effects of Husserl's early analyses of time-consciousness and intersubjectivity on his phenomenology and its accompanying conception of history has also been developed by Elisabeth Ströker in her essay "Husserl's Transcendental Phenomenology and History," in *Philosophy and Science in Phenomenological Perspective*, ed. by Kah Kyung Cho (Dordrecht: Martinus Nijhoff, 1984), pp. 171-207.

10. Aron Gurwitsch, *Phenomenology and the Theory of Science*, ed. by Lester Embree (Evanston, IL: Northwestern University Press, 1974), ch. 2, pp. 35-39.

11. Note Husserl's nicely argued rejection of this view at *LI* 58-59.

2
THE INHERITANCE

HUSSERL'S PHENOMENOLOGY CAN be read in a surprisingly thorough fashion as a response to the problem situation developed in E. A. Burtt's *The Metaphysical Foundations of Modern Physical Science*. Although much of modern philosophy is ultimately a response to the problem situation portrayed in Burtt's work (broadly: the gradual separation of the human being's experienced world from the objective world of natural science), Husserl's manner of responding to this network of problems is unique, and still remains to be explicated. To understand Husserl's response, the problems themselves must be understood; so in this chapter we will sketch the descriptions Burtt and Husserl provide concerning the metaphysical foundations of natural reductive science. In the following chapters we will see how Husserl articulates the problems to which these metaphysical foundations give rise, and how he responds to them.

2.1
GOD, CAUSALITY, AND QUANTIFIABILITY (KEPLER)

In considering Kepler it is not the laws he discovered that will concern us. Rather, we will be concerned with the beliefs and the metaphysical presuppositions that underwrote every clause and contract of those laws. It is important for us to see that not only do the positive achievements of natural science get handed down in the tradition, but likewise its metaphysical and ontological presuppositions get handed down as well.

One of the strongest motivations behind Kepler's investigations was the achievement of Copernicus, who, in turn, had been influenced by Pythagorean perspectives. Having discovered the mathematical relations intrinsic to the tuning of the lyre, the Pythagoreans had extended this intrinsic mathematical structure to the universe at large. Copernicus, with his heliocentric conception of the universe, took an important step towards instantiating this insight concerning universal mathematical harmony. By relocating the primary observational problem of astronomy, Copernicus provided a way of overcoming the plethora of *ad hoc* explanations for the motions of the planets required by Ptolemaic astronomy. His heliocentric theory of the solar system made it possible to save the phenomena (here, the observed movements of astral bodies) without appealing to a mass of aberrant calculations. In simplifying the interrelated motions of the bodies of the universe, Copernicus pushed the long-sought Pythagorean harmony into the universe at large. Although he did so chiefly by a qualitative reorientation towards astral phenomena, in so doing he set the qualitative context for the quantitative harmonization that Johannes Kepler would insist upon.

Like the other scientists of his day, Kepler's neo-pythagoreanism was expressed from within a Christian context. This was done by making a mathematician of God. If, as Kepler believed, the relations of the bodies of the universe were mathematical harmonies, then the harmonies that they expressed were the eternal harmonies in the mind of God.[1] With his thesis of a heliocentric universe, Copernicus had made it possible to produce a more unified set of mathematical relations amongst astral bodies. This high degree of aesthetic simplicity pleased Kepler, and it became his goal to dedicate his life to the "fuller knowledge of God through nature" and hence to "the glorification of his profession"[2] — the mathematical construction of the universe.

However, since Kepler believed that the mathematical relations amongst astral bodies were nearly physical manifestations of God's fully coordinated creation, and since God was the most real of all beings, the first cause and *causa sui*, it now followed (by the doctrine of "objective causality" coupled with the principle of perfection[3]) that these mathematical relations were themselves causes with the strongest possible ontological status. In other words, since these mathematical harmonies are near-physical manifestations of the most real being, they are the most complete revelation of the truest cause, and are themselves (formal and "objective") causes of lesser phenomena. Quantifiable relations were literally causes for Kepler; and indeed, they were the most fundamentally real causes of the phenomenal facts that confront the perceiving consciousness. With Kepler, then, the first natural scientific conflation of numbers with causes occurs.

Although the extension and implications of this way of thinking would appear very distinctly in Galileo, some of these implications can already be noted. When Kepler made his claims that "wherever there are qualities, there are likewise quantities, but not always *vice versa*," and that "nothing can be known completely except quantities or by quantities,"[4] he espoused the first version of a scientific *Weltanschauung* that would last a millennium. By suggesting that the underlying mathematical relations of entities were the ground and cause of those entities, he expressed the perennial need to correlate methodological-epistemic necessity with some form of onto-logical grounding.[5] This was now done by making an illicit inference about ontology upon the basis of methodological necessity. The inference went like this: If the underlying mathematical relations of entities are what is truly knowable about entities, then they must be the ground and cause (i.e., the reason "why") of those entities. If the ground and cause of entities are their mathematical qualities, then the purely phenomenal qualities of entities must have a secondary onto-logical status. This inference has, of course, now implicitly infiltrated almost all natural scientific ontologies. The psycho-logical source for this kind of inference seemed (and still seems) to lie in a metaphysical need: the need to equate the most knowable with the most real. In the natural scientific tra-dition, quantities were taken to be the exemplars of clear knowledge; hence, they needed ontological correlates. These correlates emerged with the distinction between primary and secondary qualities.

Though Kepler did not explicitly claim that primary qualities were objective, while secondary qualities were subjective, the thesis of the quantifiable as basic cause and reality (after God) makes this claim imminent for the natural scientific metaphysics. Since the quantifiable indicates a higher degree of the real, surface qualities that are not quantifiable stand closer to illusion than to reality. Though somehow necessary for the perceiving and conceiving consciousness to reach the real, surface qualities taken alone would condemn humanity to a life lived behind a veil of ignorance. This veil would soon be explicitly recognized by Galileo and Descartes as the lived-world of secondary quality experience. And indeed, if Bishop George Berkeley was to become infamous for arguing that "to be is to be perceived," others before him had already argued the equally absurd position that "to be is to be quantifiable."

2.2
QUANTIFIABILITY AND THE PRIMARY-SECONDARY QUALITY DISTINCTION (GALILEO)

The possibility of conceiving the world mathematically was not lost to Galileo. His famous statement along these lines is worth repeating once more:

> Philosophy [i.e., natural philosophy = natural science] is written in this grand book, the universe, which stands continually open to our gaze. But the book cannot be understood unless one first learns to comprehend the language in which it is composed. It is written in the language of mathematics, and its characters are triangles, circles, and other geometric figures without which it is humanly impossible to understand a single word of it; without these, one wanders about in a dark labyrinth.[6]

Husserl was, perhaps, thinking of this passage, as well as Galileo's actual work, when he wrote that ". . . through

Galileo's *mathematization of nature, nature itself* is idealized under the guidance of the new mathematics; nature itself becomes . . . a mathematical manifold" (*C* §9, p. 23).

Husserl recognized, however, that Galileo's project for the mathematization of nature, the reconstruction of the world as a mathematical manifold, immediately encountered a methodological problem. An ontologically framed solution was offered, and this led to the metaphysical and epistemological morass par excellence of modern and contemporary philosophy. The problem was the quantification of sensed qualities; the "solution" was an attempt to eliminate them.

Husserl notes that "a direct mathematization . . . in respect to the specifically sensible qualities of bodies is impossible in principle" (*C* §9, p. 34). While there is an experience of gradations of sensed qualities of which we might assess the magnitude (say, between bitterness and sweetness, roughness and smoothness, etc.), there is not an approximation towards exactness, which for Husserl is the distinguishing characteristic of mathematical articulation (*C* §9, pp. 27-28, 34). Whereas mathematical idealities provide what Husserl calls "ideal limiting poles or shapes," intuition of sensory qualities occurs in relation to no such ideal limits. One almost always operates in pure intuition with the normative, comparative, and superlative—all of which have indeterminate degrees of variation.

However, if nature is to be realized as a mathematical manifold in the manner projected by Kepler and Galileo, then sensed qualities, as integral to the *experienced manifold*, must be susceptible to some form of mathematization. Husserl refers to this issue as "the problem of the mathematizability of the 'plena' " (*C* §9, p. 34). David Carr points out that this notion of a sensible plenum (*die sinnliche Fülle*) refers to "the sensible content which 'fills in' the shapes of the world, the 'secondary qualities' that are left over after the pure shape has been abstracted" (*C* §9, p. 30, n. 7). And Husserl argues that Galileo deals with this problem by the indirect mathematization of sensed qualities via the notion of a universal correlative causality:

> . . . with regard to the "indirect" mathematization of that aspect of the world which in itself has no mathematizable world-form: such mathematization is thinkable only in the sense that the specifically sensible qualities ("plena") that can be experienced in the intuited bodies are closely related in a quite peculiar and *regulated* way with the shapes that belong essentially to them. (*C* §9, p. 35.)

This "peculiar and regulated way" is accounted for by the hypothesis of a universal correlative causality between sense qualities and their mathematical-geometrical forms:

> . . . everything which manifests itself as real through the specific sense-qualities must have its *mathematical index* in events belonging to the sphere of shapes . . . and there must arise from this the possibility of an indirect mathematization . . . i.e., it must be possible to construct *ex datis*, and thus to determine objectively, all events in the sphere of plena. (*C* §9, p. 37.)

Hence, this universal correlative causality demands a necessary connection between plenum qualities and their mathematical correlates. But, as we will see shortly, this necessary connection gets *illicitly* undermined.

Husserl notes that there had been numerous occasions in pre-scientific experience that "suggested something like the indirect quantifiability of certain sense-qualities, and thus a certain possibility of characterizing them by means of magnitudes and unities of measurement" (*C* §9, p. 37). For instance, "the ancient Pythagoreans had been stimulated by observing the functional dependency of the pitch of a tone on the length of a string set vibrating" (*C* §9, p. 37). With Galileo, however, something more occurred: such random observations were projected into a context that promised an infinite and unending number of causal-mathematical correlations for the experienced world. Although it was not obvious in Galileo's day that everything in the sphere of plena had a mathematical index, the belief that it did was projected into the world at large and became a methodological hypothesis, a regulative idea. According to Husserl this idea had the massive impact that it did because it opened, both temporally and spatially, an infinite domain of possible verifications (*C* §9, pp. 41-43). Indeed, Husserl goes on to describe the essence of natural science generally as an "unendingly hypothetical and unendingly verified" process of cognitive accomplishment. And this process, he claims, always occurs in relation to "mathematical idealities which are hypothetically substructed in advance" (*C* §9, p. 43).

The problems that will concern us emerge from the attribution of the universal causality to the mathematical index associated with the interpretation of sensory phenomena. First, let us note statements by both Burtt and Husserl that claim to depict the method and outcome of "Galilean Science."[7] Burtt describes Galileo's method in the following way:

> Facing the world of sensible experience, we isolate and examine as fully as possible a certain typical phenomenon, in order first to intuit those simple, absolute elements in terms of which the phenomenon can be most easily and completely translated into mathematical form; which amounts (putting the matter in another way) to a resolution of the sensed fact into such elements in quantitative combinations. Have we performed this step properly, we need the sensible fact no more; the elements thus reached are their *real* constituents, and deductive demonstration from them by pure mathematics . . . must always be true of similar instances of the phenomenon . . . .[8]

Husserl's analysis of the Galilean method is very similar to Burtt's. Concerning this method, he writes:

> From the very beginning . . . one is not concerned with the free fall of *this* body; the individual fact is rather an *example*, embedded from the start in the concrete totality of types belonging to intuitively given nature, in its empirically familiar invariance; and this is naturally carried over into the Galilean attitude of idealizing and mathematizing. The indirect mathematization of the world, which proceeds as a methodical objectification of the intuitively given world, gives rise to general numerical formulae which, once they are formed, can serve by way of application to accomplish the factual objectification of the particular cases to be subsumed under them. (*C* §9, p. 42.)

Most significantly, the meaning of these relations is not thought to "lie in the pure interrelations between numbers . . .; it lies in . . . the Galilean idea of a universal physics . . ." (*C* §9, p. 41). But this idea of universal physicality as a causal *modus explanans* of all that occurs is destined to cause some of philosophy's greatest problems. Let us turn to the beginning of these problems.

In his discussions of the mathematizability of the "plena" Husserl had written that:

> If we ask what is predetermined a priori by the universal world-form of geometry and mathematization with its universal causality . . . it is . . . predetermined that, in each case of real bodies, factual shapes require factual plena and vice versa; that, accordingly, *this* sort of general causality obtains, binding together aspects of a *concretum* which are only abstractly, not really, separable. (*C* §9, p. 35.)

Galileo, however, had insisted that the concretum, or the thing itself (which was foredoomed to become the thing in itself by way of Galileo's interpretation), was separable from, indeed, different from, its plenum qualities — even while plena and the "thing" maintained a universal causal correlation. This universal causal correlation had to be maintained as a hypothesis if *all* of nature was to be mathematized or at least made susceptible to mathematization in principle. But until all of it was so mathematizable *in fact*, the proclamation that the fundament of nature consisted of pure physicality (causally productive of plenum experience) guaranteed the possibility of this mathematization *in principle* precisely because the "purely" physical was already mathematizable in fact. Galileo's proclamation to this effect took the form of a rejuvenation of the distinction between primary and secondary qualities.[9]

Although Kepler had assigned a fundamental ontological status to the underlying realm of mathematical harmonies, he had not explicitly downgraded the ontological status of "surface qualities," that is, of natural phenomena as perceived. Galileo, however, who had complimented Aristarchus and Copernicus for allowing reason "to commit a rape upon their senses,"[10] did just this with his distinction between primary and secondary qualities. He announced that primary qualities were those aspects of a body that could not, under any conditions, be abstracted from that body. These qualities were the mathematically cognizable aspects of a body, particularly its weight, figure, position, and temporal relations. These characteristics were now said to constitute a body *qua* body. On the other hand, Galileo claimed, "secondary qualities," such as color, sound, taste, smell, and texture, were not inherent in bodies per se. Rather, any given body might be distinctly conceived without these qualities and still maintain all its essential attributes as a body. The mathematical qualities of a thing were thus proclaimed to be "primary" to that thing, while its qualities, which were only sensory qualities, were proclaimed to be "secondary," that is, subordinate effects of the primary.

Problems started when Galileo suggested that the former, primary qualities were objective, while the latter, secondary qualities were mere subjective experiences not at all inherent to the things themselves.[11] This position was soon extended to mean that secondary qualities were not inherent to the objective world, the world as it *really* was. Another famous set of statements by Galileo attempts to make this point:

> Now I say that whenever I conceive any material or corporeal substance, I immediately feel the need to think of it as bounded, and as having this or that shape; as being large or small in relation to other things, and in some specific place at any given time; as being in motion or at rest; as touching or not touching some other body; and as being one in number, or few, or many. From these conditions I cannot separate such a substance by any stretch of my imagination. But that it must be white or red, bitter or sweet, noisy or silent, and of sweet or foul odor, my mind does not feel compelled to bring in as necessary accompaniments. Without the senses as our guides, reason or imagination unaided would probably never arrive at qualities like these. Hence I think that tastes, odors, colors, and so on are no more than mere names so far as the object in which

we place them is concerned, and that they reside only in the consciousness. Hence if the living creature were removed, all these qualities would be wiped away and annihilated.[12]

Secondary qualities, then, those qualities which were sensory and only sensory, were conceived to be parasitic upon primary qualities. The quantifiable stuff of reality was proclaimed to be the primary stuff of reality, and immediate sensory experience was relegated to being an epiphenomenon of the relations between such corporeal bodies. This distinction, Galileo seemed to reason, guaranteed the possibility of a complete understanding of Nature. But, instead, it made such an understanding *incomprehensible*.

The transition to Descartes' role in this development can now be made by borrowing a few comments from E. A. Burtt:

> . . . in the course of translating this [the primary-secondary quality] distinction into terms suited to the new mathematical interpretation of nature, we have the first stage in the reading of man quite out of the real and primary realm. Obviously man was not a subject suited to mathematical study. His performances could not be treated by the quantitative method, except in the most meagre fashion. His was a life of colors and sounds, of pleasures and griefs, of passionate loves, of ambitions and strivings. Hence the real world must be the world outside of man; . . . the only thing in common between man and this real world was the ability to discover it, *a fact which, being necessarily presupposed, was easily neglected . . . .* man is hardly more than a bundle of secondary qualities. Observe that the stage is fully set for the Cartesian dualism.[13] [My emphasis.]

The relationship between the metaphysical foundations of natural science and what Husserl calls the "crisis of humanity" in relation to science (*C*, pt. I) now begins to appear. The real, the scientifically knowable, became that which was reducible to quantities, and quantities became the primitive facts of natural reductive science. At this juncture the lived-world of the human began to be read out of nature, and the conflation of methodological necessity and ontological "fact" had begun.[14] Husserl would express the problem in this way:

> Mathematics and mathematical science, as a garb of ideas, or the garb of symbols of the symbolic mathematical theories, encompasses everything which, for scientists and the educated generally, *represents* the life-world, *dresses it up* as 'objectively actual and true' nature. It is through the garb of ideas that we take for *true being* what is actually a *method* . . . . (*C* §9, p. 51.)

Notwithstanding all his claims to presuppositionlessness, Descartes provides a primary instance in which a method predetermines the result of an inquiry.

2.3
QUANTIFIABILITY, PRIMARY AND SECONDARY QUALITIES, AND THE EXPERIENCE-WORLD DICHOTOMY (DESCARTES)

With Descartes many of the assumptions and implications of the mathematical metaphysics of his predecessors emerge. He accepted and refined the notions of a mathematical universe and the distinction between primary and secondary qualities. From these he drew what seemed their inevitable consequence: the mind-body, or more broadly conceived, the experience-world dichotomy. Husserl summarizes the transition from the work of Galileo to the achievements of Descartes in the following words:

> [In the attainment of his method] Galileo *abstracts* from the subjects as persons leading a personal life; he abstracts from all that is in any way spiritual, from all cultural properties which are attached to things in human praxis. The result of this abstraction is the things purely as bodies; but these are taken as concrete real objects, the totality of which makes up a world which becomes the subject matter of research. One can truly say that the idea of nature as a

> really self-enclosed world of bodies first emerges with Galileo. A consequence of this, along with the mathematization, which was too quickly taken for granted, is the idea of a self-enclosed natural causality in which every occurrence is determined unequivocally and in advance. Clearly the way is thus prepared for dualism, which appears immediately afterward in Descartes. . . . The world splits, so to speak, into two worlds: nature and the psychic world, although the latter, because of the way in which it is related to nature, does not achieve the status of an independent world. . . . The splitting of the world and the transformation of its meaning were the understandable consequences of the exemplary role of natural-scientific method . . . . (*C* §10, p. 60)

Let us now note how Descartes' philosophy wrenched the world of natural science and the world of experience "worlds" apart.

Unlike the Aristotelian tradition in which he was schooled, Descartes believed in the possibility of one universal method for all intellectual research. This universal method was an analogue to his conception of the mathematical method. Like his immediate predecessors, he believed that true knowledge must be derived via mathematical apprehension. Only simple, atomic intuitions were indubitable; and simple, atomic intuitions were exemplified by mathematical intuitions. As the creator of analytical geometry, Descartes had even more reason than his predecessors to believe in the possibility of a pan-mathematical comprehension of the universe because the "successful use of analytical geometry as a tool for mathematical exploitation presupposes an exact one-to-one correspondence between the realm of numbers, i.e., arithmetic and algebra, and the realm of geometry, i.e., space."[15]

Since the human mind could have certainty only of simple, atomic intuitions, and since these intuitions were most readily had as mathematical intuitions, Descartes believed that the simple intuitions of mathematics were the key to any truly scientific comprehension. These simple intuitions were attained by an analytical reduction of phenomenal entities to their "simple natures," and the "simple nature" of a material entity means its mathematical nature.[16] Only geometry, now in the guise of algebra, could provide certainty about the particularities of the physical world.

"Matter," the ultimate constituent of material nature, now became a purely intellectual intuition of mathematical relations. In order to maintain the equation between the most knowable and the most real, matter had to be conceived of as *nothing but* a clear and distinct idea of numerical relations concerning extension, flexibility, and changeability.[17] Husserl refers to this purely mathematical-causal notion of matter as "pure corporeality" (*pure Körperlichkeit; I* II,§13, p. 31; *C* §§10, 69):[18] "pure" because it is untainted with any empirical-phenomenal elements, "corporeal" because the mathematical intuitions are supposedly indicative of the material fundament of reality. This pure corporeality, i.e., material stuff separated from any possible phenomenal experience, is what pure primary qualities must also ultimately be (*I* II, §13, p. 31). Again, then, the real world is thought to consist of primary qualities mentally had as quantifiable, simple intuitions. The lived-world of human experience (the "haven" of secondary qualities) is relegated to the status of an epiphenomenon of the truly real. From this the experience-world dichotomy emerged.

Descartes, more than his predecessors, was aware of the philosophical implications inherent in the scientific metaphysics as now conceived. If the actual world was the world of primary qualities, and if these primitive quantifiables were reached only as abstracted from secondary quality experience, then the ontological status of secondary quality experience became a problem, as did the ontological status of whatever did the abstracting from these experiences.

Kepler, Galileo, and now Descartes, had all insisted that the human mind was specifically made to know mathematically.[19] What it could know precisely were the quantifiable aspects and relations of entities, that is, their primary quality aspects and relations. Since these quantifiable relations of pure extended matter were considered representative of the truly real world, the domain of human experience that was not immediately amenable to these quantifiable relations was relegated to a secondary ontological status. What Kepler and Galileo had not recognized, however, was that if sensory experience was to be ontologically impugned because of its quantificational impossibility, then so too must the "mind," which does the knowing, be impugned for the same reasons. Descartes recognized this implication of the recent developments in scientific method and attempted to arrest it. He did so by delimiting a domain different from, but supposedly equally as real as, the domain of extended things.

Descartes claimed that "that" which does the abstracting from the realm of secondary qualities, and comes to have the clear and distinct ideas of the real world, is itself a primitive indubitable. This "other" primitive indubitable is given in the "*cogito*"; it is the thinking thing, *res cogitans*, which can have the clear and distinct ideas of extended things, of pure corporeality or *res extensae*. This thinking thing is as indubitable as any mathematical intuition because, Descartes argued, any thought verifies the being of "that" which thinks, even though that which thinks is not itself amenable to quantificational articulation because consciousness, as that which is aware of the extended realm, is not itself extended. It was, for Descartes, a nonspatial entity: the necessarily presupposed counterpart for knowledge of the extended realm of purely corporeal primary qualities. Since the thinking thing is not extended, it is conceived of as a purely intuitional, nonspatial entity, which conceives the extended world after abstracting that world's mathematical qualities from the "confusion of the senses." Sensory experience is now said to consist of "confused thoughts" that belong to the nonspatial domain.[20] And, although sensory experience is real to the extent that it is had by the mind, it nevertheless remains less real than that which is signified by the clear and distinct ideas of pure corporeality derived via those sensory experiences.[21]

As an outcome of the Cartesian analysis, the existence of an entity that carries out the mathematical-reductive procedures of natural science has been explicitly acknowledged, but this entity is itself immune to these same procedures. Consequently, the thinking thing is ontologically severed from the realm that it knows, severed from the quantifiable, extended realm of natural scientific research. The role of mind is to abstract simple mathematical ideas from the confused data of the senses, and then to conceive the real world of pure corporeality beyond those sensory experiences. The result: that which knows the world (*res cogitans*) is not itself "in" the world (as an extended corporeal thing). For that entity another mode of analysis was requisite, and the "empiricist" philosophers attempted to provide it.

2.4
THE EMPIRICIST RESPONSE (HOBBES, LOCKE, BERKELEY, HUME)

The crux of Husserl's critique of classical empiricism lies in his claim that as a naturalistic epistemological-psychology it was born to provide "a correlate to pure natural science when the latter [the psychological realm] was separated off . . ." (*C* §22, p. 84). The most important facet of Husserl's conception here is his insistence that in its very conception classical empiricism was born as a "complementary abstraction" for, and was based upon the model of, natural science (*C* §§ 22, 66). This, of course, is a documented historical fact explicitly recognized by Hobbes, Locke, and Hume.[22] But what is usually missed, Husserl argues, is the essential connection that exists between classical rationalism and classical empiricism. The essential connection (which Husserl calls the "historical-teleological connection") is to be found in the *shared underlying belief* in a domain of pure corporeality objectively existing and functioning as the causal-ontological basis for the unity of experience.

About this connection, Husserl writes: "One should not be misled by the usual contrast between empiricism and rationalism. The naturalism of a Hobbes wants to be physicalism, and like all physicalism it follows the model of physicalistic rationality" (*C* §11, pp. 62-63). Husserl's point is that from its birth classical empiricism took the presuppositions of natural reductive science for granted, and it fashioned itself after the achievements of that science. He argues that the tendency of empiricism to model itself after the natural sciences is a textually evident historical fact, while its acceptance of their presuppositions emerges most dramatically as a metaphysical premise required for the possibility of Hume's skepticism. Husserl believes that this skepticism is the inevitable result of modeling epistemology and psychology after the natural sciences, especially while basing this model upon their results. Let us develop Husserl's argument by considering the empiricist movement in terms of its historical-teleological connections.

Husserl notices that:

> . . . after the animal and human bodies have been separated off as belonging inside the closed region of nature . . . [the] naturalization of the psychic comes down through John Locke to the whole modern period up to the present day. Locke's image of the *white paper* is characteristic — the . . . psychic data come and go, somehow ordered like the events of bodies in nature. (*C* §11, p. 63)

Husserl later notes, as have many others, that Locke seems blind to the deepest epistemic problems that surface in common-sense realism. For Locke, according to Husserl, the "soul is something self-contained and real by itself, as is a body; in naive naturalism the soul is now taken to be like an isolated space, like a writing tablet, in his famous simile, on which psychic data come and go" (*C* §22, p. 85). And yet he never wonders, Husserl says, *how* these internal data can announce themselves *as* external features of the world.

Of course, Locke did recognize what Husserl would later call the problem of transcendence, that is, the problem of "reaching" the external world, to a greater extent than Husserl gives him credit for;[23] but Husserl, in pursuing the historical-teleological method established in the *Crisis*, prefers to credit Berkeley (and rightly so) with insisting that the assumption of an external world was more than problematic, it was *unjustified*.

Although in the *Crisis* Husserl provides only one short paragraph on Berkeley's contribution to the development and dissolution of empiricism (which Husserl recognizes as one and the same occurrence), this paragraph fulfills its task by capturing the historical-teleological essence of Berkeley's contribution. After recalling that Berkeley, like Locke, begins his essay from the "realm of immanent data," Husserl writes:

> Starting from here, Berkeley reduces the bodily things which appear in natural experience to the complexes of sense-data themselves through which they appear. No inference is thinkable, [according to Berkeley] through which conclusions could be drawn from these sense-data about anything but other such data. It could only be inductive inference, i.e., inference growing out of the association of ideas. Matter existing in itself, a *je ne sais quoi*, according to Locke, is [for Berkeley] a philosophical invention. It is also significant that at the same time he dissolves the manner in which rational natural science builds concepts and transforms it into a sensationalistic critique of knowledge. (*C* §23, pp. 86-87.)

Husserl is here expounding upon Berkeley's famous claim that "an idea can be like nothing but an idea"[24] and referring to a point also noted by Karl Popper, that Berkeley offers the first positivistic-phenomenalistic critique of natural scientific concepts.[25]

Berkeley's point is that if we are indeed confined to a realm of "immanent data," if the other domain is *in principle* a domain of nonexperienceable purely corporeal qualities, then all inductive inference could refer only to experiences possible within the immanent domain. Espousing an inchoate positivism, Berkeley can find no justification in the idea of "depth causality," a causality operating from behind the scenes which, a priori, makes it impossible to perceive one of the "conjuncts" of a causal relationship. Pursuing the implications inherent to representative realism Berkeley insists that we must replace the nonsensical (because unverifiable) idea of depth material causality with the recognition of "surface causality." Surface causality is causality between and amongst the appearances which is experienced as a constant conjunction between them, minus all appeals to material "occult forces." Since Berkeley's own appeal to spiritual occult forces played an insignificant role in the further development of physicalistic rationalism, we need not consider it here and can now turn to Hume.

Hume capitalized on the hard work done by Berkeley and, ironically, promoted the skepticism, atheism, and irreligion that Berkeley had written to prevent — *and for precisely the reasons that Berkeley had predicted.* Using the natural scientific domain of pure corporeality as a metaphysical and epistemological foil, Hume evolved a radical skepticism that was possible only on the basis of a preestablished belief in the necessity of a depth domain of purely material stuff.

When Descartes had attempted to establish the absolute metaphysical validity of objective knowledge, he had started to work, so to speak, from the inside out. All too quickly, however, he jumped from the domain of subjectivity to an objectivistic domain by justifying the "truth" of our experienced world (the world of "seeming" in *Meditation II*) by an appeal to a transcendent world of pure corporeality (mediated by God's veracity). But if Descartes had actually held to the project proposed in *Meditations I* and *II*, which was to work only from the indubitably given, then both the transcendent world of natural science and "God's veracity" would have been justified in relation to the truths of our experienced world and not vice versa. In violation of his own proclaimed method, however, Descartes guaranteed the truth of experience by an appeal to nature, a transcendent by definition, while simultaneously establishing the gulf between experience and nature! Husserl often refers to this event as Descartes' falsification and misunderstanding of his own greatest discovery: the transcendental domain in which "seeming" *is* certain (*CM* §10; *C* §§ 18, 19). But because of the rapidity with which Descartes appealed to the transcendently grounded truths of natural science ("truths" about which Descartes had supposedly suspended all belief in *Meditations I* and *II*), Husserl concludes that, from the first, Descartes was guided by objectivistic prejudices (*C* §19). Once more the transcendent truths of natural science became the final court of appeal for judgments on "seeming" rather than the other way round. But how does this relate to Hume?

Hume's skepticism can be viewed as a statement on the impossibility of succeeding at the project that Descartes had inaugurated and *not* carried through. More positively, it can be viewed as a systematic working out of the reasons *why* it could not be carried through within the context of Descartes' thought; broadly, within the context of the presuppositions of physicalistic rationalism. In *A Treatise of Human Nature* Hume recognized the error of Descartes and the Cartesians as the attempt to guarantee the truth of the immanent by appealing to a transcendent, which was itself epistemically suspect if one began from the immanent. Nevertheless, he implicitly acknowledged their belief in a transcendent domain of the real by starting his *Treatise* with an analysis of perceptions which, he said, "arise in the soul originally from unknown causes."[26] In relation to this belief in unknown causes, Hume would produce the greatest skepticism in the history of philosophy.

Hume produced his epoch-making skepticism by arguing that the question concerning the existence of external objects was equivalent to the question of whether perceptions had a continued and distinct existence apart from their being perceived.[27] This continued and distinct existence was shown to be an analytic impossibility in regard to the senses,[28] an illicit inference in regard to the reason,[29] and a fictionalistic prejudice that gained currency only because of the imagination.[30] For our purposes we need only mention Hume's argument with regard to reason.

Like Berkeley, Hume argued that the distinction between perceptions and objects was a fiction that, *in principle*, could never be justified. Since all causal relations capable of being observed were between perceptions (i.e., phenomena), and since phenomena were all that could be observed, then all causal inferences from objects to perceptions were unjustifiable (read: unverifiable) a priori.[31] Hume writes:

> . . . as no beings are ever present to the mind but perceptions, it follows that we may observe a conjunction or a relation of cause and effect between different perceptions, but can never observe it between perceptions and objects. 'Tis impossible, therefore, that from the existence of any of the qualities of the former, we can ever form any conclusion concerning the existence of the latter, or ever satisfy our reason in this particular.[32]

Hume even does us the favor of explicitly deriving this problematic from the primary-secondary quality distinction. About this distinction he writes that ". . . instead of explaining the operations of external objects upon the senses . . . it utterly annihilates all these objects . . . ."[33] Ironically, this annihilation of the object behind the perceptions is precisely the reverse effect of the original intention behind the distinction. As we have seen, the distinction between primary and secondary qualities was originally meant to emphasize the reality of the objects behind the perceptions, but it has finally resulted in their very annihilation! Consequently, Hume not only effected the most solvent skepticism in the history of philosophy, but the greatest *reductio ad absurdum* as well. He has shown that if the world of natural science is as the metaphysics of natural science claims it to be, i.e., pure corporeality, then we cannot get there from here.

Hume concludes section IV, book I, part I of the *Treatise* by writing that: "When we reason from cause and effect, we conclude, that neither color, sound, taste, nor smell have a continu'd and independent existence. When we exclude these sensible qualities there remains nothing in the universe, which has such an existence."[34] The cause and effect relationship Hume is referring to here is the one prescribed to the world by the metaphysics of natural reductive science where the cause lies forever buried beneath its effect.

Husserl aptly summarizes the effect and outcome of Hume's *Treatise* in the following words: "All categories of objectivity — the scientific ones through which an objective, extra-psychic world is thought in scientific life, and the prescientific ones through which it is thought in everyday life — are fictions" (*C* §23, p. 87). This results in "a bankruptcy of objective knowledge" in which all the transcendently oriented claims of cognition, the claims of objective knowledge, are finally declared "fictionalistic prejudices."

2.5
THE TRANSCENDENTAL TURN (KANT)

In his "Kant Critique" of the *Crisis* (*C* §§ 25-32) Husserl asks, "What is the meaning of the 'dogmatism' from which Kant was awakened by Hume?" (*C* §25, p. 91) Husserl answers his own question by suggesting that this dogmatism was the dogmatism of the post-Cartesians (e.g., Spinoza, Leibniz, Wolff) who had lost contact with Descartes' radical turn to transcendental subjectivity in the second Meditation. Whereas Descartes had not succeeded at bridging the gulf between reason and its metaphysical objectivities, his rationalistic successors had largely forgotten that this was a problem, instead, taking the truths of reason for granted and occupying themselves with the attempt to develop metaphysical systems and logical technologies which would explain the "that" rather than the "how" of those achievements (*C* §25, pp. 92-93). Hume's refusal to take the "that" of everyday and scientific truths for granted is what awoke Kant. Husserl writes: "Hume made him sensitive to the fact that between the pure truths of reason and metaphysical objectivity there remained a gulf of incomprehensibility, namely, as to how precisely these truths of reason could really guarantee the knowledge of things" (*C* §25, p. 92). This was Descartes' project come alive again, and Kant's genius, Husserl argues, was explicitly to make the transcendental turn in the attempt to resolve it.

In order to understand precisely how Kant's gaze was turned towards the transcendental, Husserl attempts to grasp Kant's "inwardly guiding thoughts" (*C* §25, p. 94). He suggests that they were these: Hume substituted sense-data for the everyday things we normally experience. But these "mere data of sense" could not account for either the full objects of experience or the fact that these objects can be known scientifically "through logic, mathematics, and mathematical natural science." Consequently (Husserl argues for Kant), Hume ". . . overlooks the fact that these full objects of experience point to a hidden mental accomplishment and to the problem of what kind of an accomplishment this can be" (*C* §25, p. 94).

In questioning himself about this accomplishment, Kant notes that when things appear they appear as always already organized manifolds of sense-data that are always already amenable to the laws of reason. And yet they appear in this manner *without any conscious appeal to reason* in its normative forms as used in mathematics and logic. Must we not imagine, then, a hidden and concealed, a covert reasoning function, in order to account for a mathematics and logic of nature that does give us the possibility, indeed the actuality, of knowing objects through mere sense-data (*C* §25, p. 94)? Kant, of course, thinks so and undertakes

> to show, through a regressive procedure, that if common experience is really to be experience of *objects of nature* . . . then the intuitively appearing world must already be a construct of the faculties of "pure intuition" and "pure reason," the same faculties that express themselves in explicit thinking in mathematics and logic. (*C* §25, p. 94)

This attempt to recast the pregiven world and the world of natural science as constructs grounded in subjectivity is the transcendental turn as expressed in Kant.

Part II of the *Crisis* is brought to closure when Husserl offers a broad description of the concept of the "transcendental" as it emerged in the work of Descartes and Kant. He tells us that it is guided by "the motif of inquiring back into the ultimate source of all the formations of knowledge," and this is achieved by "the knower's reflecting upon himself and his knowing life in which all the scientific structures that are valid for him occur purposefully . . . " (*C* §26, pp. 97-98). Hence, transcendental philosophy

> is a philosophy which, in opposition to prescientific and scientific objectivism, goes back to knowing and subjectivity as the primal locus of all objective formations of sense and ontic validities, undertakes to understand the existing world as a structure of sense and validity, and in this way seeks to set in motion an essentially new type of scientific philosophy. (*C* §27, p. 99.)

This "new type of philosophy," Husserl believed, would break from its natal environment only in his own transcendental phenomenological idealism. The need for its extended incubation period would, in part, point back to early problems and mistaken paths in Descartes and Kant.[35] At any rate, the Kantian critical philosophy, in its attempt to provide the epistemological basis for a new metaphysics of nature, prefigures Husserl's own transcendental turn.

2.6
OVERVIEW

These five major methodological occurrences integral to the development of the metaphysics of natural science will provide the background for our reading of Husserl's phenomenology. They are (§2.1) quantifiability (as the basis for all possible knowledge), (§2.2) the primary-secondary quality distinction (evolving from the equation of the quantifiable with the real), and (§2.3) the experience-world dichotomy (evolving from the notion of the subjectivity of secondary qualities as contrasted to the objectivity of primary qualities). From these (§2.4) the dissolution of the natural scientific metaphysics began with the empiricist movement, and this motivated (§2.5) the transcendental turn in Kant. Husserl summarizes the first three steps in this development with the following words:

> With Galileo's mathematizing reinterpretation of nature, false consequences established themselves even beyond the realm of nature which were so intimately connected with this reinterpretation that they could dominate all further developments of views about the world up to the present day. I mean Galileo's famous doctrine of the merely subjective character of the specific sense-qualities, which soon afterward was consistently formulated by Hobbes as the doctrine of the subjectivity of all concrete phenomena of sensibly intuitive nature and world in general. The phenomena are only in the subjects; they are there only as causal results of events taking place in true nature, which

events exist only with mathematical properties. If the intuited world of our life is merely subjective, then all the truths of pre- and extrascientific life which have to do with its factual being are deprived of value. They have meaning only insofar as they, while themselves false, vaguely indicate an in-itself which lies behind this world of possible experiences and is transcendent to it. (*C* §9, pp. 53-54.)

This development can now be depicted with a figure that portrays the world as conceived, and seemingly demanded, by the mathematical-reductive methods of modern physical science.

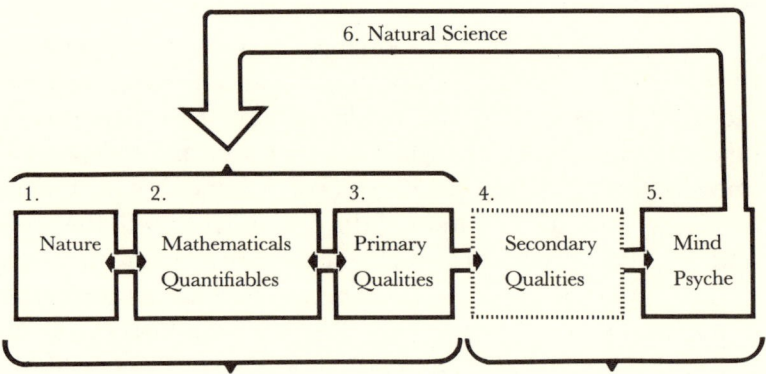

A. The Objective World   B. The Subjective World

Figure 1

The bracketed sections, (A) and (B), of this figure indicate the relations of the methodological primitives of the development we have traced. The double arrows (← →) indicate the relationship of ontological interdependence or, in fact, identity. The single arrows (→) indicate the parasitic nature of the intellect or psyche upon the world that it knows, that is, of (B) upon (A). The connection between components (4) and (5) can be thought to indicate the abstractive operations of the intellect upon sensory data where (4) is in direct connection with the real and primary realm. The dashed lines of component (4) signify the ontological-epistemic limbo where sensory phenomena reside in this world-view. Finally, component (6) indicates the intellect's "discovery" of the "real" and "primary" realm. This component, (6), became problematic with the empiricist movement, as did the entirety of domain (A) in the work of Berkeley, Hume, and Kant.

Some of the greatest philosophical problems emerged from this intertwining development of natural reductive science and the accounts given to explain the conditions for its possibility. The first attempt to do this emerged as a metaphysical-ontological dogmatism believed necessary for the validation of the achievements of natural reductive science. These "explanations" eventually led to philosophy's greatest metaphysical problems (e.g., the mind-body dualism and all the epistemic problems that follow from it), thereby producing the need for the great "critiques of reason" that would attempt to supplant such dogmatism with transcendental explanations. We are now in a position to consider the problems that followed from the attempts to provide a metaphysical and ontological grounding for natural scientific knowledge and to see how these problems persist today. After that we shall be ready to understand the sense of Husserl's transcendental phenomenological epoche and methodological reductions.

NOTES

1. Burtt, *Foundations*, p. 69. Reference to Kepler, *Opera*, I, p. 31.

2. Burtt, *Foundations*, p. 61.

3. I am here making explicit what I believe is the implicit and perhaps unconscious inference made by Kepler. The relationship between formal or "objective" causality and the "principle of perfection" is dealt with by Descartes in *Meditation III* for a more explicit backing of a similar position, i.e., the grounding of formal-mathematical causality in the *"Prima causa."*

4. Burtt, *Foundations*, p. 67. Reference to Kepler, *Opera*, VIII, pp. 147-48.

5. This tendency is explained somewhat less psychologically by Husserl's concept of doxic/ontic-certainty (*Seinsgewissheit*). This notion will emerge in numerous places as we proceed, usually in relation to the tendency of natural science to support its method-ological achievements by the postulation of ontological correlates. The issue of "ontological genesis" in natural science will be dealt with in §§5.2(c)-(d).

6. Drake, Stillman, *Discoveries and Opinions of Galileo* (Garden City, NY: Doubleday & Co., Inc., 1967), pp. 237-38. Hereafter referred to as *Discoveries and Opinions*.

7. Husserl calls all science that proceeds as a mathematical reduction to pure physicality "Galilean Science." He realizes that this appellation is historically skewed (*C* §9, p. 57), but for simplici-ty's sake uses Galileo's name (as have many others) to indicate the natural scientific tendency towards the mathematization, and, cor-relatively, materialization, of the universe.

8. Burtt, *Foundations*, p. 81.

9. While the basic arguments for this distinction date back to antiquity (to Leucippus and Democritus, c. 430 B.C.), the actual terms were coined only after Galileo, by Robert Boyle, and given their classic formulation in John Locke's *An Essay Concerning Human Understanding* (1689). Both Boyle and Locke were admittedly influ-enced by Galileo's rejuvenation of the distinction.

10. Burtt, *Foundations*, p. 79.

11. In his book *Sensations and Phenomenology* (Bloomington: In-diana University Press, 1966) Harmon Chapman argues, against Burtt and Cassirer, that Galileo never made the subjectivizing move in relation to secondary qualities, and that Descartes was the original culprit here (pp. 14-15, 27-28). I think that Chapman is wrong about this, as can be seen from Galileo's statement about to follow in the body of the text.

12. Drake, *Discoveries and Opinions*, p. 274.

13. Burtt, *Foundations*, pp. 89-90.

14. This was not the first time this correlation had been insisted upon. Plato's insistence on the necessary connection between knowl-edge and the "forms" is the historical exemplar of this occurrence.

15. Burtt, *Foundations*, p. 106.

16. In *Rules for the Direction of the Mind* Descartes defines "simple natures" in the following way: they are essences beheld as "primary and existing *per se*, not as depending on any others [i.e., on any other natures]. . . . [T]hey are just those facts which we have

called the simplest in any single series. All others can only be perceived as deductions from these . . . ." (Elizabeth S. Haldane and G. R. T. Ross, trans., *The Philosophical Works of Descartes* [Cambridge: University Press, 1969], v. I, p. 16. Hereafter referred to as *Philosophical Works*.)

Later, Descartes explicitly correlates simple natures with clear and distinct ideas, taking mathematical intuitions as the exemplary instance of these: We "shall call simple only, those cognitions which are so clear and so distinct that they cannot be analysed by the mind into others more distinctly known. Such are figure, extension, motion, etc.: all others we conceive to be in some way compounded out of these" (*Philosophical Works*, v. I, p. 16).

17. Descartes, *Philosophical Works*, pp. 154, 179. Also see pt. II, prin. VIII, from *The Principles of Philosophy*, p. 258 (also in the *Philosophical Works*), entitled: "That quantity and number differ only in thought from that which has quantity and number."

18. Jacob Needleman makes great use of this notion in *Selected Papers of Ludwig Binswanger: Being-in-the-World* (Harper Torchbooks: New York, 1967), p. 40. Hereafter referred to as *Being-in-the-World*. Note that this notion is implicit in Husserl's analysis of Galileo's method, as above, p. 23.

19. Kepler expressed this in particularly acute form when he wrote, "Just as the eye was made to see colors, and the ear to hear sounds, so the human mind was made to understand, not whatever you please, but quantity." Burtt, *Foundations*, p. 68. Reference to Kepler, *Opera*, I, p. 31.

20. Descartes, *Philosophical Works*, pp. 291, 294-96.

21. Descartes, *Philosophical Works*, pp. 255, 295-96.

22. *The English Works of Thomas Hobbes* (ed. by W. Molesworth, 11 v., London, 1839-1945). *Concerning Body*, v. 1, pp. 7, 10; *Leviathan*, v. 3, p. 71. John Locke, *An Essay Concerning Human Understanding* (New York: Dover Pub., Inc., 1959), v. I, "Epistle to the Reader," p. 14. David Hume, *A Treatise of Human Nature* (Clarendon Press: Oxford, 1975), pp. xvii, xix. Also see Hume's *An Enquiry Concerning Human Understanding* (Indianapolis: Hackett Pub. Co., 1977), pp. 8-9.

23. John Locke, *An Essay Concerning Human Understanding* (New York: Dover Pub., Inc., 1959), v. II, bk. IV, ch. III, §§ 7-15; ch. XI, §§ 1-10.

24. George Berkeley, *A Treatise Concerning the Principles of Human Knowledge* (La Salle, IL: Open Court Pub. Co., 1963), p. 33.

25. Karl Popper, "A Note on Berkeley as Precursor of Mach and Einstein," in *Locke and Berkeley*, ed. by C. B. Martin and D. M.

Armstrong (Notre Dame: University of Notre Dame Press, 1968), pp. 436-49. This is a reprint of Ch. 6 of Popper's *Conjectures and Refutations* (London: Routledge & Kegan Paul, 1962).

26. David Hume, *A Treatise of Human Nature* (Oxford: Clarendon Press, 1975), p. 7. Hereafter referred to as *Treatise*.

27. Hume, *Treatise*, p. 188.

28. Hume, *Treatise*, pp. 188-93.

29. Hume, *Treatise*, pp. 193, 212-18.

30. Hume, *Treatise*, pp. 194-210.

31. Hume, *Treatise*, p. 212.

32. Hume, *Treatise*, p. 212.

33. Hume, *Treatise*, p. 218.

34. Hume, *Treatise*, p. 231.

35. For the criticism of Descartes, see below, §4.1, and §§5.1 (a), (c), and (e). The criticism of Kant is not developed in this work, but for it see *C* §§28-32, and see David Carr, *Problem of History*, pp. 127-133.

3

THE PROBLEMS OF PHYSICALISTIC RATIONALISM

FOR HUSSERL, AS FOR KANT, the traditional division of philosophical method into rationalism and empiricism is misleading and simplistic (*C* §11, pp. 62-63). The doctrines of both schools, Husserl claims, are imbued with and guided by unexamined prejudices concerning physicalistic causality, as well as by the correlative belief in a purely corporeal world behind the scenes that is the source of this causality. Husserl calls this set of beliefs and manner of interpreting the world "physicalistic objectivism" or "physicalistic rationalism" (*C* §§10-14). It contains both empiricistic and rationalistic elements and emerged from the tradition traced in the previous chapter.

The unexamined prejudices inherent to physicalistic objectivism (especially the belief in a purely corporeal world) led in an obvious way to the problem of the veil of ideas in Locke and eventually to Hume's skepticism. From step one of their analyses, these philosophers are plagued by the problem of a purely corporeal world behind the appearances; and from step one, Husserl argues, this vitiates their claims to having achieved a radical empiricism. As was Descartes, Hobbes and Locke were guided by the belief that a physicalistic objectivism must ultimately explain the world, and, if not, then the world is unexplainable. Indeed, even Hume seemed to feel there was some need for a metaexperiential "real" world to order our impressions. If not, then as a unified phenomenal manifold, the world was an enigma.

Ultimately, then, Husserl views traditional empiricism, too, as evolving from a physicalistic rationalism. Eventually, however, in Hume's skepticism and proto-phenomenological descriptions, the first step was taken towards the emancipation from the belief in the necessity of a purely corporeal world (*C* §§23-24). The paradoxes brought out by Hume in his attempt to develop "a science of human nature" modeled upon the natural sciences "shook the foundations of physicalistic objectivism" (*C* §24), both as a means of cognizing Nature (as the natural scientific metaphysics understood it), and as a means of understanding human existence and the world in which it finds itself. When physicalistic objectivism is used as a means for doing this, the great "world-enigmas" emerge as shown in Hume's *Treatise*. These enigmas provoked the first conscious transcendental turn in the work of Kant.

In this chapter we will attempt to articulate the problems Husserl believed to result from the world-view of physicalistic rationalism. Four distinct sets of problems can be identified in Husserl's criticisms. We will label these issues (§3.1) the transformation of phenomena and natural scientific objectivity, (§3.2) sedimentation and the depletion of meaning through technization, (§3.3) the ontological reversal and the perversion of sense, and (§3.4) the riddle of cognition and the transcendence of the world.

Generally, Husserl views (3.1) and (3.2) as providing the conditions for the possibility of (3.3) and (3.4). If (3.1) and (3.2) can be correctly understood through phenomenological analyses, then (3.3) and (3.4) should dissolve as philosophical problems. This phenomenological act of dissolution will be dealt with in Chapters 4 through 6.

3.1
THE TRANSFORMATION OF PHENOMENA AND NATURAL SCIENTIFIC OBJECTIVITY

Throughout his works Husserl is fond of pointing out that the life-world, the everyday world in which each of us lives, is a world riddled with a vague but persistent typology (*PP* §7; *C* §§ 34, 36, 51, 62; *EJ* §§ 8, 26, 83). This typology is the regulated set of relations of types, kinds, and relations themselves that are expressed in ordinary language and provide the prepredicative understanding and proto-logic for the symbolic achievements of advanced predicative logic and for the mathematization of the world (*C* §§ 36, 66; *EJ* §§ 4-10).[1] These vague typological relations that hold amongst the phenomena of the life-world provide the truth fundament for all more precise typological relations and formulae, i.e., the laws of natural reductive science (*C* §§ 34, 66; *EJ* §10). Because this typological life-world is the truth fundament, the first step in the achievements of natural reductive science must be the transformation of phenomena, or, of some phenomenon, of the everyday life-world.

Unsurprisingly, then, in numerous places Husserl insists that the theoretical, manipulative, and predictive achievements of natural reductive science lie in the original possibility for the "transformation of phenomena" (*C* §34; *EJ* §10).[2] The "phenomena" referred to here are the objects, events, and relations of the life-world that always show themselves in general typological form, while "transformation" refers to their reduction or transformation through abstraction and idealization to the set of primitive facts that are said to constitute them. Such primitive explanatory facts are usually believed to constitute or explain phenomena when they give us theoretical, manipulative, or predictive power over the phenomena they refer to. These primitive facts are generally synonymous with Descartes' "simple natures" and are considered to be the simplest and most essential elements to which the phenomena of a particular science can be reduced. Most importantly, these primitive facts, as the fundamental units of natural scientific explanation, are thought to be essential for explanations because all other "essential" elements of the phenomena under question can be derived from them, and the possibility of such derivation may determine in advance the set of essential elements. The result of this, as noted in Chapter 2, is that the possibility of a reduction to and derivation from primitive facts is usually accompanied by a stripping-away and junking of all nonessential qualities with the remaining qualities seen as nonderivative. The nonessential qualities are usually classified as purely phenomenal and then thrown into the junk-heap of subjectivity.

Husserl, similar to Burtt and others, thinks he recognizes one persisting set of primitive facts for the natural sciences. These primitive facts are derived from the tradition traced in the previous chapter and, as might be expected, are the mathematical units and relations thought to be indicative of pure corporeality or pure physicality (C §12). Such mathematical formulae signify things as *res extensae*: "entities" conceived in their purely mathematical dimensions and relations. These dimensions and relations provide the "simple natures" of purely (and merely) physical things. The scope of the notion of pure corporeality, as the fundamental primitive fact and regulative idea of natural science, is much more extensive than first appears. The idea has many empirical disguises effectuated by its embodiment in different words, significations, and contexts. However, as a general reductive goal it is always the same: a reduction to nonqualitative units and/or relations. As nonqualitative, such units and relations are believed to become universally determinate for the given set of (qualitative) phenomena that they explain.

The two most striking examples of the extension of purely quantifiable corporeality as primitive fact can be found in the "life-sciences," biology and psychology (C §ll, pp. 63-64).[3] For example, in nonholistic biology the idea of pure corporeality has been instantiated in the concept of an organism as a highly complex *thing*. This organism is, at least from a methodological perspective, reducible to the primitive facts of drives, instincts, tropisms, and genes. All of these are in turn traceable to corporeal, somatic correlates, which are themselves reducible to determinate, quantitative units. It is not hard to see that these primitive facts of nonholistic biology are parallel to the primitive facts, "force" and "elementary particles," of physics proper. For all other purely physical sciences, from chemistry through biology, the extension of the same methodological ideal is obvious.

This entire process of reductive transformation was succinctly described by Ludwig Binswanger when he wrote, "Natural science never begins with just the phenomena; indeed, its main task is to divest the phenomena of their phenomenality as quickly as possible."[4] And, in fact, in Binswanger's own science the same methodological ideal has taken control. The "era of schools" in psychology[5] — the era in which psychology underwent near civil war in the battle to achieve a master paradigm — provides us with a classical instance of this occurrence taking place. Consider, for instance, just three of these historical schools.[6]

Behaviorism mathematized and corporealized psychology's subject matter by placing it in the objective realm and, initially, by viewing the mechanistics of behavior as physiologically grounded.[7] Though behaviorism has usually been viewed as a "nurture school" standing in opposition to functionalistic and physiological psychologies, this has not been the usual case. The founder of behaviorism found much in common between the methods and findings of functionalistic and physiological psychologies and his own behavioristic psychology. In the manifesto of behaviorism, John. B. Watson wrote that behaviorism's ". . . closest scientific companion is physiology. Indeed you may wonder, as we proceed, whether behaviorism can be differentiated from that science. It is different from physiology only in the grouping of its problems, not in fundamentals or in central viewpoint."[8] In its attempt to provide the world with a scientific psychology, behaviorism leaped from the domain of subjective experience and placed its "subject" in the appearing realm in order to reduce it to nonappearing facts, laws of behavior ultimately grounded in pure corporeality.

Likewise, Freudian psychoanalysis reserved the possibility for a reduction to pure corporeality by way of its doctrine of the unconscious instincts. For Freud instincts were the biologically interpreted equivalent of intentions.[9] Of importance is Freud's claim that instincts "represent the somatic demands upon the mind"[10] and that "the source of an instinct is . . . that somatic process in an organ or part of the body from which there results a stimulus represented in mental life by an instinct."[11] This corporeal interpretation of intentions opened psychoanalysis to the possibility of what Freud called "the economic approach."[12] The objective of the economic approach is the explanation of all psychic phenomena in the form of quantitative relations of instinctual forces. Freud even went so far as to write, "It may even be supposed that the disposition of all human beings is qualitatively alike and that they differ only owing to these quantitative conditions."[13] "Indeed, the decision on whether the outcome is to be illness or not always lies with quantitative factors."[14] In fact, much earlier, in his abandoned "Project for a Scientific Psychology" Freud had written: "The intention is to furnish a psychology that shall be a natural science: that is, to represent psychical processes as quantitatively determinate states of specifiable material particles, thus making those processes perspicuous and free from contradiction."[15]

Finally, even Gestalt psychology, which is renowned for its adherence to the phenomena, insisted upon the possibility of interpretative transformation to the purely corporeal. This was done with its principle of psycho-physical isomorphism. Wolfgang Köhler expressed this principle in the following words: "Our principle says that the temporal 'between' in experience goes with a functional 'between' in the sequence of underlying physiological events."[16] This means that ". . . units in experience go, i.e., always occur in a one to one relation with, functional units in the underlying physiological processes."[17] From this principle Köhler drew the conclusion that "if . . . my words represent a description of my experiences, they are at the same time objective representations of the processes which underlie these experiences."[18] Again, then, even in the formation of Gestalt psychology the possibility of reduction to pure corporeality was maintained as a methodological touchstone for psychological explanation.

In all of the foregoing cases, once the phenomenal or subjective elements of experience are stripped away, and the primitive fact of pure corporeality is reached, the natural scientist is thought to have direct exposure to the fundamental nature of Nature as constituted by primary qualities. Even in relation to psychic life this notion of pure corporeality has become the *terminus ad quem* of scientific research. And it is in this separation of the experienced phenomenal world from the purely corporeal world of natural reductive science that something like the first consistent and systematic epoche was achieved (*C* §66, p. 227). In contrast to the phenomenological epoche, however, this objectivistic epoche systematically excluded all subjectivity and thereby permitted the transformation of phenomena and a radical new form of objectivity — *natural scientific* objectivity.

When Galileo and Descartes distinguished between the subjective and the objective, declaring that only the purely physicalistic or corporeal was objective, they thus excluded or "bracketed-out" the domain of "experiential givens" (*C* §66) in order to articulate and explain the world in mathematical form. These forms served as measures of the purely physical units and relations. This bracketing-out of subjective factors meant, on the other hand, a bracketing-*in* of all the physicalistic-objective characteristics of the world, that is, a bracketing-in of the purely corporeal. Thereby a method of exclusion was directed towards the purely phenomenal while a method of orientation or direction of interest was used for the articulation of a purely physical world. This was achieved by "seeing through" and "transforming" phenomenal characteristics into mathematical form.

In his lectures on *Phenomenological Psychology* (§5, pp. 39-40) Husserl develops this line of thought by arguing that in its very initiation modern science was an attempt to realize an objectivity that "was already an artificial product of method." This artificial product was the mathematical-corporeal Nature projected by the methodological dictates of natural science. Such a preestablished interest meant that a "consistent elimination of all 'merely subjective' properties belonging to the things of immediate experience . . . belonged essentially to its method." And, in exact contrast to phenomenological procedure, this method of elimination was oriented towards the purely material, physical, and mathematical domain that was left over as a residuum after the suspension of everything mental and subjective had been achieved. This method of exclusion in the original epoche of natural science is the first step in the transformation of phenomena; it effects the theoretical shift of standpoint, which allows for the possibility of transforming phenomena while the actual transformation occurs through the processes of idealization. These processes of idealization are thought by Husserl to be the objectifying functions of the highest order (*PRS* 90). But before turning to these processes, we need to articulate the problems that Husserl thought an understanding of these processes would solve — problems brought about by ignorance and neglect of them. To do this it will be necessary to consider the notion of "objectivity," which Husserl adopts directly from his conception of natural scientific objectivity, and to show how this conception of objectivity has been traditionally related to the phenomena as they appear prior to transformation. In Chapter 5, we will return to the processes of idealization.

For Husserl, "objectivity" implies transcendence (*IP* 37-38); and transcendence, in its objectivistic sense, means anything outside of the perceiving consciousness in the now moment (*IP* 28; *FTL* §94, p. 233). The essential fact to be noted about objectivity, however, is that the "x" that transcends the perceiving consciousness (the object of objectivity) is *meant* as existing independently of consciousness.[19] Such objects, which for Husserl are a necessary element for the conception of objectivity, range from typical objects, say, a house, which exists over and above its appearing sides, to the primitive facts of natural science, say, photons and atomic particles, which exist over and above the house's appearing.

In the natural attitude, one variation of which is the natural scientific attitude, these objects of objectivity are thought to be explanatory of 'i.e., the reason for' the phenomena immediately experienced by consciousness. Such is their use in causal theories of perception. Husserl, like Hume, observes that this belief in objects, as transcendent and independent existences explanatory of immediate experience, is inherent to the natural attitude and made into an explanatory dogma by natural science. Both these interpretative perspectives, or rather, both these variations of one perspective, constantly understand, interpret, or explain immediate experience in terms of that which transcends it. And, if that which transcends immediate experience is to be believed to have explanatory power, then it must be believed to have independent existence as well.[20] Husserl claims that this existence-dictate inherent to all natural knowledge is grounded in the doxic- or ontic-certainty (*Seinsgewissheit*) of everyday understanding and that it filters up to the highest levels of scientific articulation (*EJ* §7). In sum, Husserl defines "objectivity" (as viewed from the natural attitude) in terms of transcendent, independent existence, explanatory of immanent phenomena.[21]

Since Husserl's conception of objectivity was adopted from the traditions we have considered, the meaning of the word "explanatory" in his definition has already been adumbrated, at least implicitly. An explicit rendering of its meaning will now show us how the notion of "the objective" has been traditionally related to the phenomena of everyday experience.

With hardly anything more than an appeal to God and the achievements of natural science itself, the objective, as purely corporeal stuff independent of consciousness, was claimed by the representatives of early natural science to be the source and the cause, indeed, the actual reality of the appearing phenomena. Moreover, when any "x" was claimed to be the causal source, or reality of any "y", then "x" was believed to be the explanation for "y". Transferring this claim back to our earlier analyses and Figure I, it can be seen that the subdomain indicated by component 4 was claimed to appear to the perceiving consciousness (component 5) only because it was caused by (the elements of) domain A. Physicalistic causality, as real push-pull or mechanical causality, was claimed to be the real connecting link between the objective world and the phenomena that were immediately given to consciousness. And it was knowledge of these causal connections, as causal laws, that explained the phenomena. These causal laws were supposed to have the efficacy that they did because of the pure corporeality of the objective domain, which was always dressed in the primitive concepts of the natural science at hand. In fine, the physicalistic-objective was declared the explanans of the phenomenal-subjective, the explanandum.

But here our problem arises: *how was the movement from the subjective-phenomenal to the physicalistic-objective explained?* While the notion of physicalistic causality was used to explain the phenomena, that is, to give the reasons "how" and "why" for the phenomena, the movement from the phenomena themselves to the physicalistic-objective was never appropriately considered. If the subjective phenomenon was the first-order prior experience, then was there not need for an understanding of its transformation to the physicalistic-objective? — especially if the *epistemic achievement* of physicalistic objectivity was itself to be understood? Although the processes of transformation were given some consideration by the early natural scientists, the interpretation of these processes soon became entangled with the objectivistic *results* of the processes themselves. Soon after, the problems of transformation were largely forgotten until our own century. They have become remembered now because the separation between humanity's lived-world and the world of natural science can no longer be safely ignored.

While Husserl never believed that the physicalistic, reductive manner of knowing the world was somehow epistemically flawed, he did recognize two major problems contingently related to this manner of knowing. First, this natural scientific method of explanation had been illicitly extended to all world-regions, some of which are essentially different from the purely corporeal. Consequently, this method has come to represent the only mode of real understanding. Second (and the previous point is probably the result of this), the undeniable successes and achievements of this method had almost totally blinded its practitioners and interpreters to the actual transformation of phenomena (i.e., the processes of abstraction, generalization, and idealization) and led them instead to focus upon the *results* of this method. However, the most impressive result of this method was the discovery (or postulation) of the purely corporeal domain, and this domain was then appealed to (by naturalistic psychology and naturalistic epistemologies) to explain the possibility of natural knowledge itself. But to argue in this way is to commit a *petitio principii*, and it simply adds more fuel to the objectivistic interpretation of the world in the very act of attempting to explain that interpretation. This is just one more form of what Husserl calls the "naturalistic prejudice."

Before turning to the main task of this text (which is to show how Husserl proposed to clarify, and perhaps even reverse, this tendency towards universal objectivistic explanation), we will outline the problems that helped produce and that resulted from this physicalistic rationalism. First, we will turn to what Husserl saw as the most prominent contributing factors to the forgetfulness of the transformation of phenomena. Husserl called these factors the sedimentation and the technization (*Technisierung*) of method. By obscuring the original transformation of phenomena, these factors aided in the occurrence of "the ontological reversal" (§3.3) and the "problems of functioning subjectivity," which Husserl also calls the "riddle of cognition" and the "problem of transcendence" (§3.4).

3.2
SEDIMENTATION AND THE DEPLETION OF MEANING THROUGH TECHNIZATION

In the *Crisis* Husserl identifies a set of problems inherent to the natural sciences that, in earlier works, he had often identified as problems for natural knowledge generally. These problems are the problems of *Selbstverstandlichkeit* (effectively: taken-for-grantedness), sedimentation, and meaning-depletion (*Sinnentleerung*) through the technization of methods. It is essentially as a resolution to these problems, by a restoration of meaning, that Husserl attempted to sound the death-knell for the metaphysical problems that followed from the tradition we have traced and that we will develop further in sections 3.3 and 3.4.

The primary event to be understood is the depletion of meaning in mathematical natural science; but to comprehend this event we need to understand the epistemic, genetic occurrence of "sedimentation," from which *Selbstverstandlichkeit* follows. The depletion of meaning follows from these epistemic, genetic conditions.

In Husserl's writings the term "sedimentation" has many of the connotations, in an epistemic context, which the term normally has in its geological contexts. In Husserlian language, "sedimentation" refers to the progressive layering of knowledge as it develops in a single life-history or in the history of human knowledge generally. This layering of knowledge refers to the fact that all present knowledge is based upon past knowledge, while the past knowledge upon which it is based is normally covered up by the epistemic achievements and interests that have followed it. This means that in most acts involving knowledge, the knowledge presupposed for the act will be implicit or, in Michael Polanyi's term, "tacit,"[22] while the object of the immediate cognitive act will remain at the focus of consciousness. Husserl sometimes refers to the knowledge or information that has been layered over as the "deposit" (*Niederschlag*) of knowledge that is no longer given, but nevertheless retained, and he realizes that even his pet notion of "immediate experience" is inevitably and always infiltrated by sediments of such past knowledge.

In his lectures on *Phenomenological Psychology* Husserl described the sedimentations inherent to all knowledge by writing that ". . . our opinions which stem from our theoretical or practical activities clothe our experience over, or clothe its sense with new layers of sense" (§6, p. 41). All objects of knowledge, he says, "contain sediments of previous mental activities." It is due to these inescapable sense-deposits, inherent to all human understanding, that phenomenology must enter into "genetic analysis."

Genetic analysis is the investigation backwards (*Zuruckuntersuchung*) from the given, into the layers of accumulated sense that constitute the given. Or, more colorfully stated, it is the archaeological dig into the sense-chains of understanding. By uncovering these sense-chains, genetic phenomenology can restore meaning to knowledge domains that have become severed from their intuitive, intentional, and semantic roots and can, simultaneously, dispel any objectivistic mis-interpretations of the possibility for the higher domains of cognition.

The term for the event that connects sedimentation to the depletion of meaning is *Selbstverstandlichkeit*. In David Carr's words, *Selbstverstandlichkeit* refers to modes of knowledge and understanding that are "unquestioned, but not necessarily unquestionable" (*C* §9, p.24, n.3). It refers to whatever is "obvious" because of our personal and historical inheritance; but such knowledge is so "obvious" that the sense-chains of implication constituting this obviousness are neither questioned nor investigated. This obviousness might best be referred to as the "taken-for-grantedness" of our knowledge inheritance, but, as we all know, "taken-for-grantedness" makes the "obvious" fade from sight. It might be stated generally that insofar as this taken-for-grantedness is of advanced symbolic achievements, then just so far has the emptying of the meaning of these achievements occurred: the presupposed becomes unexpressed and perhaps unknown. In order to understand how this happens, we must make a brief excursus into Husserl's theory of meaning and evidence.[23]

Husserl's most thorough presentation of his own conception of meaning is given in the *Logical Investigations*, especially in Investigations I and VI. Here, his conception of meaning involves four distinct elements. The essential elements for meaning are (1) the intentional act, which confers meaning upon (2) signs or data, which may (3) allow for the senseful manifestation of the object meant (pp.280-84), and (4) the meaning itself, which has (ideal) being independent of the particular act (p.333).

In the *Logical Investigations* Husserl states that (1) the intentional act is the carrier of meaning (pp.680-84). He denies that the object meant or the "percept" is the sole determinant of meaning because from the same percept quite different senses can be derived. Upon looking out into the garden and seeing a blackbird, "I could give expression to my percept in the words: 'There flies a blackbird!' " But I could also have remarked: " 'That is black!', 'That is a black bird!', 'There flies that blackbird!', 'There it soars!', and so forth" (p.680). In each case, from the same percept a different sense emerges.

These comments notwithstanding, however, Husserl does insist that perceptual filling does play an essential role in determining the final significance of certain types of meaning, namely, those with material content. So, he says both that "meaning cannot first have been acquired through intuition . . .," yet that "one can say in general, that in order to be quite clear as to the sense of an expression (or as to the content of a concept) one must construct a corresponding intuition: in this intuition one sees what the expression 'really means' " (p.306). In this second statement Husserl is using the word "means" (*gemeint*) by reference to element (3) above, the object meant. The object meant would thus tell us what the intentional act, manifest in the expression, really means. It is not simply the case, then, that (1) the intentional act confers meaning upon (2) signs and/or data that present (3) the object meant; but correlatively, (3) the objective meant *clarifies* (1) the meaning of the intentional act. It *displays* what (1) really means to precisely the extent that (1) does achieve some degree of "coincidence" with (3).

In the Sixth Investigation Husserl attempts to clarify this relationship between act and object by saying that when intuited the object meant "determines the meaning without embodying it" (pp.682, 684). This means that while the object meant does not determine all the nuances of a meaning, it does function to determine the degree of coincidence between the meaning and the meant. Thus Husserl writes: "If perception never constitutes the full meaning of a statement grounded in perception, it nevertheless seems to make a contribution to this meaning . . ." (p.682). And he continues: "Intuitions may indeed be allowed to contribute to the meaning of a perceptual statement, but only in the sense that the meaning could not acquire a *determinate* relation to the object it means without some intuitive aid" (p.683). In this early writing Husserl calls the conscious act either the "meaning-intention" (*Bedeutungsintention*) or the "signitive-intention," and argues that it is usually made manifest in some linguistic expression, while the appearance of the object meant is called either the "meaning-fulfillment" (*Bedeutungserfüllung*) or "intuitive-fulfillment" (*erfüllenden Anschauungen*), and has its exemplary occurrence as perception.

Even in his earliest writings, however, Husserl is aware that the relations between the meaning-intention and the meaning-fulfillment are susceptible to innumerable degrees of coincidence between signitive-intentions and their intuitive fulfillments (pp.731-36). This awareness is shown in his reference to purely signitive-intentions as "empty intentions" and by later claims that unless they are absurd such intentions admit of some degree of evidential fulfillment (*FTL* §§82-87). The ideal happening of meaning would occur as the complete fulfillment of signitive-intentions by the object they intend, precisely *as* they intend it. This "flash" of fulfilled meaning would simultaneously present us with the highest degree of self-evidence, what Husserl calls "adequate evidence," complete adequation between signitive-intention and intuitive-fulfillment (reminiscent of, though a refined version of, adequation between intellect and thing).

Later, Husserl writes that when this coincidence between signitive-intention and intuitive-fulfillment occurs, "The object is not merely meant, but in the strictest sense *given*, and given as it is meant, and made one with our meaning reference" (p.765). The achievement of the steps necessary for this ideal correlation between meaning-intention and meaning-fulfillment is called the "unity of coincidence" (*Deckungseinheit*) or the "unity of fulfillment" (*Erfüllungseinheit*). Concerning this occurrence Husserl had already written that ". . . the fulfilling content coincides with the intending content, so that, in our experience of this unity of coincidence, the object, at once intended and 'given,' stands before us, not as two objects, but as *one* alone" (p.291). Expressed in the later jargon of transcendental phenomenology, this means that the exemplary occurrence of meaning emerges as the fulfillment of some noema through a noetic act, which directs the noema towards an object, which then fulfills the precise intention and rule expectations of the noema.

"Noeses" (meaning-intentions) and "noemata" (in part, intuitive meaning-fulfillments) are eventually called by Husserl the "correlational a priori" for all possible meaning (*IP* 17; *I* §84; *C* §46). This notion of the "correlational a priori" is, in part, an expression for the inseparability of meaning-intentions and meaning-fulfillments in the constitution of determinant meaningfulness. For Husserl, the term "a priori" is here meant to emphasize the inseparability of meaning from evidence as the ground condition for an experience of meaning. The universal a priori of correlation may also be thought of as the axiom for the slogan that "consciousness is always consciousness of something," that is, for the claim that consciousness is essentially intentional and, from the first, intentionally intertwined with evidence (*FTL* §§59-60).

Although Husserl places the locus of meaning in the intentional act of consciousness, it is clear, because of his insistence on inseparability, that intuitive fulfillment also plays an important role in the functionings of meaning. This role is one of clarification via the possibility of intuitive explication. For Husserl, meanings signify "objectivities" because objects meant are an essential aspect of all meanings (*LI* 280). And, for him, all such meaning-objectivities occur in a hierarchical context, the lowest and most fundamental of which are the *perceptual* life-world objectivities constituted in the unities of coincidence between signitive meaning-intentions and perceptual meaning-fulfillments (*I* §§149-53; *CM* §58; *FTL* §§82-87; *C* §§33-34; *EJ* §§4-7). Most important for our present considerations is Husserl's oft-reiterated claim that ". . . at each of the levels in question, the primordial enters, with a new stratum of sense, into the secondarily constituted world . . ." (*CM* §58, p.134). The significance of this point is that the lower strata, constituted in the first instance by acts of perception, have both genetic and logical priority over all higher strata. This means, in turn, that the possibility of intuitive fulfillment plays a fundamental role in determining (that is, clarifying) the meaning of all and any meaning constructs, even those of the highest level (*I* §24; *FTL* §§82-87). But obviously, if this is the case, then even the highest level objectivities (the objectivities in which sense and meaning are purely "theoretical," "explanatory," and "signitive") must have hidden within themselves horizons of intuitive fulfillment, if not the possibility for an immediate unity of coincidence. Consequently, if meaningfulness is to accrue to these higher levels of sense, then the purely signitive or symbolic intentions must (1) achieve direct fulfillment or (2) have some of their horizons for the possibility of fulfillment displayed. If neither of these occurrences takes place, or rather, if the need for and possibility of these occurrences is forgotten, then the depletion of meaning has begun.

We have noted that for Husserl "meaning" involves a relation to sense-strata. It can now be said that for him the depletion of meaning occurs when there is a forgetfulness or ignorance of the connections between higher level objectivities (secondarily constituted worlds) and lower level objectivities (given in and *as* the world). Since Husserl believes that "the primordial must always enter into these higher strata of sense," any hiatus between these higher levels and the primordial realm of meaning (the life-world) can, theoretically, result in an emptying of meaning from the higher level objectivities. When any such transformation of phenomena is overlooked, the meaning of the higher level objectivities (that is, the meaning inherent to the results of transformation) is depleted. In archaeological terms, these bedrock meanings are covered-over and then over-looked.

We can now turn directly to Husserl's charges concerning "the emptying of meaning of mathematical natural science through technization" (*C* §9g), which, more particularly expressed, is "the problem of the sense of natural scientific 'formulae' " (*C* §9f).

Husserl believes that the two major historical occurrences that stimulated the emptying of meaning of mathematical natural science were, at the same time, the achievements that made the great successes of natural science possible. They were (1) the *geometrization of nature* and (2) the *arithmetization of geometry*. Each of these events is indicative of steps in sense-stratification that distance natural scientific formulae from the primordial meaning-realm of first-level world constitution, the domain where meaning-intentions and meaning-fulfillments first achieve some unity of coincidence. After attributing these historical developments to the main figures associated with them (the "geometrization of nature" with Galileo; the "arithmetization of geometry" with Vieta, Descartes, and Leibniz), Husserl claims that, with algebraization, mathematical thinking:

> . . . becomes free, systematic, a priori thinking liberated from all intuited actuality. . . .
>
> This arithmetization of geometry leads almost automatically, in a certain way, to the emptying of meaning. The actually spatio-temporal idealities, as they are presented first hand [*originär*] in geometrical thinking under the common rubric of "pure intuitions," are transformed, so to speak, into pure numerical configurations, into algebraic structures. In algebraic calculation one lets the geometric signification recede into the background as a matter of course, indeed drops it altogether; one calculates, remembering only at the end that the numbers signify magnitudes. (*C* §9, p.44)

Husserl's point is one that every freshman in algebra has experienced. In calculating the magnitude of a body, we first drop all reference to the body, calculate over numerical variables in a pure arithmetical context, and finally, when finished calculating, add the signs for magnitude to remind us what we were "really" doing. But this backward reference to the meaning fundament of these calculations is inevitably a rather empty and inauthentic reminder of the world our calculations relate to. This gradual development away from the intuited world through constantly increasing arithmetization is called by Husserl the process of "method transformation" (*C* §9, pp.45-47). To the geometrization of nature, which first accomplished the transformation of phenomena, is added arithmetization, specifically algebraization, which accomplishes the transformation of the method of geometry. With this transformation of geometry, we are now two steps from the meaning fundament (*Sinnesfundament*) of intuited actuality, two steps from the world of everyday life (*C* §9h). Step one was the geometrization of nature (i.e., the transformation of phenomena); step two is now the algebraization of geometry (method transformation$_1$).[24] Owing largely to their tremendous achievements, these new methods of natural science began to demand almost the entire interest of the natural scientific investigator. The *interpretation* of the results demanded by every new achievement in the transformation of method became an issue secondary to the further achievement of predictively and pragmatically successful method-transformations themselves. Husserl calls this new direction of interest, which focuses almost exclusively upon the mathematical-experimental methods themselves, "technization" (*Technisierung*).

Technization is seen by Husserl as an intentional focus upon "games-construction," which, as an indirect focus upon method-transformation, "becomes a technique, that is, it becomes a mere art of achieving, through a calculating technique according to technical rules . . ." (*C* §9, p.46). With each advancement in technization (that is, with each method-transformational step forward) a bit of sedimentation occurs in relation to the original transformation of phenomena; and, as one becomes more proficient in the practice of the methods of science, one also becomes all the more impregnated with the characteristics of "taken-for-grantedness" as explained above. For these reasons Husserl writes that eventually ". . . the *original* thinking that genuinely gives meaning to this technical process and truth to the correct results . . . is excluded" (*C* §9, p.46). Moreover, this problem of forgetfulness is exacerbated by the fact that with each new generation's inheritance of the new techniques — an inheritance that presupposes the processes of transformation without explicitly recognizing them — another increment in the *Selbstverstandlichkeit* of natural scientific achievement occurs as well.[25]

In his essay on *The Origin of Geometry*, Husserl gives further consideration to the issues under consideration here. He notes that the temporal location of all knowledge (within a person's life and within human history) makes the occurrence of sedimentation inevitable. Vivid self-evidence, which is coordinated with the ideal of meaningfulness arising out of a unity of coincidence (*LI* 765), always passes into the "passivity of the flowingly fading consciousness of what-has-just-now-been" (*OG* 359). This self-evidence occurs as an essential insight into the unity of fulfillment, which, however, can become materially embodied in words and symbols and then be mechanically or technically *used* without reawakening the original meaning-base of the truth-functional insight itself. And it is this later occurrence that motivates the depletion of meaning.

While the inevitability of sedimentation, and thereby the need for genetic analysis, was implicitly recognized by Husserl in his 1905 lectures on internal time-consciousness, sedimentation, as an externally grounded occurrence, was not explicitly discussed by him until some time later (though, interestingly, Part Two of *Philosophie der Arithmetik* does *carry out* genetic analyses required because of externally grounded sedimentation). This external grounding for sedimentation is recognized, in *The Origin of Geometry*, to occur via the "embodiment" of thought and concepts in written words and symbols (pp.360-62).[26] As with all other communal acquisitions constantly encountered in our everyday world, our language and symbol systems become sedimented and taken-for-granted. The original meaning of words and symbols (experienced in the "ah-ha!" consciousness of first-time understanding) is often obscured and covered over in the constantly passive and mechanical use of those words and symbols. In fact, with the continually increasing dominance of writing, this passive grasping of meaning becomes the norm rather than the exception. And since for Husserl, "meaning" emerges as evidential insight into the unity of coincidence between a signitive-intention and a fulfilling-intuition, the constant use of and reliance upon signitive-intentions alone gradually empties those intentions of their primordial meaningfulness.

This issue of embodiment, which also motivates the depletion of meaning, is broadly referred to by Husserl as the "seduction of language" (*OG* 362). But here Husserl should not be taken to mean that language is some contingent evil in relation to thoughts and understanding, but rather that language, as the carrier of meaning par excellence, constantly strains for liberation from its intuitive correlates. In approaching the attainment of this freedom, however, the evidential and meaningful correlational basis of and for language is often forgotten. This results in a "kind of talking and reading that is dominated by association" (*OG* 362), by mechanical associative habits. When this occurs, "games-meaning" becomes the dominant form of meaning (*LI* 305; *C* §9g), and almost everyone but the creators of new "games" and their always astonished initiates appropriate these meanings passively.

What Husserl calls "method transformation" is generally synonymous with the emancipation of language and symbol systems from their intuitive correlates. This, Husserl claims, occurs because of the "unavoidable sedimentation of mental products in the form of persisting linguistic acquisitions" (*OG* 362). These persisting linguistic acquisitions soon become free-floating symbol systems of various sorts and persist as depleted, though still meaningful, domains of discourse. This depletion of meaning in the founded modes of discourse occurs because, as temporally extended historical processes, the meanings inherent to these domains are genetically and logically dependent upon other meanings, which may never be reactivated in the unity of a signitive-intuitive (i.e., noetic-noematic) fulfillment. Since ". . . scientific thinking attains new results on the basis of those already attained, . . . the new ones serve as the foundation for still others, etc. — in the unity of a propagative process of transferring meaning." And "since meaning is grounded upon meaning, the earlier meaning gives something of its validity to the later one, indeed becomes part of it to a certain extent" (*OG* 363). If these earlier meanings are not reactivated, then epistemic alienation, which Husserl calls the depletion of meaning, occurs.

At this point our earlier definition of "technization" can be formulated more clearly. "Technization" refers to the symbolic-material embodiment of meaning that permits its manipulation without reactivation of the original insight upon which meaning rests. When this occurs, higher level objectivities (e.g., "theoretical entities" and purely signitive meanings) become disconnected from their intuitive correlates; and since intuition plays an essential role in the clarification of meanings, these higher level meanings remain unclarified and are thereby gradually emptied of meaning.

But an important question now arises: Why is this so-called depletion of meaning an issue anyway? What is the need for the reactivation of sense-chains if, as Husserl writes, all "grammatically coherent propositions and concatenations of propositions . . . have their own logical meaning"? (*OG* 367). In short, why do we need to reinvoke the original unities of coincidence for all truths belonging to the higher levels of sense-strata when these higher levels admittedly carry their own unities of meaning?[27]

Part of the response to these questions is that without such reactivation, false accounts for the possibility of the results of these scientific achievements, for the higher level objective meaning-systems, come to be postulated. To such false accounts many other problems accrue, such as meaning depletion and even the possibility of meaning-negation, perhaps better called "epistemic nihilism." In fact, the historical development of the scientific metaphysics traced in Chapter 2 revealed just such an occurrence, which eventually culminated in the experience-reality dichotomy of Descartes and then Hume's radical skepticism — both of which have since haunted all attempts to comprehend the knowing process.

We now propose, then, a return to our earlier account of the metaphysical foundations first supplied to the natural sciences in order to show more clearly how mistaken interpretations of scientific achievement followed from (and continue to follow from) ignorance or neglect of the sense-chains that are productive of higher level meaningfulness.

3.3
THE ONTOLOGICAL REVERSAL AND THE PERVERSION OF SENSE

When the sedimentation of meaning occurs, higher level objectivities, such as the formulae of mathematical natural science, seem to take on a life of their own because the multiple strata of cognitive achievement — that is, the many-layered, sense-bestowing acts of consciousness — are no longer experienced; and the scientific objectivities now seem to stand disconnected over and above the fluctuating appearances of daily life while *explaining* these appearances. Probably because of this, these "categorial objectivities" — natural scientific formulae — came to be correlated with, and then conflated with, true Being qua objects in themselves. The higher level objectivities were then believed literally to *re-present* a transformation of a phenomenon into its "true self," which thereby indicated the thing in itself. Conversely, once this domain of "actual things" was postulated, the tendency towards sedimentation, *Selbstverstandlichkeit*, and the depletion of meaning was reinforced because epistemic achievements were now taken to be guaranteed by something radically other than themselves — by the naturalistic guarantee *sine qua non*, the "true world." This manner of epistemic justification and world explanation, which was developed in Chapter 2, shall be referred to as "the Ontological Reversal."

Husserl develops his analyses of the historical possibility for this reversal by noting that the self-perpetuating force of Galilean science lies in the fact that its fundamental hypothesis, that nature is a mathematical manifold, is a regulative idea, demanding by its very nature an infinite number of verifications. The tremendous holding-power of this hypothesis is generated from the fact that in relationship to the experienced world it eternally remains a hypothesis and, correlatively, it demands eternal verification. Its grip on practitioners of knowledge-seeking is thereby, likewise, "eternal," owing to the labors that it places before them (*C* §9, p.42).

It is also noted by Husserl that this infinite project of mathematizing nature was itself inherited by Galileo through the relatively advanced geometry known to him, pregiven by the tradition (*C* §9, pp.27, 38,49). The neo-pythagoreanism of his day also provided the implicit force behind the interpretative idea of nature as a mathematical manifold. All this inevitably involved sedimentation of meanings, especially in conjunction with the "infinite hypothesis," which involved the constant handing-down of results upon results; and this, in turn, fueled the conditions of *Selbstverstandlichkeit*, even in the work of Galileo.

In these conditions one's tacit knowledge of the processes of idealization was overlooked, and the telic ideal of Nature as the Real, as a mathematical manifold, infiltrated all interpretations of the conditions for the possibility of natural scientific knowledge (*C* §9, pp.47-48). Furthermore, to the steadily advancing method-transformations accrued ". . . the tendency [of interpretation] to superficialize itself in accord with technization. Thus natural science undergoes a many-sided transformation and covering-over of its meaning" (*C* §9, p.48). As we have seen, this process of unrecognized meaning-shifts leads to the emptying of meaning from natural scientific formulae, and this process reaches its pinnacle when the formula-world is coordinated *in toto* with nature (*C* §9, p.48). But another major misinterpretative step is still to be taken: the conflation of the concepts "Nature" and "world."

Husserl's emphasis on the notion of the life-world (*Lebenswelt*) in the *Crisis* is well known. Here, its historical aspect proves to be of great importance.[28] While it was earlier claimed that the existence-dictates of the natural attitude (implicit in the doxic-ontic-certainty of everyday knowing) originally infiltrated the highest reaches of natural scientific explication and determined its existence criteria, it may now be claimed that with the increasing infiltration of natural scientific truth into the everyday life-world, the existence-dictates of the natural scientific attitude have, in a reverse movement, infiltrated, and now determine, the existence criteria of the natural attitude.

The extension of the ontological reversal as it creeps from the natural scientific attitude into the natural attitude *simpliciter* is well expressed in section 10 of the introduction to Husserl's *Experience and Judgment*.[29] It is there claimed that the metaphysics of the *Weltanschauung* of natural science has infiltrated and now undergirds the tacit understanding that each of us has of the everyday world. This holds even for those uninterested and uninvolved in the natural sciences. Indeed, even for those who are repulsed by the natural scientific world-view, *the pregiven world is given as mathematically determinable* in principle; it is given as the physico-material *totality* of what is. And it is implicitly believed, though rarely professed, that after the world is determined in this fashion, nothing is left over. Furthermore, intrinsic to the understanding of this mode of epistemic determination is the recognition of the control that this knowledge can provide in relationship to what is. More specifically, every individual datum, from headache to heartbreak, is recognized ahead of time as falling under the binding force of naturalized, materialized, and mathematized explanation. All this has become a matter of course and is no longer even reflected upon by the laymen of our times. The world as lived, the *Lebenswelt*, is now understood in the mode of *Selbstverstandlichkeit* as a world-Nature existing and determinable in itself.

In Husserl's view what has happened is this: the achievements of natural science, once spawned from immediate engagement with the life-world, have now infiltrated the meaning we give to that world in our first-order experience of it. The layering and condensation of the constituted meanings of natural scientific formulae, and their encasement in the life-world, obscure the sense-chains that connect life-world experience and higher level objectivities. These sense-chains are thereby "covered-up" and forgotten. This is the process of sedimentation that promotes *Selbstverstandlichkeit* and the unwitting reversal considered above.

This historically developed perspectival reversal can also be described in broad strokes by appealing to three of Husserl's standard, but often conflated, descriptive concepts. First, the ontic-certainty of the *natural attitude* lent its reifying force to the truth correlates of natural scientific research. "Objectivity" thus became one with the idea of a "non-relative truth-in-itself" (*C* 310, n. t); and, as Husserl argued throughout his career, truth in itself implies some correlation with being in itself, or at least with *real* being (*LI* 765-70; *C* 304). Second, the *natural scientific attitude* thereby became a methodological instantiation and exemplification of the reifying certainty inherent to the natural attitude, and postulated the (idea of an) entire world in itself, that is, true Nature. Finally, the reverse flow of this natural scientific attitude (aided by the immense force of its practical achievements) entered back into the life-world and its philosophies and produced a reign of *naturalism* in which the "greatest" philosophies of the age became apologies for natural science, modeling themselves after its methods and starting with the same presuppositions as they (*PRS* 79-84).

Although it was not until his last published work that Husserl explicitly tackled the historical problematics of "flowing-in," that is, the ever-incremental determination of our everyday natural attitude by the natural scientific attitude, he certainly recognized the motivation of naturalism by natural science (*PRS* 82) and natural science by the natural attitude (*IP* 13; *I* §56, p.155) long before this. In fact, as early as *Ideen II* Husserl had made mention of the reverse flow in which natural science became the determining factor for perspectives in the life-world (*I* II §§2-3, §§6-7, §62, p.282). Husserl's position, then, is that what began as a methodological procedure — the process of abstraction from the experiential to the purely corporeal — was illicitly transformed into an ontological claim, namely, that the real world *is* purely corporeal.

As David Carr points out, however, step one, the methodological procedure, involves an *abstraction from* something (namely, the world as it originally appears), while step two, the ontological claim, involves an *interpretation* of something (again, the world as it originally appears).[30] But the traditional formulation of the ontological claim forgets that it is an *interpretation* and claims instead to be a clear and distinct idea of the real world, now thought of as *Nature*, that is, as a purely material, mathematical reality, existing in itself. This is supposedly "true Being" and all else is a causally effectuated epiphenomenon.

However, the word "epiphenomenon" becomes completely misleading in this context because the would-be material fundament is precisely *not* a phenomenon, precisely *not* intuitable *in principle*. As Husserl writes, "The objective is precisely never experienceable as itself; and scientists themselves, by the way, consider it in this way whenever they interpret it as something metaphysically transcendent, in contrast to their confusing empiricist talk" (*C* §34, p.129). Even as "epiphenomena" the appearances of things that appear point to the things that appear and these are the things of the world given to us in perception, not metaphysically transcendent things in themselves.

Husserl, then, accepts the purely cognitive results of the natural scientific procedure, but he rejects what he sees as the reification and universal extension of these procedures and results. While he has no complaint with step one above, the processes of abstraction and idealization, in his writings after 1907 he begins explicitly to reject step two, the ontological interpretation of step one. His reasons for rejecting the methodological disintegration of phenomena are not due to an irrational disdain of natural scientific knowledge, however; rather, they are grounded in his belief that the ontological interpretation of (the possibility for the achievement of) natural scientific truth would deprive those achievements of meaning. Or, perhaps more accurately, it would make the meanings of those achievements *absurd*. Husserl argues that the ontological interpretation of natural scientific objectivity would, in principle, nullify the possibility for the achievement of evidential fulfillment in signitive-intuitive unities of coincidence, and thereby nullify the possibility of verifying natural scientific truth. This would occur because the ontological interpretation of natural scientific objects would make the concept "object" categorially incoherent; it would make it a conceptual absurdity.

In our previous discussion of technization and method transformation, which, we showed, tend to motivate the depletion of meaning in natural scientific formulae, no mention was made of the problem of absurdity or countersense (*Widersinn*). In the *Crisis*, however, Husserl's articulation of the problems of physicalistic-rationalism does invoke the spectre of absurdity or countersense that he deals with elsewhere, sometimes in relation to the ontological interpretation of natural scientific formulae (*I* §§ 40, 52). Generally, Husserl's position on the problem of countersensicality in natural science is this: absurdity would indicate more than an extreme case of the depletion of meaning (which is an epistemic problem of *meaning-alienation*); instead, it would be indicative of an impossible comprehension that follows from the erroneous interpretation—the ontological interpretation—of the possibility for natural scientific achievement.

For significant reasons Husserl usually speaks of countersense (*Widersinn*) or absurdity (*Absurdität*) instead of meaninglessness (*Sinnlosigkeit*) and nonsense (*Unsinn*). This is because Husserl's understanding of the latter notions place them far beyond the traffic of daily intercourse: they refer to circumstances with which we simply do not traffic. "Meaninglessness" or "nonsense" indicate, for Husserl, expressions that are really not expressions at all, for it is "part of the notion of an expression to have a meaning" (*LI* 291). Instances of such phenomena would be sign-strings such as "a round or" or ": for * suag < ." These sign-strings are literally senseless because they do not even function as empty signitive intentions; they do not carry even enough sense to emptily mean an object (*LI* 516-18, 522-23). Absurdity or countersense, on the other hand, implies some meaning because simply by virtue of possessing a formal grammatical structure a sign-string (composed of conventional signs) has meaning—though perhaps not a unified and coherent one (*LI* 516-18, 522-23). Hence, absurd or countersensical expressions would be ones such as "that thing which in no way appears" or even "p and ~p." Each of these expressions has a sense, but a sense that can never be coherently unified and fulfilled. There is, however, a significant sense in which the countersensicality of these latter two expressions differ as well.

In *Formal and Transcendental Logic* Husserl clarifies the senses of "senselessness" somewhat further by use of his depiction of the threefold strata of formal logic. He identifies the pure forms of judgment (§13), "consequent logic" (§14), and "truth logic" (§15) as these three strata. Each stratum is logically prerequisite for the following stratum if the expressions in the higher stratum are to achieve the successful constitution of sense unique to their domain. The morphology of pure judgment forms (for which Husserl had laid the foundations in *LI* IV) isolates and identifies the formal structures and combinations that allow for "the *mere possibilities of judgments, as judgments*, without inquiry whether they are true or false, or even whether, merely as judgments, they are compatible or contradictory" (*FTL* §13, p.50; also see *LI* 522). As we noted a moment ago, a sign-string which does not conform to these primitive structures, such as the string of signs "all and buts," is not an expression but is nonsense in the strictest sense.

Consequent logic (the logic of noncontradiction) presupposes the primitive sense-constraints identified in pure grammar while attempting to isolate and identify the pure forms of judgment consistency. Here, the expression "p and ~p" is recognized as inconsistent though nevertheless as having a sense. But the sense is *formally* countersensical or absurd (*FTL* §89a). It is formally countersensical because it is formally inconsistent, and it is formally inconsistent because any content whatever could fill in the constant "p" and the expression would remain contradictory. Such an expression has the sense of a contradictory expression, but this sense invalidates itself. But by virtue of the fact that it has a sense it is not non-sense, only absurd and counter-sensical.

Finally, of greatest consequence for us, is Husserl's notion of "truth logic." Truth logic presupposes the constraints of the laws of consequent logic and of the pure forms of judgment (*FTL* §§ 15, 19). This type of logic is the place where logic gears into the world and where the *contents* of expressions play a significant role in determining their sense (*FTL* §90). Here again, since successful judgments at the level of truth logic have necessarily already met the sense requirements of the pure forms of judgment and noncontradiction, unsuccessful judgments at the level of truth logic are ones that are grammatically well-formed and formally consistent, but *materially* incoherent. An instance of such an expression would be the general reference to "a thing which cannot appear." Such an expression would be countersensical because the evidential fulfillment-correlate to the signitive intention "thing" could not be achieved in principle, even though the sense of "thing" demands the possibility of such fulfillment. Here we have what Husserl called *material* countersense, for the *contents* of such a judgment do not sensibly cohere; they issue in a "material contradiction."

These distinctions allow us (1) to isolate nonsense or meaninglessness proper, which refers to sign-strings that do not meet even the primitive pure forms of judgment; (2) to isolate and identify formal absurdity and countersense, which refers to expressions exhibiting contradictory and inconsistent logical form; and (3) to isolate material absurdity and countersense, which refers to expressions whose *content* is contradictory, whose predicate ascription has no senseful relation to its own subject. These distinctions can now help us to understand Husserl's critique of the metaphysical foundations of natural science.

Whereas the depletion of meaning occurs as an event of epistemic-genetic alienation from the signitive-intuitive meaning roots of the life-world, the problem of absurdity can be described as a key source of this alienation stemming from an *interpretatively promoted material countersense* that denies, a priori, intuitive fulfillment to signitive intentions that demand such fulfillment. In other words, whereas the depletion of meaning presupposes a coherent hierarchy of meanings in order for forgetfulness or estrangement from parts of it to occur, absurdity implies that there could never be a coherent material sense of such meanings because material fulfillment for intentions that demand such fulfillment are denied, a priori. In what follows we shall see how the ontological reversal, as a manner of explaining the possibility of the truths of natural science, figures squarely into this form of absurdity.

In *Ideas* Husserl makes indirect reference to the tradition we have considered when he alludes to the problem of absurdity, which threatens natural scientific formulae when they are ontologically interpreted. In section 40 of *Ideas* he refers to the distinction between primary and secondary qualities that divides them into the geometrico-physico objective qualities and the merely subjective qualities of sense experience. This schism between measurable and nonmeasurable qualities severed the nonmeasurable sensuous qualities from the thing (in itself) and relegated them to the function of signs indicating the primary measurable qualities of the real thing — the thing that exists "in itself." This, in turn, promoted the belief that all directly experiential qualities of the bodily object were *mere appearance* and the "mere" was meant in a denigrating sense in contrast to the laudatory sense that accrued to the *actual* physico-mathematical qualities of the "true thing" known through the methods of physical science. Husserl argues, however, that insofar as the "thing" of natural science is defined purely through concepts such as atoms, ions, and energies, whose sole characteristics are those of space-filling mathematical relations, the thing of natural science cannot be the thing of everyday experience because the "thing" of natural science "transcends the whole content of the thing as present to us in bodily form" (p.116). Moreover, this natural scientific "thing" cannot even be the object that appears in the lived-space of everyday experience because this conception would cause it to crumble before the Berkeleian arguments concerning the *experiential* inseparability of primary and secondary qualities.

The cost of maintaining the ontological reading of the conditions for the possibility of natural scientific knowledge, while avoiding the Berkeleian objections, then, is to make the "thing" of natural science a *surd* that now lies outside of all ordinary experience. But for Husserl to make reality into such an ontological surd is, simultaneously, to make our knowledge of it *ab-surd* by blocking, a priori, a type of evidential fulfillment required by the very meaning of "thing." This would occur by making the "thing" nonperceivable in principle. With these difficulties in mind we can begin to see how the problem of absurdity and countersense threatens the very sense of natural scientific formulae.

It is first important to note that in none of his writings does Husserl argue about the *truth* achieved via the symbolic indexing of perceptual entities,[31] nor does he cast doubt on the *value* of such epistemic activity. His criticisms of natural science arise (as we have seen in reference to the *Crisis*) when the symbolic indices of natural scientific formulae are ontologically substituted for the perceptual things that they index. It is because Husserl accepts the validity of natural scientific achievement while rejecting the natural scientific (ontological) interpretation of those achievements that he writes:

> . . . it cannot be the intended meaning of scientific workers (especially when we do not judge them by what they say but by the real significance of their method) that the thing that appears is an illusion or a faulty *image* of the "true" physical thing. Similarly the statement that the apparent determinations are "*signs*" of the true determinations is misleading. (*I* §52, p.143)

What the scientific workers *say* that is wrong is that "the appearances are merely subjective," while what they *do* that is right is to constantly appeal to the appearances in their construction of natural scientific formulae. Husserl is admonishing us, then, to appeal to what the natural scientist does and not to what he says if we are to understand the validity achievements of natural science. For while it is factually obvious that natural scientific formulae are meaningful (though to some extent meaning-depleted), the ontological interpretative reification of these formulae (what the natural scientific worker "says" about them) threatens to make them *absurd* in their very meaning.

Husserl's reasoning in relation to this problem is as follows: if appearing "things" are thought of as merely causally effectuated signs or images for natural scientific things in themselves, then the problem of absurdity arises in natural science (*I* §§ 40, 42, 52) because the "thing" of physics would then be indicated by purely signitive intentions that, a priori, are denied the possibility of intuitive fulfillment. Or, put correlatively, the possibility of a fulfilled perceptual noema would be denied to a noetic act that by its very structure demands some such fulfillment. Under Husserl's correlational theory of meaning, the cognitive value of such *inevitably empty acts* would be zero if these acts were inevitably empty throughout the entire range of the hierarchy of evidences. In such a case cognition would face an absurdity similar to that of someone trying to gain intuitive insight into the notion of a "round-square." In fact, Husserl uses just this analogy when he says that the idea of a thing in itself is countersensical and that the idea of any such "thing" is just as valid as that of a round-square (*I* §55, p.153).

The expression "round-square," though meaningful because it can be thought (as a purely, but inevitably empty, signitive intention), could never have a fulfilled meaning because in an a priori manner the notion denies the possibility of fulfillment. Analogously, Husserl believes that a "thing," by definition and in principle, is a perceivable entity and consequently the notion contains within itself the implication of an a priori possibility of being perceived (*LI* 791; *I* §§ 43, 52, 53). But if the signitive-intention "thing" implies the a priori possibility of perception (this is an essential part of the material sense of "thing") and simultaneously the "real thing" is defined by natural science as pure corporeality severed from all perceivable qualities, then we have an absurd situation in which it is impossible a priori to fulfill the meaning of a meaningful term!

In *Ideas*, in response to the natural scientific tradition and the inherited realistic reifying naturalism of his day, Husserl began to reject the idea of the "thing of physics," the purely corporeal thing in itself, precisely because it was *not* capable of being perceived. He begins, in numerous contexts, to insist that "corporeal Being is in principle a Being that appears, declaring itself through sensory perspectives" (*I* §53, p.150). Given this claim, he maintains that "it is thus a fundamental error to suppose that perception . . . fails to come into contact with the thing-itself . . . [;] it belongs to the meaning . . . of a thing . . . to be perceivable . . ." (*I* §43, p.124). Whence, the beginning of Husserl's conscious rejection of the metaphysical presuppositions of natural science. This rejection was essentially connected to his turn to transcendental-phenomenological idealism, which in its turn motivated his revisionary critique of the philosophy of natural reductive science.

To summarize: the ontological reversal is seen by Husserl as a tendency in naturalistic thought to replace and explain (away) the thing of appearances (that is, the thing of the life-world) by the mathematically substructed, purely material thing in itself of natural science. By appealing to a transcendent domain, with the aid of a causal inference, scientists began to view the thing itself as an epiphenomenon of the thing *in* itself. As early as the *Logical Investigations* Husserl had called this postulation of a transcendent material realm "the metaphysical presupposition of natural science" (*LI* 59), and although he ignored this realm in the phenomenological analyses of the *Logical Investigations*, he also seemed to give this domain some degree of credence because he *delimited* phenomenology in relation to it (*LI* 264).[32]

In *The Idea of Phenomenology* and then more clearly in *Ideas*, however, Husserl begins to reject the metaphysical presuppositions of the sciences of nature; for the first time, he explicitly puts them "out of play" with the phenomenological epoche due to his suspicion that if we are to overcome the problems of physicalistic rationalism, they must be so neutralized. But this neutralization poses a new problem, this time for the practicing phenomenologist. In *The Idea of Phenomenology* Husserl broaches this problem when he writes that:

> All cognition of the natural sort . . . is cognition which makes its object transcendent. It posits objects as existent, claims to reach matters of fact which are not "strictly given to it," are not "immanent" to it . . . . So the question is: how can the mental process . . . transcend itself? . . . How can cognition posit something as existing that is not directly and truly given in it? (pp. 27-28)

In the next section of this chapter we will note how the ontological reversal has made the riddle of transcendence "the central problem of the critique of cognition" (*IP* 28).

3.4
THE RIDDLE OF COGNITION AND THE TRANSCENDENCE OF THE WORLD

In section 2.4 it was noted how the traditional empiricists had responded to the philosophy of natural science by postulating a self-enclosed domain of subjectivity correlative to the purely corporeal domain of natural science. Although this psychic domain was postulated by both Locke and Hume as a complementary abstraction to the purely corporeal domain of natural science, the complementary abstraction soon swallowed up its natural scientific exemplar. Owing to his continuing implicit insistence on the need for a purely material world to account for experience, the result of this, in Hume's epistemology, was a radical skepticism that "shook the foundations of objectivism." Indeed, as Husserl never tired of pointing out, it shook the foundations of philosophy itself by shaking the belief in philosophy as foundational science. The problem that caused this crisis in philosophy was "transcendence," dubbed by Husserl "the riddle of cognition" (*IP* 26-27). On Husserl's view, the problem emerged from the empiricist tradition because the empirical arguments for representational realism, which were themselves motivated by the unexamined presuppositions of natural science, left it unclear how cognition could reach the objective domain.

Surrounding Husserl's criticisms of traditional empiricistic and positivistic philosophies is his more general criticism of the naturalistic attempt to deal with the problem of cognition in the guise of a natural scientific epistemology. Any epistemology that either bases itself upon or models itself after the natural sciences would be an example of this. About such approaches to the problem of knowledge Husserl had written, "To follow the model of the natural sciences almost inevitably means to reify consciousness— something that from the very beginning leads us into absurdity . . ." (*PRS* 103). All such natural scientific attempts in epistemology, he argues, commit a *petitio principii*. For instance, ". . . the favorite ploy of basing the theory of knowledge on the psychology of cognition and biology" (*IP* 19) inevitably assumes the existence of the transcendencies integral to these natural sciences. But the possibility of the cognition of such transcendencies is precisely the fundamental question to be resolved! To explain our understanding of the world by an appeal to the world that we (think we) understand is to beg the essential questions of epistemology. Whenever the results of natural scientific thinking are appealed to in order to explain the truth or validity of our cognitions, the truth and validity of these cognitions are already presupposed. Consequently, Husserl argues throughout his career that philosophy, as radical epistemology, must be fundamentally different from all naturalistic types of investigation.

This point returns like a leit-motif in Husserl's epistemology; at one point he writes, ". . . it is nonsensical not only at the start but also in general to borrow from the sphere of transcendence, in other words, to try to found the theory of cognition on psychology or on any science whatever of the natural sort" (*IP* 26). And in *Philosophy as Rigorous Science* he refers to "the absurdity of a theory of knowledge based upon natural science . . ." (p.88). Later in his career, in *Formal and Transcendental Logic*, Husserl ties this problematic to the tradition we traced in Chapter 2. He there criticizes the Cartesian tendency to reify consciousness as the *res cogitans*, the tendency to make of the self a substantial reality. He argues that:

> . . . a realism that [starts] from this first real [the reified ego], projects hypotheses and probability-inferences to carry it over into a realm of transcendent realities . . . [but] such a realism *misses the actual problem and does so in a countersensical manner*, since everywhere it presupposes as a possibility that which, as a possibility, is itself everywhere in question." (§93, p.228)[33]

Nevertheless, Husserl argues, even if we should allow the *petitio principii* that inevitably occurs when naturalistic modes of thought attempt to epistemologize, the riddle of cognition would still remain untouched:

> . . . *the theory of knowledge can never be based upon any science of the natural sort, no matter what the more specific nature of that*

science may be. [To show this] we ask: What will our opponent do with his transcendent knowledge? We put freely at his disposal the entire stock of transcendent truths contained in the objective sciences, and we take it that those truths are not altered by the emergence of the puzzle of how a science of the transcendent is possible. What will he now do with his all-embracing knowledge? How does he think he can go from the "that" to the "how"? That he knows for a fact that cognition of the transcendent is actual guarantees as logically obvious that cognition of the transcendent is possible. [But] can he solve it even if he presupposes all the sciences, all or any cognition of the transcendent? (*IP* 29)

Husserl's answer here is obviously "no"; and, at this point, his position should recall the transcendental idealism of Kant. Husserl, unlike Descartes and Hume, does not ask, "What do I know?" Rather, like Kant, he says, "This is what I know. Now, *how* do I know it?" But Husserl realizes that the "this" *that* I know cannot help me to understand *how* I know it, at least not as long as these facts refer to radical transcendencies. He thus continues his rhetorical questions:

Consider: What more does he really need? That cognition of the transcendent is possible he takes for granted, even as analytically certain in saying to himself, there is in my case knowledge of the transcendent. What he lacks is obvious. He is unclear about the relation to transcendence. He is unclear about the "reaching the transcendent" which is ascribed to cognition, to knowledge. Where and how can he achieve clarity? . . . As long as the object is, and remains, something transcendent, and cognition and its objects are actually separate, then . . . his hopes for reaching a solution . . . by way of falling back on transcendent presuppositions are patent folly. (*IP* 29-30)

The riddle of cognition may now be given new light by referring back to Figure I.

While natural scientific explanation functions to explain the physicalistic actuality of phenomena by arguing that domain A is the source, cause, and reality of domain B, it can go no distance towards explaining the cognizing or knowing of the objective domain. That is, it does not and cannot explain how component 6 of our figure is a possibility without begging the fundamental questions of epistemology, the questions concerning the achievement and the validity of our knowledge of transcendencies. Indeed, the naturalistic prejudice towards physical causality as the *modus explanans sine qua non* makes such an explanation all but impossible and makes its possibility incomprehensible. It was just this dilemma, Husserl suggests (*IP* 30), that led Descartes to postulate potentially subsisting innate ideas that were *causally* activated by the realm of pure corporeality.[34]

But this proposed solution to the problem of knowledge is actually an escalation of the naturalistic fallacy because it now appeals to transcendencies in both domains. The one set consists of purely material causal forces; and the other, of potentially subsisting innate ideas. Thus, by Husserl's lights, the problem of knowledge remains untouched, and untouchable *in principle*, by what he sees as the apologetic epistemologies based upon the sciences of nature. Let us now develop another perspective on Husserl's position here.

In the *Logical Investigations* Husserl had spoken of the sciences that require "explanatory metaphysical hypotheses" for theoretical completion (p.59). There, he did not reject such hypotheses as absurd or even problematic, but he did consciously abstain from appealing to any such hypotheses in his own phenomenological explications of conscious life (pp. 263-66). On the other hand, Husserl's teacher, Franz Brentano, had explicitly accepted the metaphysical presuppositions of the natural scientific tradition and taken the position that the real object was the object of physics. The metaphysically postulated world was considered by him to be *the real*, while the object that appeared was the intentional object, yet an object still conceived to be causally effectuated by the object in itself of physics. Indeed, Brentano had made it a point to insist that:

> The *phenomena* of light, sound, heat, spatial location and locomotion which [the natural scientist] studies are not things which really and truly exist. They are *signs* of something real, which, through its causal activity, produces presentations of them. They are not, however, an

adequate representation of this reality, and they give us knowledge of it only in a very incomplete sense. We can say that there exists something which, under certain conditions, causes this or that sensation. We can probably also prove that there must be relations among these realities similar to those which are manifested by spatial phenomena of shapes and sizes. But this is as far as we can go. *We have no experience of that which truly exists, in and of itself, and that which we so experience does not truly exist.*[35] (Emphasis mine; with translation changes.)

Husserl's criticisms of sign and image theories of perception that we considered earlier can now be seen, in part, as aimed at his own mentor because Brentano, too, had accepted the metaphysical postulations of the natural scientific tradition. Indeed, this early influence helps explain the continuity exhibited between Husserl's earliest writings where he did not explicitly consider the historical and metaphysical foundations of natural science and his later writings where he did. From the start, he had inherited this tainted history, at the very least, osmotically.

Brentano's position may be read from the following variant of Figure 1:[36]

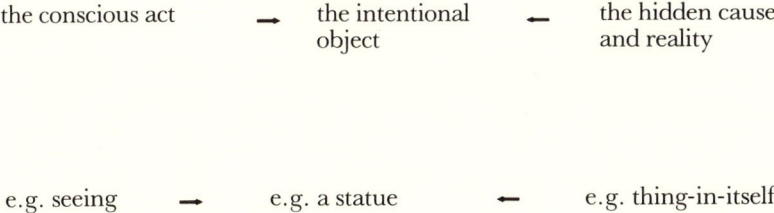

| the conscious act | → | the intentional object | ← | the hidden cause and reality |

| e.g. seeing | → | e.g. a statue | ← | e.g. thing-in-itself |

Figure 2

If we recall that Brentano was working primarily qua psychologist, and not qua philosopher, in *Psychology from an Empirical Standpoint*, it is understandable why the "hidden cause" remained an unknown in Brentano's work without it seeming to bother him. As a natural scientific psychologist the realm of objective reality had to be retained as a naturalistically presupposed cause. For Brentano the descriptive psychologist, however, outer perception thereby became a *Falschnehmung* by definition; it functioned to provide a sign that something was "out there," though this sign provided no real correspondence between intellect and thing.

For Brentano intentionality provided no bridge between cognition and reality. "Intentionality" was a working concept limited to the immanent psychological sphere alone. And, most bizarre, the bridge between cognition and reality was again believed to come from the side of "reality"; and again, it was presumed to be a corporeally effectuated causal bridge! This is why Brentano can be legitimately spoken of as an epistemological realist and a psychological idealist; and why, after complimenting him for his rediscovery of intentionality, Husserl writes, "Unfortunately, in the most essential matters he remained bound to the prejudices of the naturalistic tradition . . . " (*C* §68, p.234).

With these new perspectives in mind, it should now be easy to see how the ontological reversal is related to the great "riddle of cognition" — the transcendence of the world. As Husserl's philosophy developed so did his notions of "immanence" and "transcendence."[37] These concepts came to possess an internal dynamic relationship that demands constant recognition if we are to understand Husserl's critique of the natural scientific metaphysics. Within the overall context of his thought there are two significations for each of these notions, and at one point the meanings intersect.

Throughout most, if not all, of his career Husserl accepted the concept of immance (immanence$_1$), which allowed for some psychical content to be "in" consciousness. Examples of this would be sensations, feelings, and in general kinaesthetic experiences of consciousness (*LI* 309-10, 569-76,

861-62). These contents of body-consciousness were said to be really (*reell*) in consciousness and, once synthesized, were said to allow for the appearances of an object (*LI* 310, 861; *I* §41, p.119). More important for our purposes, however, is the "immanence of the transcendent" (immanence$_2$), which refers to the appearances of objects of which we are conscious even while these appearances are not contained "in" consciousness as are apples in a sack (*LI* 861). This immanence$_2$ refers to that which appears immediately to consciousness in its everyday life as the "multiple manners of appearance" of a thing (*FTL* §61, p.163). Yet, as intentionally implicative of objects themselves, such appearances are experienced as outside of consciousness. That is, they are real *for* but not really *in* consciousness (*I* §41, p.118; *FTL* §62, p.166).

It is this second kind of immanence, immanence-in-transcendence, that forces Husserl to recognize that the concept of transcendence is an ambiguous one (*IP* 27; *FTL* §62, p.166), because the first meaning of transcendence (transcendence$_1$) refers to the same experience, though with different emphasis, as does immanence$_2$. Transcendence$_1$ refers to the one identical object qua appearance that stands over against consciousness while it is, nonetheless, simply the flipside of the synthetic functionings of consciousness (*LI* 310, 861; *I* §42, p.122; *FTL* §61, p.164). Intentionally speaking, however, this object-appearance is not "in" consciousness in the sense of immanence$_1$, nor even in the sense of an "implicative appearance" as per immanence$_2$. It is not a sensation nor even just an implicative appearance, but simply the appearance *of a thing* (*LI* 310, 861; *I* §41, p.119). Here we might note that the famous concept of "intentionality" refers particularly to a melding of immance$_2$ and transcendence$_1$.

Finally, transcendence$_2$, as might be guessed by now, is where the riddle of cognition becomes acute (though it is also an issue for transcendence$_1$ and immanence$_2$). Transcendence$_2$ refers, for example, to the transcendent object of natural science, which has been postulated as the correlate of natural scientific knowledge (*I* §41, p.117, §47, p.133, §52, pp.146-48). This means that transcendence$_2$, as an epistemic event, refers to the natural scientific thing in itself which *in principle* does not and cannot appear to consciousness, while, nonetheless, it is systematically appealed to, to explain the coherent succession of perceptions that do appear to consciousness (in the experiences of $immanence_1$, $immanence_2$ and $transcendence_1$) (*I*§47, p.133). Husserl refers to this "thing" as the "thing" of objective Nature as opposed to the thing referred to in $immanence_2$-$transcendence_1$, the thing of everyday experience.

The different notions of immanence and transcendence line up as shown in Figure 2.

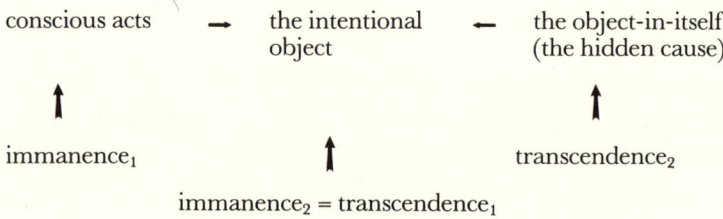

Figure 3

In relation to Figure 1, they would be portrayed in the following way:

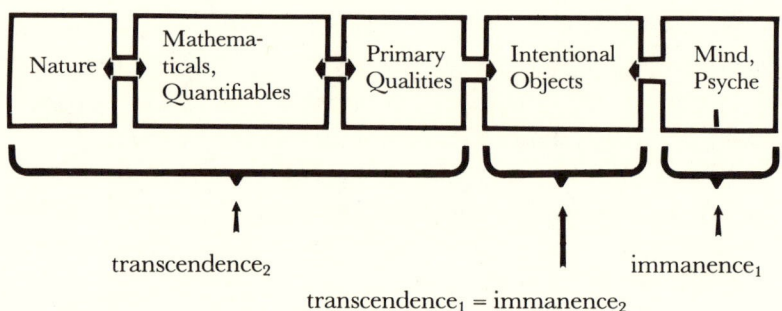

Figure 4

Husserl's distinctions may be further clarified by comparing Figure 4 to Figure 1. Component 6 of Figure 1 is left off in Figure 4 because we now see that it is precisely component 6 that indicates the *problem* of transcendence. For reasons we have noted, Husserl rejects the naturalistic/theological "resolution" to the riddle proposed by Descartes and his followers. In fact, with his arguments pointing to the a priori impossibility of naturalistic attempts to resolve the problem, Husserl seems to have believed that the problem itself was never clearly grasped, and hence was never given its proper solution. The change of component 4 in Figure 4 in relation to Figure 1 occurs because of Husserl's belief that the idea of "secondary qualities" was already a fiction based upon the natural scientific metaphysics (*C* §9, p.30, n. *). The postulation of these secondary qualities was just another instance of the so-called radical empiricism gone rationalistic. Finally, for similar reasons, the causal arrow connecting components 4 and 5 is now changed to the arrow of intentionality, which indicates the most primordial instance of consciousness in transcendence.

3.5
OVERVIEW

A very general overview of the argument of this chapter can now be given.

Since the highest level objectivities (symbolic meaning systems) necessarily occur as symbolic formulae, a gradual alienation between these formulae and the origin of their meanings in signitive-intuitive correlations tends to occur. Owing to the technologies of cognition these higher level objectivities can be effectively cognized and *used* without reactivating the hierarchically interconnected processes and layers of evidence that make them valid as interpretations of our experience. This covering-over can occur in an individual person's life or in an expansive social-historical development. Whenever such forgetting of the sources of our meanings occurs, the higher level objectivities appear as possessing an awesome aura of power. This occurs because they seem to stand disconnected over and above the flux of appearances in which we live our daily lives, while still managing to explain these appearances. Probably because of this, they came to be correlated with, and then conflated with, true Being qua objects in themselves. These higher level objectivities were then believed to literally *re-present* a transformation of a phenomenon into its "true self." The postulated "true thing" or "domain of the real" became the *modus explanans* for all that appeared, that is, for all phenomena prior to "transformation." This transformation of effect for cause we have called "the ontological reversal."

Finally, because of the ontological reversal, the riddle of cognition arose: if all objectivity is transcendent objectivity, then how is knowledge of objective truths possible? How, in particular, is natural scientific truth possible? These are the problems that continually motivated Husserl's phenomenology after 1905.

NOTES

1. Aron Gurwitsch credits his student Lester Embree for the neologism "proto-logic." Gurwitsch correctly points out that the term is more explicit in conveying the logicality inherent to everyday experience than is Husserl's own term, "prepredicative experience" (*vorprädicative Erfahrung*). Gurwitsch, *Phenomenology and the Theory of Science*, p. 30, n. 48.

2. To my knowledge Husserl never explicitly uses the locution "transformation of phenomena," but his criticisms of the ontological interpretation of nature are in reference to the idea of literal transformation. (See, for instance, the general comments on this process made by Husserl and Burtt on p. 19 above.) The locution, like that of "primitive facts," is borrowed from J. Needleman, *Being-in-the-World*, p. 32ff.

3. Jacob Needleman extends Husserl's analysis in his introduction to Ludwig Binswanger's work. We are borrowing from Needleman and extending the analysis still further.

4. Needleman, *Being-in-the-World*, p. 156.

5. c. 1880-1950. See, e.g., Duane Schultz, *A History of Modern Psychology* (New York: Academic Press, 1975), pp. 7-11. Since the 1950's a gradual merging of behavioristic and functionalistic psychologies has occurred, providing a relatively stable, if not totally satisfactory, paradigm for psychology.

6. I believe that the interpretative theme of the analyses that follow could be applied to all the major schools of psychology if one were to evaluate their attempts to make psychology a natural science. Though we cannot do so here, this would prove a very interesting and enlightening study of the necessary sacrifices that any "science of the psychic" must make in order to become a *natural* science.

7. This brief analysis will focus upon the founding of behaviorism in the works of John B. Watson. In the more recent work of B. F. Skinner the emphasis on the "objective realm" is maintained while the reduction to "inner" physicalistic causes is not. See, e.g., Skinner's *Science and Human Behavior* (New York: The Free Press, 1953), pp. 27-29.

8. John B. Watson, *Behaviorism* (New York: W. W. Norton & Company, Inc., 1970), p. 11.

9. Sigmund Freud, *Introductory Lectures on Psychoanalysis* (New York: W. W. Norton & Company, Inc., 1977), p. 40.

10. Sigmund Freud, *An Outline of Psycho-Analysis* (New York: W. W. Norton & Company, Inc., 1969), p. 5.

11. Sigmund Freud, "Instincts and Their Vicissitudes," contained in *A General Selection to the Works of Sigmund Freud*, ed. by John Rickman, M.D. (New York: Doubleday Anchor, 1957), p. 71.

12. Sigmund Freud, *Introductory Lectures*, pp. 275, 356, 374-75, 378, 418.

13. Sigmund Freud, *Introductory Lectures*, pp. 374-75.

14. Sigmund Freud, *Introductory Lectures*, p. 402.

15. Sigmund Freud, *The Standard Edition of the Complete Psychological Works of Sigmund Freud*, ed. by James Strachey (London: The Hogarth Press, 24 vols., 1953-1974), v. 1, p. 295.

16. Wolfgang Köhler, *Gestalt Psychology* (New York: Mentor Books, 1975), p. 39.

17. Köhler, *Gestalt Psychology*, p. 39.

18. Köhler, *Gestalt Psychology*, p. 40.

19. In this discussion of "objectivity" we shall not mention its most essential facet for Husserl; namely, intersubjectivity. For our purposes the "objects" of objectivity (or, noematically phrased, the correlates of objectifying acts) are of primary importance.

20. This position comes into conflict with the beliefs of operationalists and instrumentalists, and Husserl himself may have problems in relation to some of his own doctrines here. We will consider these problems in Ch. 5 §5.2(c)-(d).

21. The meanings inherent to the term "objectivity" change somewhat for Husserl throughout his philosophical development. In his earlier writings, while still "transcendentally naive," he tends to presuppose the naturalistic conception just stated. Consequently, early on, phenomenology is only a descriptive psychology (*LI* 262). After the turn to phenomenological transcendental idealism, however, roughly with the appearance of *IP* in 1907 and *I* in 1913, "objectivity" came to be understood as a constituted sense within the domain of subjectivity. With this development phenomenology becomes "universal philosophy," part of which deals with science, its objects, and its degree of objectivity.

22. Michael Polanyi, *The Tacit Dimension* (New York: Anchor Books, 1967). Also see Polanyi's *Personal Knowledge: Towards a Post-Critical Philosophy* (Harper Torchbooks, 1964). In the preface to the Torchbooks edition Polanyi makes explicit reference to the background of this notion in phenomenology (p. x).

23. We will develop Husserl's theory of meaning only insofar as is needed to understand the manner in which the issues of technization, sedimentation, and the depletion of meaning relate to the crisis in the sciences. For a more thorough development of Husserl's theory of meaning see J. N. Mohanty, *Edmund Husserl's Theory of Meaning* (The Hague: Martinus Nijhoff, 1969).

24. A complete phenomenological history of mathematics would trace each occurrence of method transformation that motivated the depletion of meaning and would thus help to restore meaning to the results of these methodological achievements. This restoration of meaning would be achieved by the revelation of the relation of each method of transformation to its methodological progenitor until eventually these methods were reconnected to the life-world and the original transformation of phenomena. For an instance of work along these lines see John J. Drummond, "The Perceptual Roots of Geometric Idealizations," *Review of Metaphysics* 37 (June 1984): 785-810.

25. Note that these historically and socially induced conditions of *Selbstverstandlichkeit* are very much like those made famous by Thomas Kuhn, *The Structure of Scientific Revolutions* (Chicago and London: University of Chicago Press, 1970), Ch. III and V.

26. It is this line of thought, from this essay, that activated Derrida's thought in *Of Grammatology*, trans. by Gayatri Chakr-

vorty Spivak (Baltimore & London: The Johns Hopkins University Press, 1976). Also see Derrida's introduction to his translation of Husserl's work, *Edmund Husserl's L'Origine de la géométrie* (Paris: Presses Universitaires de France, 1962); and his *Speech and Phenomena*, trans. by David B. Allison (Evanston: Northwestern University Press, 1973).

27. While there are some problems with Husserl's assumptions about the value of genetic versus static phenomenology that revolve around this point, I will not develop them here. For a statement of them see my essay "Husserl's Phenomenology and Possible Worlds Semantics: A Reexamination," *Husserl Studies* 3 (1986): 191-207, esp. pp. 198-200.

28. On this theme see David Carr, *Phenomenology and the Problem of History*, esp. Chs. 5, 6, and 7. The concerns of this work overlap with Carr's at various points. However, whereas he is chiefly concerned with the problems *of* history for Husserlian phenomenology, our chief concern is with the relation of Husserl's phenomenology *to* the problems *in* this history. (See §4.5 below for a comparison of the present work with Carr's.)

29. This introduction was actually written by the editor of *EJ*, Ludwig Landgrebe, who was Husserl's assistant at the time most of the work was composed. Husserl, however, gave his full approval to this introduction. See editor's foreword, p. 7.

30. Carr, *Phenomenology and the Problem of History*, p. 123.

31. Hans Wagner makes a problem of Husserl's silence on this point in his essay, "Husserl's Ambiguous Philosophy of Science," *The Southwestern Journal of Philosophy*, trans. by J. N. Mohanty, v. 5, no. 3 (1974): 169-86.

32. Husserl's gradual evolution away from this limited concept of phenomenology parallels his growing understanding of the scope of the phenomenological epoche and reduction. For two readings of Husserl along these developmental lines see Theodore De Boer, *The Development of Husserl's Thought*; and, Philip J. Bossert, *The Origins and Early Development of Edmund Husserl's Method of Phenomenological Reduction*. Also see Ch. 4, §4.2 of this work.

33. Husserl's argument here is developed by Suzanne Cunningham in her defense of Husserl against Rorty's insinuation that he is a representational realist [*Synthese* 66 (1986): 273-89]. Another well-developed statement of Husserl's criticisms of naturalistic epistemologies can be found in James R. Mensch, *The Question of Being in Husserl's Logical Investigations* (The Hague: Martinus Nijhoff, 1981), pp. 18-25.

34. Descartes, *Philosophical Works*, pp. 442-43.

35. Franz Brentano, *Psychology from an Empirical Standpoint* trans. by Antos C. Rancurello, D. B. Terrell, and Linda L. McAlister (New York, Humanities Press, 1973), p. 19. I add emphasis to the word "phenomena" here because Brentano is referring to light qua color, sound qua auditory effect, etc. (See *PES* at p. 19, n. 11. Also pp. 9, 19, 47, 48, 60, 67, 70, 98, and 107.) Throughout *Psychology from an Empirical Standpoint* Brentano's phrase "physical phenomena" is problematic because, as we have argued and as Brentano recognizes, the "purely" physical is precisely *not* the phenomenal.

36. This figure is a slight modification of Theodore De Boer's in *The Development of Husserl's Thought*, p. 42. My analysis of the relation between Husserl and Brentano owes much to De Boer's work.

37. For an extended reading of this development see Rudolf Boehm, *Vom Gesichtspunkt der Phänomenologie* (The Hague: Martinus Nijhoff, 1968), pp. 141-85.

4

EPOCHE AND REDUCTION

IT IS WELL KNOWN THAT from the time of *Ideas* the problem of the "way into phenomenology" became crucial for Husserl.[1] If a way into phenomenology could not be clearly explicated, then the hopes for a pure phenomenology would not be fulfilled. Hence, Husserl had proffered or suggested at least five ways into phenomenology by the end of his working life. These were "the Cartesian way" (*I*), "the way from psychology" (*C* III B), "the way from the pregiven life-world" (*C* III A), "the way from logic" (*FTL*), and, rarely mentioned, "the way through the critique of the positive sciences" (*EP* 259-74). These last three ways have been collated and called the "way from ontology,"[2] because the regional or material ontologies of the natural sciences and the formal ontologies of logic and mathematics are derived, in Husserl's view, from the fundamental ontology of the *Lebenswelt*. Hence, all these can be referred to as "ontological ways."

In any case, none of these paths into phenomenology was ever considered an outrightly mistaken path by Husserl, though, as a perpetual beginner, he was never fully satisfied with his articulation of any of them. It is perhaps for this reason that he continually searched for new ways into phenomenology. David Carr has even suggested that we might be tempted to speak of "the historical way" into phenomenology.[3] Whenever he suggests this, however, he immediately denies it as a real possibility by insisting that the implications of historical reflection constitute a *necessary fore-investigation* for all and any "ways" into phenomenology.[4] We shall argue, for reasons inherent to the entire project of this text, however, that Carr's position needs to be modified on this point, and that the historical approach of the *Crisis* is a satisfactory way into phenomenology in that it provides the *raison d'être* for transcendental phenomenology. The relation of the position developed in this text to Carr's position shall be dealt with in section 4.5 of this chapter.

Husserl's disenchantment with the most famous and most often used path into phenomenology — "the Cartesian way" (*C* §43) — has also been noted by Carr and others.[5] The reasons for this disenchantment were, we will argue, due more to Husserl's own initial lack of clarity on the "ways" into phenomenology than to an inherent deficiency of the Cartesian way itself. Indeed, it is not only true that each of the ways into phenomenology is compatible with the others, but also that if the "Cartesian way" is read as *essentially connected* with both the historical way and the way from natural science, the Cartesian way becomes much more comprehensible because it is then seen to be motivated — even in Descartes — by the historical problems we have traced. In this chapter, we shall attempt to demonstrate the truth of these claims by showing how the natural scientific way, the historical way, and the Cartesian way combine to provide a more comprehensible way into phenomenology.

Since we have followed the historical analyses of the metaphysical foundations of the natural scientific tradition and discovered the problems evoked by these foundations, and since it was Descartes himself who ultimately laid these foundations, thereby creating the problems they evoke, we are, then, in a perfect position to use the historical way, the natural scientific way, and the Cartesian way as our entrance into pure phenomenology. Such an entrance will give us a fuller sense of Husserl's phenomenological epoche and its corresponding reduction, while it simultaneously provides us with the beginnings of the reconstructive aspect of Husserl's critique of natural reductive science.

Moreover, if our suggested way is convincing, we should be able to see that while the critical position that David Carr develops in *Phenomenology and the Problem of History* is acceptable as a critical evaluation of the problem that history poses *for* phenomenology, it is nonetheless incomplete in its recognition of the *positive light* that the historical analyses of the *Crisis* can cast upon Husserl's lifelong project *of* phenomenology.

The positive light these historical analyses cast upon Husserl's phenomenology will be developed in section 4.4 of this chapter, where we will attempt to provide a fresh perspective on the phenomenological epoche and its associated reductions. This perspective is actually one suggested by Husserl in numerous places, though never clearly developed by him, and largely suppressed or forgotten by Husserl's followers. Along the lines hinted at by Husserl we will suggest that on the basis of our historical analyses we make two explicit acts of epoche and reduction of what has often been called the first epoche and reduction—the phenomenological reduction. This procedure will involve making an explicit distinction between the suspension of natural scientific Reality and the natural scientific attitude that goes with it, and natural reality and the natural attitude at which Husserl more generally aims the epoche and reduction. This strategy can be justified by the development of Husserl's thought, and, more importantly, by the fact that it offers a clearer view of the nature and aims of Husserl's phenomenological methods.

4.1
HUSSERL'S ANALYSIS OF DESCARTES' SIGNIFICANCE

The meditations on history that first emerged in *Erste Philosophie*, and then later in the *Crisis*, led Husserl to an explicit recognition of the dual role played by Descartes in determining the sense of modern intellectual history. Descartes was the primal founder not only of the modern idea of objectivistic rationalism, but also of the transcendental motif that explodes it (*C* §16). With this claim Husserl means to suggest that Descartes was simultaneously shocked by the visions of the objectivistic domain *and* the transcendental domain. On Husserl's view, however, Descartes erred when he went on to justify the latter domain by an appeal to the former. But before he did this, Husserl argues, he had already suggested why the objective domain could never suffice as a mode of epistemic justification for the truth achievements of natural science. Husserl hints at this point by writing that at the very moment that Descartes inaugurated the idea of a universal philosophy modeled after a universal physicalistic mathematics, he also inaugurated the perspective that would ruin this model — and he inaugurated it precisely in order to justify the model! The perspective was that of transcendental philosophy which, Husserl claims, seemed to follow "a hidden teleology of history" that would eventually uproot the very physicalistic rationalism that it was initially planted to protect (*C* §16, p.74).

We have already seen how this hidden teleology "exploded" in the absurdity of Hume's skepticism, and how this explosion grew out of Hume's original acceptance of "unknown causes," such as those of physicalistic rationalism. When this original acceptance of causes that are unexperienceable in principle had to be rejected, the entire edifice of physicalistic rationalism seemed to crumble with it. But now let us backtrack in history once again and see how Descartes played the double role the grounding of all knowledge (*CM* §8; *C* §17). But most important for Husserl, the transcendental domain only emerged with his relation to the objectivistic domain.

Husserl now argues that the traditional distinction between "empiricism" and "rationalism" gives the history of philosophy a false sense. He claims, instead, that the true sense of modern spiritual history lies in the struggle between objectivism and transcendentalism (*C* §14). The dual role played by Descartes in the historical development of philosophy can be seen in this light: he was a champion of both perspectives.

Husserl locates Descartes' discovery of the transcendental domain in the first two *Meditations*, especially in *Meditation II* (*EP* 63-70; *CM* §§1-2; *C* §17), where Descartes returns to the transcendental ego as the apodictic Archimedean point for the grounding of all knowledge (*CM* §8; *C* §17). But most important for Husserl, the transcendental domain only emerged in its concrete fullness with Descartes' recognition that the *cogito* was always given as a relation to *cogitata* (*CM* §8; *PL* 12, 14; *C* §§ 17, 50). The importance of this discovery cannot be overemphasized because here we have in inchoate form the original signitive-intention/intuitive-fulfillment theme, the original noetic-noematic theme, and the recognition that consciousness is always consciousness of something — that is, that consciousness is essentially intentional (*C* §20). In short, according to Husserl, in the *Second Meditation* Descartes gains the first glimpse of the *correlational a priori* for all possible meaning, and by Husserl's lights, for all possible knowledge as well.

Husserl calls Descartes' suspension of belief in objectified validities the "Cartesian epoche," and depicts the corresponding discovery of the correlational a priori when he writes that ". . . during the universal epoche, the absolutely apodictic self-evidence 'I am' is at my disposal. But within this self-evidence a great deal is comprised. A more concrete version of the self-evident statement *sum cogitans* is: *ego cogito — cogitata qua cogitata*" (*C* §17, p.77). The importance of this extension of emphasis is extreme for Husserl because it makes it explicit that:

> In the epoche, all . . . determinations, and *the world itself*, have been transformed into my *ideae*; they are inseparable components of my *cogitationes*, precisely as their *cogitata*. Thus here we would have, included under the title "ego," an absolutely apodictic sphere of being rather than merely the one axiomatic proposition *ego cogito* or *sum cogitans*. (*C* §17, p.78)

Throughout his writings after the transcendental turn in *Ideas*, Husserl also makes this point more generally and more radically by writing that "the epoche changes nothing in the world" (*PL* 12) and that after applying the epoche "[w]e have literally lost nothing, but [rather] have won the whole of Absolute Being" (*I* §50, p.140).

The notion which Husserl understands to emerge in *Meditation II*, when Descartes claims that seeing and thinking that one sees amount to the same thing, is the idea of transcendence in immanence. This is the idea indicated by transcendence$_1$ and immanence$_2$, given in Figures III and IV, which are indicative of indubitable givens insofar as they are referred to *as and only as* they are given. And, when Descartes claims, also in *Meditation II*, that any object of immanent-transcendence tells me about me as well as about it, Husserl sees the first inchoate recognition of the correlational a priori for all possible meaning and experience. With this latter position of Descartes all the world becomes the world-for-me, all experience becomes *my* experience. For Husserl this is the beginning of a methodological procedure that would deem it necessary to base all ontology upon epistemology and all epistemology upon phenomenology. Simultaneously, by virtue of the epoche, all phenomenology becomes transcendental "egology." The power of this discovery lies in understanding the world as a correlate of consciousness.

Husserl had recognized this vast range of the Cartesian sphere early on. For instance, in the *Logical Investigations* he had written that:

> Not only is it self-evident that I am: self-evidence also attaches to countless judgments of the form *I perceive this or that*, where I not merely think, but am also self-evidently assured, that what I perceive is given as I think of it, that I apprehend the thing itself, and for what it is—this pleasure, e.g., that fills me, this phantasm of the mind that floats before me, etc. All these judgments share the lot of the judgment 'I am' . . . . (p.544)

The "Cartesian Epoche," then, promotes confinement to and immersion in the *certainty of seeming*. This domain is not really "confined," however, for it refers to the vast domain of immanently transcendent experience (immanence$_{1-2}$ and transcendence$_1$) as it is had by the perceiving and conceiving consciousness. Eventually, in *Ideas*, Husserl makes this point when he writes that ". . . the world as *immediately* given me, through spontaneous tendencies to turn towards it and grasp it, are included under the one Cartesian expression: *cogito*"

(§28, p.93). For the individual experiencing, the range of this cogito is the range of the world.

This transcendental domain that we have termed the "certainty of seeming" is called "certain" because all that is given here is taken *as and only as* it is given, only *as* consciousness experiences it, while it is "seeming" because what is given is taken *as* a doxically indexed appearance and *may or may not* refer to a reality beyond. However, it is precisely this *idea* of a "reality beyond" that led Descartes away from his great discovery and thus resulted in his failure to make the transcendental turn (*CM* §10; *FTL* §93; *C* §§18-19). Husserl locates the source of this failure in Descartes' physicalistic presuppositions: "Descartes himself presupposed an ideal of science, the ideal approximated by geometry and mathematical natural science. As a fateful prejudice this ideal determines philosophies for centuries and hiddenly determines the *Meditations* themselves" (*CM* §3, p.7). Somewhat later in his own "Meditations," Husserl refers back to this point and writes:

> Unfortunately these prejudices were at work when Descartes introduced the apparently insignificant but actually fateful change whereby the ego becomes a *substantia cogitans*, a separate human "*mens sive animus*," and the point of departure for inferences according to the principle of causality—in short, the change by virtue of which Descartes became the father of transcendental realism, an absurd position, though its absurdity cannot be made apparent at this point. (*CM* §10, p.24)

This absurdity, however, had already been made apparent in *The Idea of Phenomenology* and *Ideas* without reference to Descartes, and would be made yet more obvious years later in the *Crisis*.

Husserl suggests that the reasons for Descartes' failure to make the transcendental turn, that is, his failure to remain within the domain delineated by the epoche, stem from his mathematical and physicalistic prejudices. Husserl speculates that Descartes was "dominated in advance" by the Galilean desire to develop a universal mathematical-physics and by the belief that such a physics could be developed. This resulted in Descartes' belief in a rigid distinction between the sensible, experienceable world and a domain of purely mathematical, material being knowable through pure thinking alone. This, in turn, promoted the relegation of the sensuous domain to the status of a "pointer" that indicated the mathematical-material domain, which in turn could clarify the confused and unreliable sensuous one (*C* §18, p.79). But all of these beliefs, Husserl correctly argues, should have been put out of play via the Cartesian epoche. They were not, and this reveals that Descartes' "radicalism" was guided in advance by hidden goals.

The teleological force of these hidden goals emerges in still another form: namely, in Descartes' general neglect of the ego-cogito once discovered. Husserl points out that in neglecting "the task of systematically investigating the pure ego," Descartes reveals that its discovery was for him ultimately a *means* meant only to function in the relay to another yet more important *end*. This "end" was, of course, the priority of foundations for the new natural scientific methodologies. And once secured, the analysis of the ego could be left to one of them, namely, to naturalistic psychology (*C* §19, p.82). But this, Husserl claims, marks the true absurdity of Descartes' "transcendental realism" (*C* §19, p.82). This absurdity occurs when transcendental experience is recognized as the indubitably given (as so recognized by Descartes), while *this doxastically indexed reality of experience and appearance* is "explained" via an appeal to a nonexperiential reality, causally connected to and declared constitutive of experiences and appearances. But since as a procedural and methodological perspective *appearance becomes the real* with the application of the epoche, the realistic mode of "explanation" is absurd for one working within its constraints. In fact, when we considered Husserl's criticisms of naturalistic epistemologies, we were already seeing why a "transcendental realism" is absurd. It commits the inevitable *petitio principii* of the naturalistic epistemologies generated by acceptance of the ontological reversal.

Husserl gives us a critical summary of the two paths sighted and the one path taken by Descartes when he writes:

Thus, in truth, there begins with Descartes a completely new manner of philosophizing which seeks its ultimate foundations in the subjective. That Descartes, however, persists in pure objectivism in spite of its subjective grounding was possible only through the fact that the *mens*, which at first stood by itself in the epoche and functioned as the absolute ground of knowledge, grounding the objective sciences (or, universally speaking, philosophy), appeared at the same time to *be* grounded along with everything else as a legitimate subject matter *within* the sciences, i.e., in psychology. Descartes does not make clear to himself that the ego, his ego deprived of its worldly character [*entweltlicht*] through the epoche, in whose functioning *cogitationes* the world has all the ontic meaning it can ever have for him, *cannot possibly* turn up as subject matter *in* the world, since everything that is of the *world* derives its meaning precisely *from these functions* — including, then, one's own psychic being, the ego in the usual sense. (*C* §19, pp.81-82)

Even the ego, as empirical ego, Husserl claims, is a constituted unity of sense. Descartes' error was to reify this ego in all of its dimensions and to bestow upon it a thing-like status; to make of it, even after the epoche, a "bit of the world" (*FTL* §93, p.227). Because of this the ego, too, seemed a physicalistically constituted thing and was not recognized as that which constituted the very sense of "physicality" and physicalistic rationalism itself.

We will now turn away from the wrong path taken and turn towards the transcendental-phenomenological epoche as it emerged in Husserl's writings.

4.2
THE TRANSCENDENTAL-PHENOMENOLOGICAL EPOCHE

Of all the concepts that were generated in Husserl's search for a pure phenomenology, the concepts of the transcendental-phenomenological epoche and reduction are high among those that caused and continue to cause the greatest problems. Many of Husserl's early followers and most of his later students abandoned the ship of phenomenology precisely where these concepts begin, and, by Husserl's lights, they thereby abandoned the ship of phenomenology *in toto*. In the author's preface to Boyce Gibson's English edition of *Ideas,* Husserl had written that ". . . those who set aside the phenomenological reduction as a philosophically irrelevant eccentricity . . . destroy the whole meaning of . . . my phenomenology" (p.16). Indeed, from the time of the 1907 lectures on *The Idea of Phenomenology* until the end of his life, Husserl tried again and again to clarify this concept. Many of his successors still think that he never did.[6] In this chapter we will develop one rather neglected strand of Husserl's comments on the concepts of epoche and reduction. In so doing we hope to clarify their functions in Husserl's phenomenology a bit more fully than did Husserl himself.

Our guiding claim is that the effect of the first act of epoche can be depicted as follows:

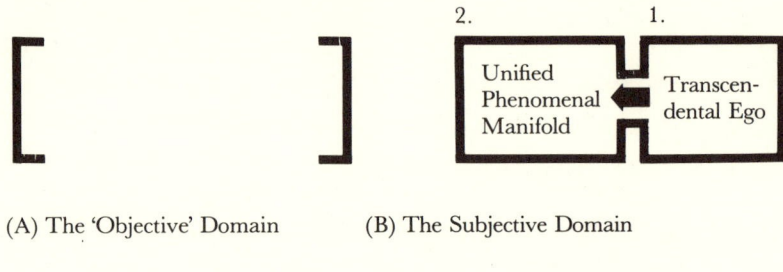

(A) The 'Objective' Domain   (B) The Subjective Domain

Figure 5

Broadly conceived, this means that the first application of the transcendental-phenomenological epoche *disconnects* domain A as radical transcendence, transcendence$_2$. It "brackets-out" the transcendent domain, which has traditionally been posited as really and independently existing, claiming to be the cause of domain B. With the first epoche, as we are interpreting it, immanence$_1$, immanence$_2$, and transcendence$_1$ remain largely unaffected. However, some transformations in our figure have occurred; these will be dealt with as we proceed.

This depiction of the epoche is metaphorical, of course, because it takes Husserl's metaphor of "bracketing" (*Einklam-*

merung) to heart. But the notions of epoche as "the suspension of belief in transcendencies" (*IP* 2-5, 31; *I* §§ 31-32) and reduction as the ensuing "change of attitude," or "shift of standpoint" (*I* 7; *C* §§ 39, 41), which follows from the suspension, are not metaphors; rather, they refer, respectively, to phenomenologically *enactable* and phenomenologically *experienceable* modes of consciousness. In this section of Chapter 4 we will deal with the *act* of bracketing, that is, the suspension of belief in transcendencies, as the implications of that act grew ever more extensive in the development of Husserl's thought. Later, in section 4.4 of this chapter, we will deal with the corresponding *event* of reduction, that is, with the shift of standpoint from the natural scientific attitude and the natural attitude to the corresponding levels of the phenomenological attitude.

(a) Epoche as a Limiting Concept (*Logical Investigations*)

In *The Idea of Phenomenology* Husserl broaches the concept that would later become known, in part, as the "phenomenological epoche." This concept is called "the principle of epistemological reduction" (*IP* 31), and, viewed closely, even this concept is foreshadowed in the "principle of presuppositionlessness" of the *Logical Investigations* (*LI* 263-66).

In the "Prolegomena to Pure Logic," which begins the *Logical Investigations*, Husserl had spoken of "sciences of reality which require metaphysical hypotheses for their completion" (§5). Later, when he speaks of "'freedom from presuppositions' as a principle in epistemological investigations" (p.263), he is largely referring to just such metaphysical presuppositions. He there argues that the "pure theory of knowledge" must keep itself free from questions that "concern the justifiability of accepting 'mental' and 'physical' realities which transcend consciousness" (p.26). This includes statements having ontological implications as made by natural scientists, and especially those statements that implicate a radically transcendent world over and above the phenomenal nature to which natural science correlates its formulae. In short, Husserl argues, we must abstain from all questions "as to the existence and nature of 'the external world' " (p.26).

Here, when Husserl disallows consideration of the idea of a transcendent world (transcendence₂) opposed to our own experienced world, he brackets it out *as an issue* for phenomenology. He does so because in the first edition of this early work he still conceived of phenomenology as a descriptive psychology (*LI* 262). At this stage of his development the "epoche" is, in its germinal form, only a limiting concept which demarcates the bounds beyond which phenomenology as descriptive psychology or as pre-transcendental philosophy cannot and need not go. In turning to *The Idea of Phenomenology*, however, we will see that with the first move towards phenomenology as a universally applicable philosophy, the naturalistic notion of an external world begins to be recognized as a problem that must be dealt with. If it is not dealt with, then phenomenology can hardly be considered a universally applicable philosophy that provides *non-metaphysical* foundations for the sciences. Hence, it is only after the *Investigations* that the problem of an external world could no longer be ignored, and could no longer be "kept apart from the pure theory of knowledge."

(b) Epoche and the Extension of the Immanent
    (*The Idea of Phenomenology*)

In *The Idea of Phenomenology* when Husserl introduces the "first step in the phenomenological orientation," he does so in reference to the "objective sciences" (pp.1-3). He writes that the natural sciences as well as the sciences of culture (*Geisteswissenschaften*), and even the formal sciences of mathematics and logic, bank upon cognition of the transcendent. As he puts it, they are involved in the "doubtfulness of transcendence." And with this our old problem arises: "How can cognition reach beyond itself? How can it reach a being that is not to be found within the confines of consciousness?" (p.3).

As we noted earlier, because all natural and natural scientific knowledge relies upon some positing of transcendencies, all attempts to explain *cognition* on the basis of natural and natural scientific facts result in a *petitio principii*. The reduction is needed, according to Husserl, to avoid this error:

> . . . if we are to avoid this confusion . . . we need
> *phenomenological reduction.*
>
> This means: everything transcendent (that which is
> not given to me immanently) is to be assigned the index
> zero, i.e., its existence, its validity is not to be assumed as
> such, except at most as *the phenomenon of a claim to validity.*
> (*IP* 4)

This notion of a "phenomenon of a claim to validity" means that while our acceptance of the existence of any object used as an explanatory postulate must be suspended, the *belief* in the object *qua object of belief* may be maintained. In fact, it *must* be maintained if phenomenological analyses are to focus upon the *constitution of objectivity*, because these beliefs are intrinsic to the very sense of the objectivities constituted.

However, in *The Idea of Phenomenology*, Husserl has the tendency to express the effect of the epoche in a misleading way. For instance, he writes:

> . . . an epistemological *reduction* has to be accomplished in
> the case of every epistemological inquiry of whatever sort
> of cognition. That is to say, everything transcendent that is
> involved must be bracketed, or be assigned the index of in-
> difference, of epistemological nullity, an index which indi-
> cates: the existence of all these transcendencies, whether I
> believe in them or not, is not here my concern; this is not the
> place to make judgements about them; they are entirely ir-
> relevant. (p.31)

What tends to be misleading in Husserl's description of the reduction is that *he is not actually speaking about "epistemic nullity," but rather about existential-ontological nullity* in relation to epistemic claims. The "index of indifference" does not refer to the epistemic achievements of objectivity considered as doxic noema, but rather, it refers to the existential-ontological *postulation* of objectivities that are then used as supports for cognitive claims and explanations of experience. The epistemological reduction is a reduction *to* what we experience in cognition, and an *existential-ontological nullification of* the transcendencies that we cannot experience in a glance (as in the case of ordinary objects), or of those transcendencies that we have *never* experienced, and which, *in principle*, we can never experience (as in the case of natural scientific objects.) While in *The Idea of Phenomenology* Husserl's examples of such transcendencies are confined to the prior type of transcendencies (transcendence$_1$), his initial undeveloped distinction between natural and natural scientific cognition portends the more explicit distinction that will later emerge.

The epistemological reduction can be read as the beginning of Husserl's attempt at an *epistemological reversal* that will function to provide an epistemic revaluation of the ontological reversal effected by the natural scientific tradition in philosophy. To understand just how radical this epistemological reversal is, we must consider the issue of the scope of the phenomenological epoche.

The *cogitata* of what is now component 2 in Figure 5 are not "secondary qualities," but rather, that domain signifies the intentional object, or, generally, the unified phenomenal manifold in which each of us lives. Once the idea of a purely corporeal world of atomistic "primary qualities" is bracketed-out, the claim that we experience "secondary qualities" or "sense-data" is seen as absurd and simply not the case (*PRS* 105; *C* §9, p.30, n.*). In fact, since the phenomenological reduction is the shift of standpoint that follows from the phenomenological epoche, in making it we can discover how sense-data explanations of the world, or indeed, of consciousness, exhibit the effects of the ontological reversal noted above.[7] Once the presuppositions that led to the postulation of secondary qualities are submitted to the conditions of the epoche (that is, when domain A is bracketed-out), then the shift in standpoint occurs. What we see, *qua* philosophers, literally changes; a *reduction* to pure experience, to "pure consciousness," occurs. We no longer experience the "flatland world" given to us by the classical empiricists, or even more recently, by the sense-data theorists.[8] As a result of this reduction we rid ourselves of ". . . the completely mistaken opinion that 'sense-data' constitute what is immediately given" (*C* §9, p.30, n.*). Instead, we begin to see the a priori harmony, the gestalt-like unification, of all experience. Furthermore, through this first act of epoche and its ensuing reduction, which rids us of the fallacy of atomistic secondary qualities as immediately given, we shall eventually rid explanations for the possibility of natural scientific truth of what is ultimately ". . . a bad theory regarding a good procedure" (*PRS* 105). The "bad" theory concerns the ontological distinction between primary and secondary qualities used to explain the results of the "good" procedures used in natural scientific investigation.

In *The Idea of Phenomenology*, which represents the first inchoate turn towards transcendental phenomenological idealism, Husserl considers the extension of the sphere of phenomenological investigation via a consideration of intentionality (pp.43-51). The sphere of investigation becomes the sphere that is *bracketed-in*, the sphere of "cogitata" or "appearances." And, already in *The Idea of Phenomenology*, Husserl claims that "phenomenological reduction does not entail a limitation to the investigation of the sphere of genuine (*reell*) immanence, to the sphere of that which is genuinely contained within the absolute this of the *cogitatio*" (p.48). He thereby argues that the "genuinely (*reell*) immanent" (immanence$_1$) can by no means limit the range of phenomenological investigations. The *intentio* of mental processes captures within themselves, in a certain sense, the object they intend, and this brings immanence$_2$ and transcendence$_1$ within the range of phenomenological consideration. Here again Husserl has included the *cogitatum* as an essential component of all and any *cogitationes*. The "objective" thereby appears within the domain of subjectivity as bracketed-in by the epoche, though it appears deprived of its ontological, causal, and explanatory status. And although these points lead Husserl to claim that the sphere of phenomenological analysis is a domain in which "nothing which is meant fails to be given" (p.48), that which is "given" is not always given so clearly as he initially believed. In fact, in his introduction to *The Idea of Phenomenology* Husserl had already expressed some worry over the implications that such "hidden transcendencies" (in immanence) had for phenomenological investigation (p.8). In order to understand how the recognition of such "hidden transcendencies" motivated Husserl's turn to phenomenological transcendental idealism, we must turn to some of Husserl's later texts.

(c) Epoche as an Act Which Implicates the World (*Ideas, Cartesian Meditations, Formal and Transcendental Logic*)

In *Ideas, Cartesian Meditations,* and *Formal and Transcendental Logic* Husserl's claim that there is "no limit to the sphere of genuine (*reell*) immanence" (*IP* 43) is recognized to implicate even the cogitatum "world" (*I* §47, p.135; *CM* §§ 8-9, 28; *C* §17, p.78). The comprehension of what is involved in the sphere of genuine immanence comes to be referred to as the "winning of a new region of Being" (*I* §33, p.101); and Husserl writes that with the attainment of this region we "have literally lost nothing but have won the whole [of] Absolute Being, which, properly understood, conceals in itself all transcendencies, 'constituting' them within itself" (*I* §50, p.140). Insofar as this new region of Being implicates the cogitatum "world," it is indicated by domain B in figure 5. The cogitata of the domain of everyday experience are thus implicated by the phenomenological domain of pure consciousness that persists after the first act of phenomenological suspension. Moreover, because all belief in the traditionally presupposed domain of pure corporeality is now suspended, the domain of everyday conscious experience is experienced anew. Once more, as may have been the case before the natural scientific revolution, the philosopher begins, Husserl believes, to understand consciousness and the world as they show themselves in their intrinsic unification. But this intrinsic surface unification begins to suggest to Husserl that nothing lies beyond the domain disclosed by the first epoche, that nothing outside of it is *needed* to provide such unification and that, instead, everything is an implicate of the conscious activities that go on within it.

Husserl expresses this consequence of the phenomenological epoche when he writes that:

> Consciousness considered in its "purity," must be reckoned as a *self-contained system of Being*, as a system of *Absolute*

Being, into which nothing can penetrate, and from which nothing can escape; which has no spatio-temporal exterior, and can be inside no spatio-temporal system; which cannot experience causality from anything nor exert causality upon anything, it being presupposed that causality bears the normal sense of natural causality as a relation of dependence between realities. (*I* §49, p.139)

The all-implicative facets of this "self-enclosed system of Being" (which is also vividly described by Husserl at *CM* §41, p.84, and *FTL* §99, p.250) are the various levels of "phenomenological residua" that persist after the transcendental-phenomenological epoche. But if this domain is truly self-enclosed and contains everything within itself, then the epoche is no longer simply a limiting concept; it becomes instead a methodological device for the clarification of world-experience, world-disclosure, and world-delineation; and, at deeper levels (as we will see) for epistemic-ontological world-transformation.

At this juncture the following questions begin to arise: If "nothing is lost" by the application of the epoche, then *what* is bracketed-out by the epoche? From the time of *Ideas* Husserl's answer is a resounding "nothing!" (§49, p.139; *C* §52, p.176). But what is the actual sense of Husserl's claim that "nothing is lost" to epoche? By saying that nothing is lost by the application of epoche, does Husserl thereby become a simple metaphysical idealist? In order to understand why he does not, a more complete understanding of Husserl's epoches and reductions, and eventually of his theory of constitution, must be achieved.

4.3
EXCURSUS: GRADING THE REDUCTIONS. CLARIFYING HUSSERL

We now submit that in the theory of phenomenological epoche and reduction as presented and developed in *Ideas,* Husserl does not distinguish sharply enough between the positing theses of the natural attitude and the positing theses of the natural scientific attitude. But on the basis of insights developed in his later works, especially in the *Crisis* and *Experience and Judgment*, Husserl did explicitly distinguish between the epoche and reduction corresponding to each of these positing attitudes. Relevant to these distinctions are the corresponding distinctions and genetic relations that pertain to Husserl's notions of the natural attitude, the natural scientific attitude, and the philosophical naturalism that were noted earlier. Let us recall the first two.

The natural attitude originally lent its reifying force (concerning the independent existence of ordinary objects) to the natural scientific attitude. The natural scientific attitude thereby postulated a yet more transcendent "real world" continually existing in itself independently of all human experience and even of all *possible* human experience. Eventually, with the increasing influence and importance of the natural scientific *Weltanschauung*, the existence criteria inherent to the natural scientific attitude came to determine the kind of beliefs that are inherent to the natural attitude — the attitude that had *originally* motivated the existence claims correlated to natural scientific discoveries.

Now, in *Ideas*, Husserl blends the epoche of the natural scientific attitude (which concerns theories about objects) and the epoche of the natural attitude (which concerns the objects themselves). The fact that Husserl speaks about a series of "graded reductions" in *Ideas* (§33, p.103), and even devotes a chapter to the special domains that "fall" to the epoche, does not alter this fact. Quite the contrary, it is precisely by focusing upon the separate domains of knowledge that are to be suspended by epoche that Husserl bypasses the opportunity to perform a layered or graded set of reductions and performs instead something more akin to a "branching" set of reductions. The "branching" use of epoche occurs when different acts of epoche are used to suspend judgments and beliefs based upon different (or separate) domains of knowledge, such as a distinct epoche of the formal sciences, of the psychological sciences, and/or of the physical sciences. And this is how Husserl proceeds in *Ideas*. A non-universal layered or graded reduction, however, would occur *within* a branched act of epoche and proceed by reaching ever epistemically deeper (with each new act of epoche and reduction) into the constitutive origins of that knowledge domain. It is this second method of approach to phenomenological analysis that will be developed as we proceed.

Perhaps Husserl's tendency to blend the two distinct types of positing theses in *Ideas* — those of the natural attitude and those of the natural scientific attitude — can also be accounted for by the fact that it was only in *Ideas II* that he seemed to recognize the "reverse flow" of the natural scientific attitude into the natural attitude (§§2-3, §§6-7, §62, p.282). That is, it is there that he began to recognize the *internal influence* that our natural scientific inheritance inevitably had on even our naive interpretations of experiences and concepts relating to the lifeworld. In any case, by the time of the *Crisis* Husserl was well aware of the differences in these kinds of positing theses, and there he made it explicit that the *first step* of the phenomenological epoche must be the epoche of (the positing thesis of) the objective sciences (§35).

In the next section of this chapter we will interpret the theory of transcendental phenomenological epoche and reduction, especially as presented in Part II of *Ideas*, in terms of the multi-step strategy suggested above. This strategy seems important because only a strict distinction between the suspension of the positing thesis of the natural scientific attitude and the suspension of the positing thesis of the natural attitude will allow us to distinguish between two notions of "corporeality," one of which Husserl rejects as nonsensical, the other of which will form the lowest stratum of subject matter for constitutional analyses in the phenomenology of material nature.

4.4
THE PHENOMENOLOGICAL SHIFT OF STANDPOINT

In part (a) of this section we will interpret Husserl's theory of epoche and reduction in terms of the epoche of and reduction from the positing theses of the natural scientific attitude, transcendence$_2$. In part (b) we will interpret epoche and reduction in terms of the epoche of and reduction from the natural attitude per se, transcendence$_1$ and immanence$_2$. In each instance we will also comment briefly on how these levels of epoche and reduction relate to the issue of Husserl's idealism.

(a) At the Level of the "First" Reduction: The Suspension of Natural Scientific Nature

In the *Crisis* Husserl makes it explicit that in the performance of the epoche the first step will be "the epoche of [the positing thesis of] the objective sciences" (*C* §35). This means that the "world" we are left with after this epoche is domain B in our Figure, the domain that includes immanence$_1$, immanence$_2$, and transcendence$_1$, while belief in radical transcendence, transcendence$_2$, is suspended. Husserl also makes it clear that the reason we are not *simply* in this domain from the start is due to "our schooling in the traditional objectivistic metaphysics" (*C* §36, p.140). He argues that owing to the blinding interpretative force of this tradition we must first explicitly separate the a priori structures of the life-world from the objectivistic a priori structure that the natural sciences plant into this world. There is also evidence that Husserl recognized these various degrees of transcendence in *Ideas*, even though he is at times unclear about their individual relationships to the procedural techniques of epoche and reduction. Let us try to clarify the presentation of epoche and reduction in *Ideas* in terms of the graded series of reductions that emerged more explicitly in the *Crisis*.

Although in *Ideas* Husserl tends to blend the positing thesis of the belief in the world as it gives itself to us, as it is *there* for us, with the positing thesis of natural science (i.e., the positing thesis of a *fact world*), he does, nevertheless, clearly direct a number of statements about the epoche and reduction towards the positing thesis of the natural sciences. In section 41 of *Ideas*, for instance, entitled "The Real Nature of Perception and its Transcendent Object," Husserl distinguishes between "the physical thing as determined by physics, that utterly transcendent thing" and the thing of everyday sensuous appearances. Here, by reference to the "thing of physics" Husserl is referring to objects within the domain we have earlier identified as transcendence$_2$ and then, with his reference to the thing of sensuous experience, he is referring to objects within the domain we have identified as transcendence$_1$-immanence$_2$. Furthermore, immediately after making the distinctions just noted, he specifically insists upon "excluding the whole of physics and the whole domain of theoretical thinking," in order to focus more clearly upon the domain of ordinary objects in their modes of givenness. And, when introducing the phenomenological epoche, he writes that he will "disconnect" all sciences that relate to the natural world, especially insofar as the truth of these sciences is understood "as a truth *concerning the realities* of this world" (*I* §32, p.100). As we have noted, the truths of natural science that relate to the realities of *this* world do so by positing their own radically objective realities. These are the realities consisting of *purely quantifiable corporeality*, precisely *not* admitting of sensory exhibition. And it is this domain, in particular, that Husserl here insists upon bracketing.

In Chapter 3 it was noted that Husserl saw the problem of absurdity threatening the interpretation of natural scientific formulae *if* these formulae were conceived to be indicative of real things of which phenomenal things and events were mere signs or images. In section 40 of *Ideas* he claims that if such be the case, then the Berkeleian objection holds good—"namely, that extension, this essential nucleus of corporeality and all primary qualities, is unthinkable apart from secondary qualities" (p.116). The absurdity in the conception of all natural scientific formulae would follow simply because these formulae *are in fact thinkable* apart from "secondary qualities" or, more generally, apart from sensory experience. Husserl argues by means of this reductio that since natural scientific formulae are neither absurd nor meaningless (however much some *interpretations* of them are), these formulae cannot be indicative of real things, that is, of pure unexperienceable corporeality, of which appearances are mere signs or images.

As early as the *Philosophie der Arithmetik* (1891) and then more clearly in "Psychological Studies for Elementary Logic" (1894), Husserl had distinguished between genuine presentations (*eigentliche Vorstellungen*) and nongenuine presentations (*uneigentliche Vorstellungen*). "Genuine presentation" referred to that which showed itself in direct sensory presentation, the *thing itself*, while nongenuine presentation referred to signs and symbols insofar as they pointed to or indicated genuine presentations (*PA* 190-95; *SW* 133-34). These latter Husserl came to call *representations* (*Repräsentation*; *SW* 134) because he noted a "dangerous ambiguity" in speaking of both things and symbols as "presentations." This dangerous ambiguity that troubled Husserl emerges in the sign and image theories of perception, or, more generally, in representative realism.

For Husserl it is phenomenologically evident that perception *presents* us with the things themselves (*I* §24, §39, p.115, §43, §45, p.129), that images *reflect* or *portray* the things themselves (*I* §43, §90, p.243), and that signs and symbols *point to* or *indicate* the things themselves, images, or even other signs and symbols (*I* §§ 43, 52). Because the eidetic essence of these phenomena is evident in "originally giving experience" (*originär gebende Erfahrung*) (*I* §24),[9] sign and image theories of perception are absurd from the moment they are asserted because they *reverse* these definitions. This reversal of definition occurs because sign and image theories of perception reduce presentation to *re-presentation*, and this tendency is a direct outgrowth of the naturalistic tradition and its physicalistic style of explanation.

Husserl's arguments on this reversal of sense (*I* §§ 40, 42, 52) are rather convoluted, but based upon the phenomenological "axioms" (or definitions) given above, they amount to this: Signs and images point to things, but are not themselves things in the sense of material objects. However, all forms of image and sign theories (that is, all forms of representative realism) claim that "things" (in the phenomenologically defined sense) *are* images or signs that somehow point to the real things, the things of natural science. But, from the phenomenological perspective, this reversal of sense results in absurdity on a number of fronts: (1) it makes things nonperceivable in principle, and (2) it thereby makes signs that do not and cannot point (because the "real" things, the "things" of natural science, are no longer there for the pointing). Likewise, (3) it makes images that do not and cannot reflect or portray (because there are no intuitive *things* to reflect or portray). The reversal of signs, images, and things would thus turn things into signs and images, and make the things disappear! But, since nothing else *which can present itself in sensory intuition* is "known *for which* the intuited might serve as a 'sign' or 'image' " (*I* §43, p.123), the intuited, presented object *is* the thing *of* which images may be made and *to* which signs may refer, but it itself is not an image or a sign. Theories of perception, then, which are based upon or governed by the metaphysics of natural science, result in the following absurdities. They give us "signs" that do not signify (point), "images" that do not reflect (anything), and "things" that do not appear (ever)! Ample reason, it seems, for Husserl to conclude that something has gone awry.

Keeping in mind that these sign and image theories of perception are essentially connected with the natural scientific conception of the world, as purely corporeal Nature explanatory of the appearances, we will now argue that the sense of the first epoche and reduction is a return to everyday experience as it might be had prior to its infiltration by the metaphysics of natural science.

Once the natural scientific world is placed within the epoche (which means that once the positing thesis of the natural scientific attitude is placed within the epoche), the view that perceptual things are signs or images of purely corporeal things has no *raison d'être*. Moreover, what may have seemed like a rampant idealism on Husserl's part may now be read as a return to realism, but a "realism" taken in its pre-philosophical sense as acceptance of the sensory given as real. When Husserl speaks about "unperceived reality" in *Ideas*, he distinguishes between (1) realities *not perceived in fact* and (2) would-be "realities" *not perceivable in principle*. The former, which he refers to as "things" (*Dinge*), are said to be perceivable as the "things of the world that surround me" and are part of this world even when not perceived in fact (§45, p.129). When not immediately perceived, they nevertheless remain as part of the *sense* of the world because their existence is directly motivated by that which is experienced. On the other hand, Husserl argues, any concern with things that are *not motivated* by what we experience is "groundless," while the postulation of "things" not perceivable *in principle* is nonsense (§45, p.129). Entities of type (1) would thereby indicate for Husserl the "things" that we have placed in component 2 of Figure 5, things that are perceived and whose perceivability is motivated by what is perceived, while those "things" Husserl refers to as type (2) would indicate the "entities" that the natural scientific metaphysics located in domain 'A' of that figure, "things" unperceivable in principle. Insofar as this domain of unperceivables is conceived of as a region of real "things," then Husserl comes to view domain A as nonsense. And, the interpretation of this domain as a realm of "real things" is precisely the interpretation that the natural scientific metaphysics gave to this region. So, after the first act of epoche, this region is bracketed-out of consideration as an explanatory ontological posit.

At the start of section 47, entitled "The Natural World as Correlate to Consciousness," Husserl provides an argument as to how at least one level of the epoche could be understood as the suspension of the natural scientific world *alone*. He there argues that human experience as it actually is compels us to pass beyond the things of intuitive experience and to place at their basis a purely physicalistic reality. However, he continues, it is fully conceivable "that our intuitable world should be the last, and 'beyond' it no physical world at all." In other words, our intuitable world might lack a consistent mathematical determinacy that would preclude the possibility of physicalistic sciences such as those we have developed. And yet even if this were so, Husserl concludes, " 'things' might still present themselves as similar to the things we know, maintaining themselves continuously in appearance-patterns as intentional unities."

It is the effectuation of just such a perspective, we would

like to suggest, that Husserl has in mind much later when, in the *Crisis*, he emphasizes that we begin phenomenological procedures with an epoche of the natural scientific domain (§35). This epoche would suspend the metaphysical domain of natural science and thereby "reduce" consciousness to an experience of everyday realities as they presumably appeared before the metaphysics of natural science had infiltrated "naive" everyday experience. While Husserl extends his arguments in *Ideas* §47 to encompass the domain of object-transcendence (transcendence₁), and hence intimates even more fully the distinction between two levels of epoche and reduction, we will postpone consideration of these arguments until a bit more has been said about the "first" level of reduced experience.

It can now be argued that at the first level of reduction Husserl is able to say, nonidealistically, that with the epoche and reduction we achieve "the detachability in principle of the whole natural world from the domain of consciousness," and that with this detachment "nothing is thereby altered in the Absolute Being of experiences . . ." (*I* §46, p.132). Nothing is altered because the suspension of the natural scientific world and its corresponding reduction to the things themselves gives us the world that we strayed from in theory though never lost in everyday life. At this level of reduction we are simply returned to the ordinary first-order world of pretheoretical experience.

When Husserl next considers the system of possible experience as a system of possibilities *motivated* by an intentional consciousness, he contrasts this to the natural scientific idea of naturalistic and physicalistic causality normally thought to be explanatory of experience. He writes that ". . . the pure phenomenological sphere [of intentionally motivated possibilities, provides] . . . a contrast . . . to the concept of causality which was related to the transcendent sphere of reality . . ." (*I* §47, p.134, n. 1). This contrast theme, given only a note in *Ideas I*, is developed much more extensively in *Ideas II*, where Husserl identifies "motivation" as the guiding concept for understanding the personalistic world-attitude, while "causality" is given that position in relation to the naturalistic world-attitude (§56). Moreover, in *Ideas II* Husserl explicitly assigns "motivation" and the personalistic attitude reductive priority over the causal-naturalistic vision of reality (§§62-64). In any case, in *Ideas I* we have at least the beginnings of Husserl's own recognition of his epistemic reversal, which will attempt to explain the unified phenomenal manifold by way of the act of intentionality rather than by way of the transcendently generated force of causality.

If the first epoche and its corresponding reduction is as we have described, then a fresh perspective can now be taken of Husserl's "idealism," at least at the level of the first reduction. Consider now the passage we referred to earlier, which is probably responsible more than any other for Husserl's appellation as an "idealist":

> Consciousness, considered in its "purity," must be reckoned as a *self-contained system of Being*, as a system of *Absolute Being*, into which nothing can penetrate, and from which nothing can escape; which has no spatio-temporal exterior, and can be inside no spatio-temporal system; which cannot experience causality from anything nor exert causality upon anything, it being presupposed that causality bears the normal sense of natural causality as a relation of dependence between realities. (*I* §49, p.139)

At the level of the first reduction, this claim leaves us the world as experienced because "consciousness considered in its purity" is consciousness *as* the domain of experiences and possible experiences (*I* §39, p.114), which *is* the spatio-temporal network *within which* all causal relations between realities occur (*FTL* §99, p.250). This network is called "the world." Hence, when Husserl claims that ". . . over and beyond this [realm of purified consciousness] is just nothing at all" (*I* §50, p.139), he simply intends (at the level of the first reduction) to exclude the positing thesis of "things in themselves." In terms of this reading, the initial effect of Husserl's first epoche and reduction is simply to divest theoretical entities of their ontological status and to deny epistemic explanatory power to the interpretative framework that contains those entities. This first epoche and reduction returns us, that is, it reduces consciousness, to awareness of the things themselves (*die Sachen selbst*) and brackets-out the so-called things in themselves (*Ding an sich*) of the natural scientific metaphysics. In fact, insofar as Husserl suspends the existence-postulates of the metaphysical-world of natural scientific "things," he effects the opposite of an idealism; he effects a *phenomenological common-sense realism,* which means a realism that is nevertheless aware of the transcendental realm ultimately constitutive of the objective world.

Husserl's perspective on the effects of this first reduction can be summarized by his claim that ". . . the meaning which 'Being' bears in common speech is precisely inverted" (*I* §50, p.139). If, in *Ideas,* he had separated the two levels of the phenomenological reduction more systematically, he might have written that "the meaning which 'Being' bears in *scientific* speech is precisely inverted." But soon after he makes the same point when he writes, "It is not that the real sensory world is 'recast' or denied, but that an absurd interpretation of the same . . . is set aside" (*I* §55, p.153). The *interpretation* of the world that is set aside is the natural scientific meta-ontology that Husserl has also called "physicalistic objectivism."

The first epoche and reduction, then, has returned us to the things themselves and inverted the natural scientific meaning of "Being." This is the major preliminary step for the achievement of phenomenology *as* phenomenological transcendental idealism. This move *begins* the inversion of the "meaning of 'Being'." Constitutional analyses of the constitution of this meaning will be required to complete the inversion. Eventually, however, the implications of this initial act of epoche will allow Husserl to write that as "applied, phenomenology supplies the definitive criticism of every fundamentally distinct science, and in particular . . . the final determination of the sense in which their objects can be said to 'be' " (*I* §62, p.166). This statement is a clue that Husserl's epistemological reversal, which will compensate for the ontological reversal effected by the natural scientific tradition, will eventually attempt to *reassign* the values for "Being"—but it will attempt to do so without needing to postulate a world of insular things in themselves that would be used to justify the truth achievements of natural science even while they usurped the *sense* of the world.

(b) At the Level of the "Second" Reduction:
The Suspension of the Object-World

In the *Crisis* Husserl writes:

> Our historically motivated path . . . has led us . . . to the postulate of that novel universal science of subjectivity as pregiving the world. . . . the first step which seemed to help at the beginning, that epoche through which we freed ourselves from all objective sciences as grounds of validity, by no means suffices. In carrying out this epoche, we obviously continue to stand on the ground of the world . . . . (*C* §38, p.147)

Here, Husserl clearly recognizes the role and the limit of the first level of phenomenological epoche and reduction. Its role is to return us to the life-world as unaffected by the natural scientific metaphysics; at the same time its limit is this world of everyday life as manifest through its things and involvements. But Husserl's pure phenomenology does not stop where existential phenomenology does. This limit is still too world-bound, Husserl believed, to resolve the great enigmas generated by the metaphysics designed to explain natural scientific achievement. To resolve these enigmas there was need to take yet another step in phenomenological investigation. This next step Husserl would describe as a step below the ground of the world, a step he sometimes called a step towards the "mothers" (*I* III §15, p.69; *C* §42, p.153). Reference to "the mothers" is Husserl's way of alluding to the mysteries of constitution via Goethe's *Faust*, where the "mothers" refers to the keepers of the keys to the mystery of existence and Being.[10]

This ground below the ground of the pregiven life-world was conceived by Husserl to be the beginning of the transcendental realm proper and is the domain that he usually had in mind when speaking of the epoche and reductions. For most of his career, however, Husserl referred to the attainment of this realm without distinguishing the preliminary step from it, suggesting that the transcendental domain could be reached and brought into phenomenological focus in one fell swoop. The criticisms Husserl would aim at the Cartesian way in the *Crisis* (§43) would take issue with just such an attempt to focus upon the domain of constitutive intentionality with one radical act of epoche and reduction. Owing to the difficulties encountered in such early approaches to the transcendental domain, however, Husserl was led to the final explicit recognition of the preliminary epoche and reduction that we have developed above; with it, one is launched directly into the domain of constitutive intentionality, and it becomes nearly impossible to explicate clearly. This difficulty occurs, in part, because the stratified objectivities that are the consequent of intentional syntheses are *reduced through* without reflection upon the many-layered acts that initially gave these strata their sense. Hence, as Husserl writes, with the Cartesian reduction the transcendental ego appears "empty of content."

Interestingly, however, it was Hume whom Husserl credits with first recognizing some of the concrete layers of constitutive consciousness encountered in phenomenological reduction (*EP* I 156-57; *FTL* §100, p.256), and it is Hume to whom we can appeal to help explicate the second level of phenomenological experience. Drawing a comparison between Hume and Husserl will give this level of epoche and reduction a ring of historical familiarity. It should also help us to relate the second level of epoche and reduction to some of the historical issues developed earlier.[11] We will then further explicate these notions by an appeal to the *Crisis* text, and once more compare these results with some of Hume's work.

At the level of the first reduction, suspension of existence positing belief involves the suspension of an "existence," which would have been existence as a sign-signified relationship, a relationship between "secondary qualities" and "real existence," primary qualities. The reality status that was bracketed-out when natural scientific "objects" were suspended was an extraordinary, a posited, "existence" over and above that immediately posited by the scientifically naive natural attitude (which, however, had itself finally been infiltrated by the natural scientific attitude). The existence positing belief that must be put in abeyance at the level of the second reduction, on the other hand, is the existence-positing belief of the common-sense natural attitude where "existence" refers to things as they appear to be to an attentive consciousness. Consequently, the difficulty of performing the second reduction is that the existence-criterion adhering to ordinary objects seems inseparable from the experience of the objects themselves. This is brought out by the ontic-certainty (*Seinsgewissheit*) of ordinary experience where any object 'x' is equivalent to " 'x' exists" and " 'x' exists" merges seamlessly into 'x'. The second level of epoche and reduction demands, however, that some such "seam" be created between any given experienced thing and its existence.

Three different though related claims made by David Hume can now help us understand the difficulties involved in achieving the second level of reduced experience. Recall Hume's arguments that:

> 'Tis . . . evident that, the idea of existence is nothing different from the idea of any object, and that when after the simple conception of any thing we wou'd conceive it as existent, we in reality make no addition to or alteration on our first idea.[12]

This statement remakes our point that in the natural attitude there is a seamless conceptual connection between the objects of experience and their existence. In Husserlian language this is to say that the perception of ordinary objects or object-contexts carries with itself the sense of the actuality of the objects or object-contexts; that is, the sense of their being "simply there" (*I* §103, p.273).

Hume makes the implications of his claim stronger when he argues that the cause for our belief in the existence of the objects of our impressions are these impressions themselves and nothing besides.[13] The objects of our perceptions are thereby made one with the idea of their existence. Consequently, Hume can later argue that: "We may well ask, *What causes induce us to believe in the existence of body?* but 'tis vain to ask, *Whether there be body or not?*"[14] Asking this latter question would be in vain because nature has made us such that *we have no choice but to believe* in the existence of the objects because the objects of our perceptions are *one* with the idea of their existence.

Now, when Husserl asks that we suspend belief in the existence of objects of our own perceptions (*I* §32; *CM* §§7-8; *PL* 7), he seems to ask us to do what Hume claims is impossible; that is, to separate our belief in the existence of objects from our perceptions of these objects. Does this mean that Husserl's second level of reduced experience is impossible to achieve? Or rather, does it point to a problem in Hume? Showing how the latter is the case will help us reach an understanding of the second reduction.

Hume, of course, denies that there is a legitimate distinction to be made between perceptions and objects.[15] Consequently, when he claims that "existence" is *internal* to every perception, this "existence" must be one with the perception itself because there is no distinction between the perception and that which exists. Husserl, on the other hand, recognizes that there is a legitimate distinction to be made between our perceptions and the objects *of* our perceptions; therefore he can distinguish between perceptions and the existence of the objects *intentionally implicated* by those perceptions.

As in the *Idea of Phenomenology*, Husserl is aware that the ". . . word 'phenomenon' is ambiguous in virtue of the essential correlation between *appearance and that which appears*" (*IP* 11). "Appearance" refers to the perception *just* as it is perceived, e.g., a side or an "adumbration," whereas "that which appears" refers to *the object* intentionally implicated by the appearance. For Husserl, then, the object qua (complete) object is not equal to the perception; hence, suspension of belief in the object's existence is not equal to separating the existence of the object from our perception of it. Belief, or better, doxic-certainty (*Glaubensgewissheit*), is always maintained in relation to what is perceived *as* it is perceived. This is revealed in the

Cartesian reduction. But this doxic-certainty in relation to the perceived as such, in relation to the appearance, does not necessarily imply doxic- or ontic-certainty in relation to *that which appears* "in" and "through" the appearing. The existence of any object is not guaranteed by the certainty of its *manners of appearing*. Appearances do, of course, give us reason to believe that an object exists, but at the level of the second reduction this is always a judgment that can only *impute* a relation between perception and its object because the object itself is either the transcendent existent intentionally implicated by, or physicalistically productive of, the perception itself.

When Husserl asks us to suspend existence at the level of the second reduction, then, he asks us to suspend belief in the existence of *objects* that might or might not exist over and above the appearances of "them." He draws a line between the perceived as it is perceived and the existent usually thought to be productive of it, the object itself or the thing itself. Hence, he can agree with Hume that the perception of "x" and the existence of "x" are internal correlates, but he can also suspend judgment on the existence of any object because at the level of the second reduction the "object" is something other than the perception *per se*. In fine, since Hume radically conflated perception and object, he concluded that existence is internally inherent to perception and could not be separated from it.[16] On the other hand, with his recognition of consciousness as always *intentionally implicative* of further perceptual possibilities, Husserl could legitimately distinguish between perceptions and the "existing" object intentionally implied in every perception.

This is the discovery that took Husserl "aback" in *The Idea of Phenomenology* (p.8) because it was revelatory of the "hidden transcendencies" packed into every given perceptual experience. Likewise, this is one of the sources (within his own works[17]) of Husserl's notion of "horizon." Hence, in *The Idea of Phenomenology*, the extension of phenomenological investigation through a consideration of intentionality occurs (p.43). It occurs in part because even the thing itself, meant here in the sense of an ordinary object, is recognized to be a regulative idea in the Kantian sense (*I* §143). That is, it is understood to be an inexhaustible sense-constituted objectivity *implied in* the "immanent" appearances, which, *qua* "thing," is never *fully given* in experience.

If, with these points in mind, we turn to the *Crisis*, Husserl's second act of epoche and its corresponding reduction can be shown to both complement and correct Hume's reduction of things to perceptions.

Husserl describes the reduction following the second act of epoche as a change of interest or attention (a shift of standpoint) from the "what" of perception to the "how" of perception (*C* §§38-39). The "what" of ordinary perception refers to the full object that appears after the first epoche of and reduction from natural scientific Reality. This return to the "what" is the reduction to everyday intentional objects (the things themselves) after the natural scientific garb of ideas (*Ideenkleid*) has been bracketed-out. In the natural involvement of everyday living, these things referred to by the "what" are usually expressed as nouns; they are objects as encountered in the value and praxis-laden activity of everyday life.

Just as the epoche of natural scientific objects effected a shift of seeing back to the things themselves, so, stepping deeper into the transcendental realm, the suspension of the belief in objects over and above perceptions *per se*, effects a reduction (shift of seeing) to the manners of givenness of those (presumed) "objects." In a sense, the existence-positing of the naive natural attitude ("naive" in that it occurs prior to the metaphysical existence-positing of the natural scientific attitude) has also functioned as an *Ideenkleid* of sorts because ordinary living is so consistently saturated with goal and object-orientation that these "objects" existing over and above perceptions of them have absorbed, and hence hidden, the *manners* in which they are necessarily given (*C* §38). This new reduction to the "how" of appearances indicates a shift of interest from that which appears to the appearing itself and would presumably be described primarily in the language of verbs, adverbs, and adjectives.

By now it should be apparent that Husserl's "suspension of existence" is often an elliptical locution that means "the suspension of belief in an existent transcending the immediately experienced." Within the epoche, meaning within the consciousness whose experiences are bracketed-*in* by the epoche, "existence" remains, and it remains unaffected by the suspension of the ontological energetics that tend to be conceptually melded into transcendencies; but, insofar as it does remain unaffected, ". . . the meaning which 'Being' bears in common [and natural scientific] speech is precisely inverted" (*I* §50, p.139). This is because in common speech, the language of the natural attitude, "Being" or "existence" always means more than our perception of "it."

If the world of this second reduction is now compared to Hume's world of perceptions, it will be seen how, with the procedure of epoche and reduction, as *conscious and systematic philosophical tools*, the possibility arises of describing the constitution of the world out of the perceptual flux in which it is "originally" given.

Hume's world of impressions and ideas reminds one of the "Flatland World" described in E. A. Abbott's *Flatland: A Romance of Many Dimensions*.[18] The reason for this is that the theory of perception and "objects" developed in the *Treatise* seems to deny the possibility of the "third dimension." "Objects" are reduced to perceptions, to *just* what is perceived, and they are *nothing but* what is perceived. Consequently, Hume is convinced that a belief in objects existing over and above perception is a fictionalistic prejudice that must be accounted for *as* a fictionalistic prejudice.[19]

Hume's manner of accounting for this belief in the existence of objects is by an appeal to the coherence and constancy of our perceptions, which seem to cohere in a constant way even when we do not directly observe the changing sequence of these perceptions.[20] It is in these analyses of consciousness that Husserl spots the first *concrete* proto-phenomenological analyses in the history of philosophy. Hume had "suspended" the world of transcendencies (epoche), reduced the world to a set of experiences (reduction), and attempted to "explain" the beliefs of the natural attitude (i.e., belief in the continued and distinct existence of objects) by an appeal to the inveterate characteristics of consciousness alone (constitution) (*FTL* §100, pp.256-57). But, while Husserl would later attempt to justify and explicate the foundations of knowledge by appealing to very similar analyses (plus some), Hume had developed a radical skepticism concerning knowledge in relation to the same! How had things turned out so differently?

We submit that Hume's belief, expressed early in the *Treatise*, that "perceptions arise in the soul from unknown causes,"[21] prevented him from recognizing the full range and potential of the intentionalistic and constitutional analyses that he inaugurated in that work. Because he presumed *causes of perception* that could never be known, appearances or perceptions were viewed atomistically; that is, they were not viewed as inherently connected *among themselves*,[22] but in need of a "real" connecting principle that would be supplied by a causal source. However, since the would-be causal source was unknowable in principle, the "real" connection among appearances could never be found. At most, there was only a mere expectation of future appearances.

From Husserl's perspective, however, the act of suspending belief in reality simultaneously suspends belief in the sources of all causal explanations; it suspends belief in all pure corporeality. Thereby, all appeals to causal explanations and all *possible* causal explanations are also denied conscious consideration; they are placed in abeyance. But, most important, with this conscious methodological act of suspending belief in transcendencies, the reduction that follows it is revelatory of *motivated possibilities*, that is, perceptual possibilities immediately present to consciousness. These possibilities are said to be *intentionally implicated*, and they are present in every perception of any "actual" object. The objects of the world that survive after epoche$_1$ are constituted by these intentional implications which are displayed only after epoche$_2$. We will turn to these constitutional considerations in the next chapter.

In response to Hume's claim, then, that "there is no satisfactory theory to explain the principles that unite our successive impressions in our thought or consciousness,"[23] Husserl would claim that there is indeed such a principle — it is the principle of intentionality, which, in relation to any perception of a "real" object, is intentionally implicative of further possible perceptions as a system of motivated possibilities. And, as Husserl came to recognize (and as Hume had supplied the conceptual machinery to recognize), implicative intentionality itself grows from primitive principles of "passive association" (*EJ* §16), which themselves supply the primitive "horizonal structure" for the developed forms of induction (*EJ* §8, p.32). Hence, Husserl eventually argued that the possibilities that are motivated by each and every perception come to be predetermined on the basis of past associative structures, and thereby their variational scope establishes the strict essential necessity of eidetic lawfulness. It is this eidetic law that then permits and reinforces the certainty that is available in our understanding of the world. So, by Husserl's lights, just as Descartes had paved the way *to* transcendental consciousness and then had become blinded by his physicalistic prejudices, similarly, Hume inaugurated the first constitutional analyses and then chose *not to trust their explanatory consequences* owing to his own residual beliefs in physicalistic objectivism.

Prior to these realizations, however, in *The Idea of Phenomenology*, Husserl's growing understanding of intentional implication or motivated possibilities had led him to write that even after the phenomenological reduction there is a distinction between appearance and that which appears. This difference showed itself even in the domain of pure givenness; hence, even in the domain of true immanence. With the recognition of this "otherness" always embedded in the purely given, Husserl wrote, "we are taken aback." We are "taken aback" because "the *cogitationes*, which we regard as simple data and in no way mysterious, hide all sorts of transcendencies" (*IP* 8). This identify-in-difference between appearance and that which appears occurs at the level of the second reduction. In relation to every thing-appearance (*Dingerscheinung*) there is a set of motivated possibilities (read: intentionally implied possible perceptions) indicative of that *object* that appears *in and through* the appearance. This proto-logic of intentional implication occurs, of course, in both the noetic and noematic facets of consciousness and eventually flowers into Husserl's notions of the act and object horizons.

Equally important for our general concerns is a distinction we have already put to use at the level of the first reduction. We refer to Husserl's contrast between the purely phenomenological sphere whose *modus explanans sine qua non* is the notion of intentionality and its motivated possibilities, as opposed to the naturalistic sphere whose *modus explanans sine qua non* is the notion of physicalistic causality (*I* §47, p.134, n. 1; *I* II §56). This contrast provides the key to understanding why interpreting Husserl's second reduction as we have suggested does not result in a Humean skepticism, put us in a Humean "flatland," or confine us to a realm of mere "sense-data."

While the idea of causally produced perceptions enforces the belief that these perceptions are atomistic or discrete (because the "real" connection between perceptions is necessarily lost behind the perceptions themselves), the recognition that all perceptions are intentionally implicative of other possible perceptions allows the unity of even the "how" of appearances to emerge (because the "real" connection between perceptions is now found within the experiences of the senses, within the domain of pure experiential consciousness). Within Husserl's second reduction, then, we still have a *unified* phenomenal manifold of appearance, though it is no longer one obscured by the full-blooded objects of daily encounter. Nevertheless, within the "how" of every appearance, the "that" of "that which appears" still remains, but it remains only as intentionally implicated.

It is for these reasons, too, that Husserl might have made his infamous statements in *Ideas* (§49), *Cartesian Meditations* (§41), and *Formal and Transcendental Logic* (§99) concerning the absolutely self-contained and self-sufficient system of consciousness. At the level of the second reduction, natural causality is experienced as intentionally constituted. The source for the sense of natural causality in the domain of the things themselves lies within intentionally implicated motivated possibilities revealed at this second level of reduction. But even at this level of reduction, the things of the world are implied because the second act of epoche promotes a reduction *from* them while every intentional act motivationally *implies* them. Again, then, Husserl seems to escape the charge of "idealism" in any traditional sense of the term. At the level of the second reduction, the statements referred to above refer to the discovery that causality is a constituted *sense* that is rooted in the deep structures of consciousness and that this *sense* does not enter consciousness from a Nature that is insulated from it. To further articulate the actual sense of Husserl's "idealism," however, his theory of constitution will have to be considered. This will be done in Chapter 5.

We have noted in this section that the distinction between appearance (the perceived qua perceived) and that which appears (the object) allowed Husserl to bracket existence at the level of ordinary experience and yet maintain the reality of the perceived as such. This was contrasted to Hume's equation of perception *per se* and existence qua object. This same distinction saves Husserl from becoming a subjective idealist, and, conjoined with the idea of intentional implication or motivated possibilities, it saves Husserl's second reduction from becoming a Flatlander's perspective on a set of perceptual atoms. The discovery of implicative intentionality "fluffs-out," so to speak; it adds a "depth dimension" to the would-be flatland of the second reduction. Within the second reduction, the "object" is always maintained in the act and object horizons of consciousness that signify the inescapable implicative surplus of the reduced perceptions had within the second level of reduction.

Owing to the implicative intentionality inherent in consciousness, then, Husserl can "have his object and suspend it too."[24] The act of "bracketing-out and yet retaining" is made possible because epoche works; that is, with the suspension of belief in a causally efficacious world, the "how" of appearances is seen as a constantly connected manifold and not as a series or collection of discrete perceptual atoms. This latter idea is a phenomenologically perverse one originally motivated by unexamined prejudices (*C* §9, p.30, n. *) concerning which Husserl eventually criticizes himself for having once held.[25]

The recognition of intentional implication, then, makes even the world of the second reduction inherently implicative of a world of real, that is, ordinary, objects. This kind of transcendence, the transcendence of things (transcendence$_1$), Husserl will always reserve as the far noematic pole of intentionality; and it will always indicate for him the only real world. This world and every single thing in it will always be transcendent to consciousness; but not radically transcendent (transcendence$_2$) because its aspects are always at least potentially perceivable. And although this as-yet-inchoate discovery of constitutive intentionality saves Husserl's reductio from becoming a reduction to the sense-data of an atomistic flatland and allows for the second level of suspension of world-positing belief, we will see in Chapters 5 and 6 that, paradoxically, it is also the reason that it is so difficult to achieve the phenomenological attitude and even more difficult to remain in it for long.

4.5
Two Views on Phenomenology and History

It was mentioned at the start of this chapter that in his work *Phenomenology and the Problem of History*, David Carr denies that Part II of the *Crisis* can be read as providing a historical way into phenomenology. We will now consider Carr's position on this issue and then the one developed in this book. The outcome of this comparison will reveal that although Carr's claim should be modified somewhat, because he suppresses the possibility of reading Husserl's phenomenology as we have done here, his general argument on the *problematic* relationship between phenomenology and history and the reading presented in this book can compatibly coexist. Indeed, they shed light upon one another.

(a) David Carr's View: Phenomenology and the Problem *of* History.

David Carr argues that the truly unique element of Husserl's final work is not the use of the concept of the life-world, as has often been claimed, but rather, it is the importance

Husserl gives to the role of history in the practice of phenomenological method.[26] He argues that this new role for history cannot be thought of as one that provides another way into phenomenology, because Part III of the *Crisis* is explicitly devoted to ways into phenomenology and history is not mentioned as one of these ways.[27] In fact, Carr insists that Husserl sees a much stronger role for history in relation to phenomenology: "The historical route is not a merely possible but a necessary one, and the idea seems to be that whichever of several parallel alternatives [i.e., paths into phenomenology] is chosen, it must be accompanied by historical reflections."[28]

After making these general claims, Carr reveals the sources, in Husserl's own work, for the problems posed by the acknowledgment of the historicity of all understanding.[29] The problem that history poses for phenomenology arises from Husserl's discovery of temporalized intersubjectivity and the realization that this leads inevitably to the communal and individual sedimentation of meanings. These sedimented meanings become acquisitions that each of us inevitably inherits as part of our selves; and this makes the ideal of phenomenological presuppositionlessness, of phenomenological epoche, a seeming impossibility.

At this point Carr emphasizes an important distinction.[30] In *Ideas* Husserl had distinguished between a "philosophical epoche" and the "phenomenological epoche" proper. He had written that, "Expressly formulated [the epoche] consists in this, that we completely abstain from judgment respecting the doctrinal content of all preexisting philosophy, and conduct all our expositions within this abstraction" (*I* §18).[31] This would contrast with the phenomenological epoche proper because, whereas the "philosophical epoche" brackets-out what is *explicitly* known in advance — a procedure that is perhaps not too difficult — the phenomenological epoche would attempt to bracket-out all the *implicit* presuppositions inherent to the natural attitude, and that is a far greater task.[32]

However, Carr argues, the ultimate effect of Husserl's earlier analyses of temporality and intersubjectivity is to make the philosophical epoche as problematic and difficult to achieve as is the phenomenological epoche[33], because the historicity of each and every consciousness must now be recognized — especially the consciousness of the philosopher performing the epoche. Since the philosopher, too, has a historical inheritance of the problems, concepts, and methods of past philosophy (*C* §7, p.17), these problems, concepts, and methods must be revealed, i.e., made explicit, in order for their full suspension to be made possible. Carr argues that this suspension can be made possible only by a kind of "historical reduction,"[34] expressing his perspective on this suspension when he writes, ". . . [T]he process of bracketing is identical with coming to awareness of [these] underlying presupposition[s] which otherwise remain hidden."[35] Making these philosophical and historical presuppositions explicit is the process of "historical reduction."

After developing Husserl's critique of the philosophical tradition,[36] Carr argues that Husserl's criticisms of Kant in the *Crisis* (*C* §§25-32) are in reality disguised criticisms of his (i.e., Husserl's) own early conceptions of the "world."[37] Husserl's criticisms of Kant had focused on the claim that Kant had accepted the natural scientific idea of Reality constituting the world and had developed his transcendental philosophy with the aim of justifying and grounding the notions of natural science, which he (Kant) had already accepted as the correct account of "world" and "reality" (*C* §§28-32). But likewise, Carr argues, until the time of the *Crisis* Husserl himself tended to describe the "surrounding-world-about-me" as "the totality of objects that, on the basis of actual experience, are knowable in correct theoretical thinking" (*I* §1, p.46).[38] By "correct theoretical thinking" Husserl meant natural scientific thinking, and consequently, he too was guilty of the belief — though to a lesser extent — that it was natural science, i.e., physicalistic objectivism, that gave us the first and most fundamental knowledge of the world.

Husserl's *Crisis* can thus be read, Carr argues, not only as a critique of the philosophical tradition for the purposes of overcoming it with a transcendental-phenomenology, but also as a critique of Husserl's own presuppositions as they lay hidden in his earlier works. And these necessarily hidden presuppositions lead to the general problem expressed by the title of Carr's book.

The problem *of* history arises for phenomenology because the philosophical-historical analytic motivates Husserl's new concept of the life-world,[39] and this new concept of the life-world, the historically and culturally "relative" world in which each of us lives, makes the possibility of radically presuppositionless transcendental philosophy more problematic than ever.[40] Although Husserl claims that the structure of the purely perceptual life-world is not itself relative (*C* §36, p.139), he does, as Carr notes, make comments that seem to suggest otherwise, namely, comments concerning the "flowing-in" and internalization of cultural achievements and perspectives into the direct experiencing of the life-world.[41] For example, each of us inherits a communal language and a communal culture,[42] a culture that determines our goals, projects, and ways of *experiencing* the world. In short, we inherit a world that molds our consciousness, perhaps even our strictly perceptual consciousness if such there be, and these factors may well make the radical phenomenological reduction, the reduction to pure experience, impossible.[43] The innocence of perception that Husserl has striven for from the birth of his phenomenology may be an impossible innocence because of our birth into a life-world always already riddled with meanings. All these factors lead Carr to paraphrase Merleau-Ponty's famous remark that "the most important lesson which the *historical* reduction teaches us is the impossibility of a complete reduction."[44]

The problems that historical-cultural relativity and the problem of "flowing-in" pose for phenomenology, then, are precisely those that have led continental philosophy in general away from transcendental philosophy into existentialism, hermeneutics, and postmodernism — all of which revolt, to use Gadamer's phrase, against Husserl's "prejudice against prejudices" (*das Vorurteil gegen die Vorurteile*).[45]

(b) The View Taken in This Work: Phenomenology
    and the Problems *in* History

Most of the problems for Husserlian phenomenology seen by David Carr as arising from Husserl's recognition of the historicity of all human consciousness do, in fact, arise. Husserl himself may have recognized this and may, as Carr argues, have realized that historical analysis must form a necessary fore-investigation for all radical phenomenological investigation. Husserl, however, also perceived another role for his historical-teleological investigations, a role that is suppressed in Carr's analyses. This is the role we have tried to develop and will continue to develop as it reveals the *raison d'être* for the *structure and project* of Husserlian phenomenology. Whereas Carr focuses upon the problems that historicity poses *for* phenomenology, we have focused upon the problems *in* history that are the historical sources demanding the telic end that phenomenology is, or at least, that Husserl hoped it would be.

Carr notes,[46] and now we emphasize, that Husserl himself saw his historical investigations in a light more sweetly colored than the light cast upon them by Carr's analyses. In a note to the first sentence of the *Crisis,* Husserl writes:

> The work . . . makes the attempt, by way of a teleological-historical reflection upon the origins of our critical scientific and philosophical situation, *to establish the unavoidable necessity of a transcendental-phenomenological reorientation of philosophy*. Accordingly, it becomes in its own right, an introduction to transcendental-phenomenology. (*C* §1, p.3, n. 1) (My emphasis)

We have tried to make this "introduction to phenomenology" clearer than did Husserl by showing how Husserl's phenomenology can be read precisely as this "unavoidable necessity" that is demanded in response to the problems of physicalistic rationalism.

Showing how the historical analyses of the *Crisis* provide a way into phenomenology, and why Carr's perspective on the positive side of the historical analyses is incomplete, involves taking a perspective on two sides of the same issue.[47] On the one hand, the historical analyses of the *Crisis* provide a way into phenomenology because they may lead the reader to recognize "the unavoidable necessity of a transcendental phenomenological reorientation in philosophy," and, on the other hand, these studies help one to understand the *structure* and *project* of phenomenology, as well as the need for phenomenology, *as* a response to the problems of uncritical physicalistic rationalism. In providing the critical basis for the interpretation of scientific naturalism, Husserl's *Crisis* effects its positive goal, and at the same time accomplishes an introduction to phenomenology by demonstrating the need for it as a foundational (reconstructive and critical) approach to the natural sciences.

Although Carr is right in insisting that the epoche of and reduction from the natural historicity of culturally burdened consciousness adds one more difficult dimension to phenomenological analysis, does it really do anything more than to make an "infinite project" a little more infinite? In the practice of natural science, there will always be presuppositions to analyze and new concepts to relate to the phenomenological conditions for intelligibility, and these presuppositions and concepts will constantly flow into the life-world itself. For these reasons, it is impossible to complete the historical reduction, as Carr has claimed, but surely no more so, as Merleau-Ponty noted, than it is to complete *any* phenomenological reduction. All presuppositions have other presuppositions, and this is why phenomenology is an infinite task. But while one more duty added to this task may make a change for phenomenological investigators, the infinite project remains the same—infinite. A complete reduction is not necessary for the existence and well-being of phenomenology.

Finally, there is an important facet of complementarity between Carr's work and this one, though it emerges in each work from diametrically opposite directions. Whereas Carr focuses upon the chronological development of Husserl's concept of "world" and argues that it involves an ever-incomplete movement from a world-concept that is infiltrated by natural scientific constructs, to a pure concept of world as "pre-theoretically lived,"[48] we have focused upon the reverse implications of this development for Husserl's work and argued that if he had separated the different kinds of positing theses earlier (i.e., the positing thesis of the natural attitude and that of the natural scientific attitude), the concepts of "world" and "Nature" would have been clarified earlier on. Interestingly, Husserl's criticisms of Kant along this line may, once again, have been a disguised criticism of himself. In *Formal and Transcendental Logic* he writes of Kant: "If he had proceeded radically, he would first of all have had to divide the problems into two groups: those concerning prescientific Nature and those concerning scientific Nature" (§100, p.265). This, of course, was what Husserl himself had eventually to do. After such broad but important distinctions, it was still necessary to distinguish the various strata of experience within each domain; but again, a graded system of reductions could accomplish this. Such simple procedural distinctions could have prevented enormous debate and misunderstanding of Husserl's project for phenomenology, and indeed, they still can.

4.6
The Cartesian Way Reconsidered

Husserl's own criticism of the "Cartesian Way" into phenomenology is given in the *Crisis* (*C* §43), though doubts about this way had emerged much earlier in his Winter Semester Lectures of 1910/11.[49] In the *Crisis* he writes that the Cartesian Way is a "much shorter way" into phenomenology than are any of the others, but ". . . it has a great shortcoming: . . . it leads to the transcendental ego in one leap, . . . it brings this ego into view as apparently empty of content, since there can be no preparatory explication . . ." (*C* §43, p.155). The point of Husserl's criticism is twofold.

First, the method of suspension by doubt implies, in the Cartesian vein, a *restriction* to the *indubitably* given. And second, the indubitably given, in the Cartesian manner of thinking, is the *immediately given* and nothing besides. Phenomenologically considered, however, the immediately given is the "how" of the "manners of givenness," and if the restriction to the indubitably given qua immediately given is enforced, then the "how" of the appearances cannot legitimately point beyond to, i.e., intentionally implicate, the "what," or the transcendence-in-immanence, which shows itself in the appearing.

The Cartesian Way would give us the "how" of appearing without a prior reduction through the "what," and would push us back to the transcendental ego "in one fell swoop," making the ego a place holder empty of implicative content. The tremendous range (indeed, the "world-wide" range) of implicative intentionality would not be seen to lie "within" the ego itself. Restricting the notion of certitude to what is *immediately and indubitably* given would certify the "how" of a phenomenon — its mode of appearance — without implicating the "what," that is, without acknowledging (the *idea* of) the thing manifest through the appearances.

Furthermore, it is the always implicit idea of the "what" implicated by the appearances that lends the doxic modification to the Husserlian notion of "certainty," and it is this doxic modification that keeps the Husserlian notion of certainty from becoming an otherworldly, classical Cartesian epistemic certainty. Also, without the doxic-ontic component inherent to the intentionally implicated aspects of reduced experience the intentional implications and motivated possibilities would not emerge, and even if they did, they could not be admitted because by their very nature intentionally implicated motivated possibilities point *beyond* the immediately and indubitably given to outlying spatial and temporal horizons. Hence, as we have already noted, whereas the Husserlian epoche suspends anything like classical Cartesian certainty concerning the transcendent object, it nevertheless always retains a doxic-ontic reference to that object, and necessarily so, by way of intentional implication.

Husserl's criticism of the Cartesian Way, then, can be read as an implicit criticism of his own tendency not to explicitly grade the reductions in his earlier works. His early laxness in distinguishing the reduction from natural scientific Reality and the reduction from the natural world — or, correlatively, his laxness in distinguishing between the epoche of natural scientific Reality and the epoche of the natural world — led to the Cartesian realm in one fell swoop. Moreover, the Cartesian realm was, in most cases, thought of as the indubitably given *as* immediately given, and this tended to obscure the implicative range, and hence the extensiveness, of the transcendental-phenomenological domain with its unique revelations of the doxic supports of ontic certainty. Finally, this tendency discouraged recognition of the "fallibilistic" strain in Husserl's philosophy.

However, we can now note how the combination of the historical way with the way through the critique of the natural sciences makes the Cartesian Way an acceptable way into phenomenology, albeit in a significantly more restricted manner than Husserl originally conceived.

When Husserl speaks of "the way through the critique of the positive sciences" (*EP* II 259-274), he sometimes means a critique of the concrete ontologies of the natural sciences, e.g., (in broadest form) the ontologies of "things," of "spirit" or "psyche," and of "culture" (*EP* II 259-74; *PP* §7; *I* II; *I* III §14; *C* §§ 37, 51), and sometimes he means the metaphysical "ontology" of the *natural physical sciences* as depicted by the metaphysical foundations of natural science, e.g., the "a priori ontology" of bare nature (*blosse Natur*) and pure corporeality (*I* II §11; *PP* §§ 17, 19, 25, 44; *C* §§ 9, 10, 12, Apx. II, pp. 305-6). We have, of course, entered Husserl's phenomenology by way of his critique of the metaphysical ontology of the natural physical sciences; that is, by way of his critique of the ontology of bare nature and pure corporeality. This way is essentially connected with the historical way because the historically inherited problems of philosophy were spawned by the acceptance of this metaphysical ontology. When this metaphysical ontology is recognized as the first item that must be suspended by the epoche, then the phenomenological procedure first reduces consciousness to the life-world itself or to the concrete ontologies of the life-world (*C* §38, p.147, §51). Thereby, the reduction to the world of the "what," to the things themselves as accepted and given in everyday living, occurs (*C* §38, p.144). For these reasons, *it is only after this reduction that the Cartesian reduction can be made to function appropriately*. Only after the first reduction does the Cartesian reduction reveal phenomena in an undistorted manner as intentionally implying *worldly* phenomena.

The Cartesian Way is the way of the second reduction. It places us in the deeper phenomenological realm, the realm strange to everydayness, in which the "how" of appearances in their manifold overlappings are revealed. The transcendental-phenomenological epoche and reduction was so troublesome for Husserl's phenomenology because it was originally presented as the Cartesian epoche and reduction without mediation of a "way through ontology." With one fell swoop Husserl tried to take his readers to the realm of the "mothers," thereby seeming to sever them from the world still intentionally implicated by the realm of reduced givens.

Husserl's criticisms of the Cartesian Way may also have been motivated by his realization that the very locution was misleading because the Cartesian reduction seemed to place the world in doubt by equating the indubitably given with the immediately given. With his recognition of intentional implication and motivated possibilities, Husserl had to break this equation and radically extend the sphere of the "immanent," that is, of the indubitably given *in a doxic sense*, because it was seen to be much more than the immediately given. Moreover, the indubitability of this givenness would prove not so indubitable as Husserl initially believed, largely because it was no so immediate as he initially believed. Again, recognition of these phenomena were behind Husserl's being "taken aback" by the discovery of "hidden transcendencies" (*IP* 8).

With the new system of graded reductions, however, the Cartesian Way can be read as the way into the *second* level of purified phenomenological experience. Since the Cartesian realm would then be entered only with the object realm as its horizon (as the constituted layer of Being surrounding it), the radical range of the immanent (qua transcendence-in-imma-nence) would be recognized even in the Cartesian reduction. Consequently, if our arguments have been cogent, the Cartesian Way may still be maintained — albeit in a new and clarified form — as *part of*, as the second step of, actual phenomenological practice.

4.7
INTERPRETATIVE CAVEATS AND CONFESSIONS: NOEMA AND FURTHER LEVELS OF REDUCTION

By now at least two idiosyncratic features in our reading of Husserl's epoche and reductions have probably been noticed. First, there seems to be a nearly total neglect of Husserl's all-important notion of the "noema"; and secondly, many further, deeper, levels of epoche and reduction seem to have been neglected in our reading. We will respond briefly to these issues here, though the second idiosyncratic feature of our reading will not be fully defended until Chapter 5 in section 5.1(b).

(a) Noema: Abstract Entity and Embedded Sense

It may seem that the reading of Husserl here offered is either completely ignorant of what has become known as the "percept-concept" or, correlatively, the "Gurwitsch-Føllesdal" debate over the notion of the noema[50] or that it simply ignores the Føllesdalian reading and adopts a variant of the Gurwitschean. The first possibility is not an actuality; the second possibility, at least procedurally, is. The importance of this exchange to the recent literature on Husserl, however, demands at least brief explanation from those who would attempt to maneuver around it.

The absence of a very explicit position concerning this debate stems from the belief that the notion of the noema has been allotted an importance in Husserl scholarship reaching far beyond that which is justified for an understanding of Husserl's overall philosophy. There are a number of reasons for this. Among these reasons are, first, the central importance of *Ideas I* in the Husserlian corpus for Husserl's logistic notion of sense.[51] Second, and correlative to the first point, there is the relative neglect of Husserl's other works (with the exception of the *Logical Investigations*) by many philosophers — works where the notion of the "noema" plays a very minor role, if any role at all. Third, there are Husserl's own statements (in *Ideas I*) that seem to give the noema central importance for his thought (§96, p.257). Fourth, the notion of the noema as an *abstract* sense through which reference is achieved is of particular importance to certain traditions in philosophy for shedding light on certain problems intrinsic to those traditions. Examples of such problems are the failure of the principles of the "substitutivity of identity" and "existential generalization" in intentional contexts. And finally, the territorialism of philosophers (a universal trait among carnivores, it seems) has promoted a reaction by the self-appointed acolytes of Husserl to what appears (and perhaps is) a rather one-sided plundering of Husserlian insights that revolves around the Føllesdalian interpretation of the noema. Apart from this sociological and historical defense of the approach adopted in this text, however, the following two points should also be made.

First, there is reason to suspect that *both* readings of Husserl's notion of the noema are partially correct, that both can be supported by appeals to Husserl's texts, and that the readings are *not* exclusive of one another. To some extent the Føllesdalian versus the Gurwitschean reading of Husserl's notion of the noema seems to be dictated by the interpreter's thematic interests: broadly, those of logic, mathematics, and formal semantics versus those of perception.[52] If one is interested in pursuing Husserlian investigations in the former areas, as are Føllesdal et al., then there is a tendency to emphasize the "concept" reading of the noema; while if one is interested in pursuing Husserlian investigations in the phenomenology of perception, then there is a tendency to emphasize the "percept" reading of the noema, as we have done. Neither of these approaches to the noema, however, is necessarily limited to these specified areas of interest because there is certainly a "logic of perception" to be understood just as there are "aspectival" or constructional facets of mathematics and logic to be understood. In defense of the potential breadth of the Gurwitschean reading, Husserl's "constructionism" in mathematics and logic leaves room for an "aspectival" reading of ideal entities,[53] while, in defense of the breadth of the Føllesdalian reading, Husserl's extensive concerns with logic and mathematics leave room for extensive use of the "abstract" notion of noema in the area of perception as well as in the area of the formal sciences.

Generally, then, our position is that the exchange over the notion of the noema is largely one of those classical philosophical debates generated by "strong misreadings" that invoke a "clinamen" (to use Harold Bloom's terminology[54]) precisely where it suits the purposes of the particular investigator's concerns. Less jargonistically stated, the debate seems often to commit the "either-or" fallacy when the "both-and" option will, we suspect, be quite apparent to our successors. It also seems to be the case, however, that Husserl himself was never explicitly aware of the possibility of this double reading of his notion, partially relative to domains and methodologies of application. Hence, it cannot be denied that he planted the seeds for the various interpretations. To this extent the debate over the notion of the noema has been a valuable and important one, for it has, once again, forced an awareness of the richness of Husserl's writings—writings that offer insights as well as concrete investigations that lead in so many directions.

A couple more comments can now be made about this issue. Research offered by Donn Welton, as well as arguments suggested by Jaakko Hintikka and myself, can lend further support to the suppression of direct concern with the notion of the noema even while permitting a fairly deep understanding of Husserl's work. Welton has shown, in effect, that as Husserl's thought developed from *Ideas* to the *Analysen zur passiven Synthesis*, where there was an increasing emphasis on perceptual problems as opposed to mathematical-logical ones, there was, correlatively, a gradual displacement of the work done by the notion of the noema (as an abstract rule accounting for the syntheses of perspectives), by an appeal to bodily kinaesthesia, movement, etc., as they (the bodily kinaesthesia) unified perspectives across time.[55] This reading of Husserl, in relationship to what has been called the "perceptual noema," seems to limit the need to appeal to the abstract and purely logistic notion of the noema for an understanding· of Husserl's theory of perception. The most famous and most developed form of such a phenomenology occurred, of course, in the works of Merleau-Ponty. The "proof" of this alternative interpretation of Husserl, however, can only be in the "pudding," and part of that pudding is being made here.

Finally, let us offer one other perspective on the issue of the "perceptual noema." Insofar as one remains object-oriented after the reductions, the "noema" remains invisible as a *functioning* abstract entity. That is, insofar as reflection and the reductions are *not* collapsed, then reduction (*still prior to phenomenological reflection*) leaves us staring at the given, and the *work* normally done by the noema is revealed via *its blending* with the object-aspect, or appearance, as now present to consciousness.[56] In its embedded form, the noema functions to motivate or intentionally implicate the object *in toto*. Here, the purposes of phenomenological analyses of perceptual experience would simply be defeated if a wedge dividing "percept" from "concept" were driven between noema and object. All this points to the simple *prereflective revelatory role* of reduction as we have been developing it in this work. As we will see more fully in the next chapter, in this phase of phenomenological experience, phenomenological description cannot be totally separated from sensory appearances.

In fine, we are suggesting that the Gurwitschean interpretation of the noema tends to read it as revealed after *object-oriented* reduction, but prior to the reflexive act in which consciousness *makes an abstract object* of the senses that it previously used to reach or implicate the objects with which we normally live. At this level of reduced experience, the noema works as an *embedded sense*, embedded in the appearances of the object. On the other hand, the Føllesdalian interpretation of the noema reads it as an object-sense largely *abstracted from* the appearances of the object, and this object-sense can only appear in phenomenological *reflection* as a *reflected meaning construct*. It is in this sense of "appearance-independence" that the Føllesdalian reading of the noema has the greater scope, but this reading does miss the empirical, psychological, and *experiential* flavor of much that Husserl wrote. It also misses what might be called the "experiential shift" as it occurs in relationship to ordinary, everyday perception. It was Gurwitsch's contribution to emphasize this experiential, gestalt-like shift somewhat at the expense of totally purified phenomenological reflection proper, while it has been Føllesdal's contribution to emphasize the importance of phenomenological reflection proper; that is, to emphasize the logical Sinn-analytic that is possible in relation to any experienced object, somewhat at the expense of the experiential aspects of phenomenological reduction. Finally, the analyses developed here can be understood to operate within the recognized and prescribed scope of the Gurwitschean "appearance-implicative" reading of the noema. But again, insofar as this noema "appears" as blended in the appearances of the object, it does its work without needing explicit mention.

(b) Further Levels of Reduction

It may also seem peculiar that the analyses of the phenomenological reduction carried out in the previous sections stopped at what we have identified as the second procedural step in phenomenological practice; that is, at the experiential domain of appearances. Surely, in most of his work, Husserl identified strata of constitutive content much deeper than that of the appearances of objects. It might be revealing, then, to offer a model along the lines of interpretation that we have developed thus far that portrays the relationships between epoche, reduction, and the deeper layers of constitutive content that we have not mentioned, but which are often mentioned by Husserl. In Chapter 5.1(b) we will argue that owing to his increasing recognition of the constitutive powers of time-consciousness, Husserl was eventually led to soften his claims about the content of the constitutive strata that lay beneath the appearances of objects. But before doing that it might be enlightening to show how the theory of graded reductions, with an object-orientation, could be used to enhance our understanding of Husserl's initial vision of the contents of the reduced domain that he hoped to use to gain an understanding of natural knowledge and its objects.

In section 4.4 we showed how, with the suspension of natural scientific Nature, the object-orientation of consciousness was reduced to an experience of ordinary life-world objects. Then, with the suspension of belief in the existence of life-world objects, consciousness was reduced to an experience of the appearances of those objects. In each case we also argued that Husserl avoided being forced into the adoption of a foundationalistic sense-data theory. Nevertheless, we suggested that Husserl was guilty of approaching some such position in his earlier writings. It is chiefly (though not entirely) in the context of these earlier writings that Husserl would have placed the greatest importance on the deeper strata of constitutive content that would (presumably) be revealed by the further acts of epoche and reduction. The model at right and ensuing comments should provide some clarification on the relations between epoche, reduction, and these deeper strata of constitutive content.

Thus far we have offered a number of descriptive arguments that have attempted to articulate the logical, analytical movement from $epoche_1$ to $reduction_1$ (4.4a) and $epoche_2$ to $reduction_2$ (4.4b). These relations are now portrayed in the upper two levels of Figure 6 as is the constitutive content of each level of reduction. In section 5.1 we will attempt to articulate the phenomenological structure of the *synthetic, constitutive movement* from the experiential domain of $reduction_2$ (the domain of appearances) back to the life-world and its objects; and then, in section 5.2 we will attempt to articulate the phenomenological structure of the constitutive movement from the experiential domain of $reduction_1$ (the life-world and its objects) back to the natural scientific domain of realities and idealities. In this section, however, we will simply give the briefest statement possible of the layers of constitutive content *below* the

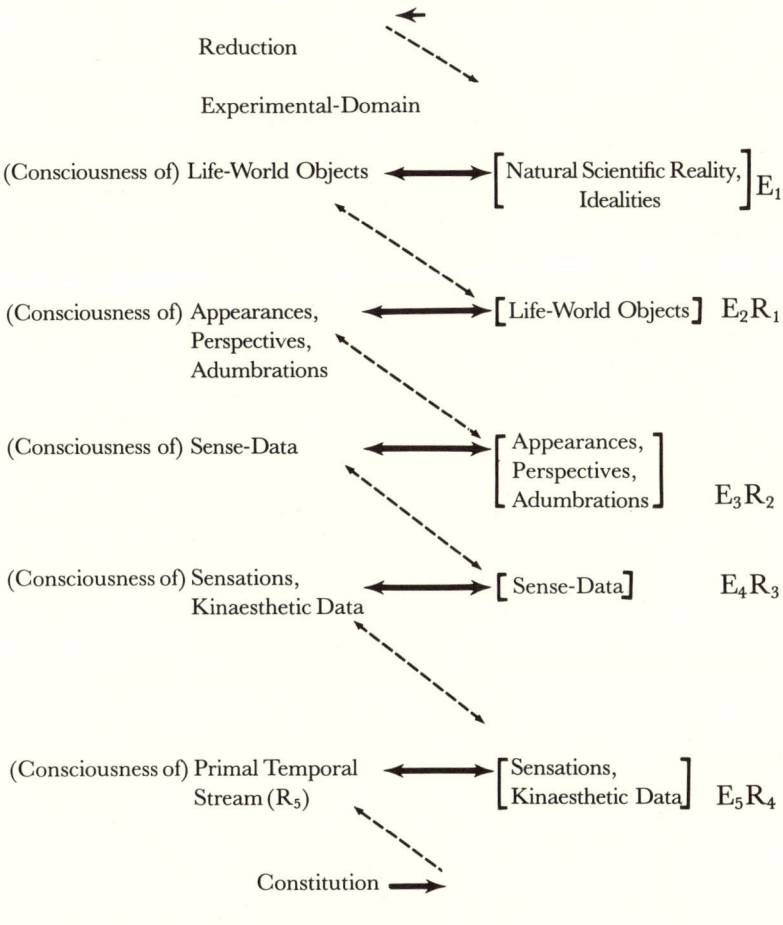

Figure 6

phenomenological focus on appearances; though, again, for reasons that will become apparent in section 5.1(b), we will not develop an argument for the *possibility* of reducing to these constitutive strata. Our reading of Husserl to follow will attempt to nudge him away from commitment to, or at least extensive concern with, such constitutive contents.

In the *Logical Investigations* (pp.309-10, 569-76, 861-62), *The Phenomenology of Internal Time-Consciousness* (§40), and *Ideas,* (§85) Husserl often struggled with the place of notions like "primal sensory data." Presumably, in terms of our interpretation, by working analytically with epoche and reduction, that is, by suspending doxic immersion in the appearances of objects, one would become acquainted with "sense-data." These sense-data, not terribly unlike those of G. E. Moore and Bertrand Russell, would be something like "a patch of yellow" or an uninterpreted sound.[57] Some of these kinds of phenomena, like the appearances of objects and unlike most sensations and kineaesthesia, would be made fully distinct from the consciousness of them. They are, presumably, extremely focused parts of appearances — "qualitatively singular parts" might be their best description — which combine synthetically to constitute the appearances of objects that, in turn, allow consciousness to constitute objects per se (*LI* 310, 861; *I* §41, p.119).

Next, some kinds of "sense-data" and most "sensations" would presumably represent the levels of reduced experience where the act and object (or "noetic" and "noematic") sides of conscious experience would begin to blur. This is because at this level of reflected experience, difficulties of distinction arise between the more primitive or "nondistantial" sensory modalities and the more advanced or "distantial" ones. For instance, it is difficult if not impossible to distinguish the *sensation* of the hotness of something to the touch from the *sense-datum* of "hot." Or again, whereas (arguably) it seems sensible to speak of the sense-datum "yellow," it is not at all clear that it makes sense to speak of the sensation of yellow or of "yellow sensations." In short, the distinction between sensing and sensed begins to collapse at the same time that our language about "sensations" and "sense-data" does.[58] And this is not because our language is insufficient to portray certain experiences of consciousness, but rather, because our language evolves precisely to portray such distinctions where and when they are had, and they simply *are not had* at these would-be "deep" levels of reduced experience.[59] Treading lightly in this metaphysical morass, Husserl often refers to such levels of "experience" as *abstractions* from the experiences of appearances of objects (*LI* 309f; *I* §85; *EJ* §16, p.72), rather than as unique levels of actual, reduced experience.

In any case, once the doxic focus on sense-data is

suspended, reduction to pure sensations and kineaesthesia would presumably be achieved. Here, consciousness *is* body-consciousness; and hence, consciousness and its sensational-kinaesthetic object can, at times, become one and the same. The sensation of pain, for instance, can become an object of consciousness as in the case of minor pains, or consciousness can *become a sensation of pain*, that is, it can *be pain* through and through, in the case of terrible pain. At the level of kinaesthetic sensations, body-consciousness and world meet with full emphasis placed upon prereflective body-awareness.[60] Growing out of this first-order dimension of *contact*, sense-data arise, then appearances, then things, and finally the Nature of natural science. Sense-data, in theory, would thus be the first distantial act of object-constitution via the objectification of sensations and kineaesthesia.

Finally, the final act of epoche and the lowest level of reduction would bring us to the primal temporal stream. Here consciousness *is* absolute consciousness, and it *is* just the self-constituting flow of temporality.[61] There is, presumably, no deeper experiential domain of data than this one (hence, it marks the nadir of the phenomenological reductions), and all else is constituted from this set of data (hence, it marks the beginning, the source point, of constitutive intentionality).

As mentioned earlier, for reasons that will be developed in section 5.1(b), we have refrained and will refrain from developing or arguing for the possibility of these further reductions in any greater detail. In what is to follow we will attempt to blend these deepest levels of constitutive content with the levels of content we have distinguished earlier. We will not argue for the complete elimination of such "deep level" contents, but we will suggest that their importance is minimal for an understanding of our knowledge-constituting achievements, and therefore it is appropriate that their role grew ever smaller in Husserl's thought.

NOTES

1. See especially *EP, Zweiter Teil*, entitled: *Theorie Der Phänomenologischen Reduktion* (Den Hague: Martinus Nijhoff, 1959). Cf. also R. Boehm's Introduction, pp. xxx-xxxvii.

2. Iso Kern, *Husserl und Kant* (Den Haag: Martinus Nijhoff, 1964), p. 218.

3. Carr, *Phenomenology and the Problem of History*, pp. 64-65; "Husserl's *Crisis*," p. 130.

4. Carr, *Phenomenology and the Problem of History*, pp. 65-66; "Husserl's *Crisis*," p. 130.

5. Carr, "Husserl's *Crisis*," p. 127; see also, Guido Küng, "The Phenomenological Reduction as Epoche and as Explication," *The Monist* 59 (1975), pp. 72, 74; and Ludwig Landgrebe, "Husserl's Departure from Cartesianism," in *The Phenomenology of Edmund Husserl*, ed. by Donn Welton (New York: Cornell University Press, 1981), pp. 66-121.

6. See for instance J. N. Findlay's introduction to his translation of *LI*, p. 10. And Richard Schmitt, "Transcendental Phenomenology: Muddle or Mystery?" *Journal of the British Society for Phenomenology* 1 (1971): 19-27.

7. For an interpretation of the epoche and reduction as a motivated relation (as we are applying them here), see Philip J. Bossert, "The Sense of 'Epoche' and 'Reduction' in Husserl's Philosophy," *Journal of the British Society for Phenomenology* 5 (1974): 243-55. Also see my discussion on "The Existential Foundations of Phenomenological Reduction," in the same journal, 17 (1986): 193-97.

8. We shall see, however, that the reduction to the second level of phenomenological experience does, at first, seem to threaten Husserl, too, with something like a reduction to mere sense-data as a "given"—albeit a "reduced" given. See below §4.4(b). For an insightful comparison of E. A. Abbott's *Flatland* with Husserl's phenomenological reduction see Philip Bossert's essay "Plato's Cave, *Flatland* and Phenomenology," in *Phenomenology in Practice and Theory*, ed. by William S. Hamrick (Dordrecht: Martinus Nijhoff, 1985): 53-66.

9. I have been following Boyce Gibson's translation of *Ideas* throughout this text; however, Husserl's "principle of principles," "*originär gebende Erfahrung*," is probably better rendered as "originally giving experience" than as Gibson's "primordial dator intuition."

For a much less literal, though very suggestive translation, see Erazim Kohak, *Idea & Experience* (Chicago and London: University of Chicago Press, 1978), p. 197, n. 10, where it is rendered "primary synthetic awareness," signifying the synthesizing awareness that always grows with experience.

10. See Goethe's *Faust*, Pt. II, line 6216, passim.

11. For extended considerations of Husserl's philosophical relation to Hume see R. A. Mall, *Experience and Reason* (The Hague: Martinus Nijhoff, 1973) and Richard T. Murphy, *Hume and Husserl* (The Hague: Martinus Nijhoff, 1980).

12. David Hume, *A Treatise of Human Nature* (Oxford: Clarendon Press, 1975), p. 94. Also see, pp. 66-68, 94, 102, 187, 623-24.

13. Hume, *Treatise*, p. 201.

14. Hume, *Treatise,* p. 187.

15. Hume, *Treatise,* ibid.

16. Hume, *Treatise*, pp. 211, 214, 216-17, 241.

17. A notion very similar to that of "horizon," the concept of the "fringe," had already been developed by William James in his *Principles of Psychology* (New York: Dover Pub., Inc., 1950), see esp. Ch. IX, "The Stream of Thought." Husserl had read parts of this work and had thought highly of it. See his comments in *"Persönliche Aufzeichnungen,"* ed. by W. Biemel, *Philosophy and Phenomenological Research* (Buffalo: New York) 16 (1955-56), p. 295.

18. E. A. Abbott, *Flatland: A Romance of Many Dimensions* (New York: Barnes & Noble Books, 1963). As mentioned earlier Philip Bossert puts this story to interesting and revelatory use in his essay " 'Plato's Cave', *Flatland* and Phenomenology," contained in *Phenomenology in Practice and Theory*, ed. by William S. Hamrick (The Hague: Martinus Nijhoff, 1985), pp. 53-66.

19. Hume, *Treatise*, p. 188.

20. Hume, *Treatise*, p. 194 ff.

21. Hume, *Treatise*, p. 7.

22. Hume, *Treatise*, pp. 233, 252, 259, 263, 636.

23. Hume, *Treatise*, p. 636.

24. In a series of discussions with Jaakko Hintikka on the nature and possibility of this second reduction, it was consistently claimed by him that Husserl was attempting to "have his cake and eat it too." The adage is apropos because the problem surrounding the deep levels of phenomenological reduction is the possibility of "suspending the object and having it too (still)." But it is precisely Husserl's discovery of implicative intentionality that demands the coincidence of this "reducing and yet still retaining" because each act of epoche and each event of reduction reveals that the object *in*

toto is still *intended*. The consequence is that when Husserl suspends the object he must *necessarily* still intend it too.

25. For Husserl's criticisms of sense-data theories see *PL* 13; *FTL* §100, pp.256-57; *C* §9, p.30, n.*; and especially Mss. B I 13 I, p.8 (see below, p.244), cited in Robert Sokolowski, *The Formation of Husserl's Concept of Constitution* (The Hague: Martinus Nijhoff, 1964), pp. 179-80.

26. Carr, "Husserl's *Crisis*," p. 127.

27. Carr, *Phenomenology and the Problem of History*, p. 65; "Husserl's *Crisis*," p. 130.

28. Carr, "Husserl's *Crisis*," p. 130.

29. Carr, *Phenomenology and the Problem of History*, Ch. III-IV; "Husserl's *Crisis*," p. 131-36.

30. Carr, *Phenomenology and the Problem of History*, pp. 115-17; "Husserl's *Crisis*," p. 137.

31. Carr, *Phenomenology and the Problem of History*, p. 63.

32. Carr, *Phenomenology and the Problem of History*, pp. 115-17.

33. Carr, *Phenomenology and the Problem of History*, pp. 117-18; "Husserl's *Crisis*," pp. 137-38.

34. Carr, *Phenomenology and the Problem of History*, pp. 117-20; "Husserl's *Crisis*," p. 138.

35. Carr, "Husserl's *Crisis*," p. 137.

36. Carr, *Phenomenology and the Problem of History*, pp. 120-32; "Husserl's *Crisis*," pp. 139-42.

37. Carr, *Phenomenology and the Problem of History*, pp. 142-61, 168-72; "Husserl's *Crisis*," pp. 142-43, 145.

38. Carr, *Phenomenology and the Problem of History*, p. 144; "Husserl's *Crisis*," p. 143.

39. Carr, *Phenomenology and the Problem of History*, p. 182.

40. Carr, *Phenomenology and the Problem of History*, pp. 172-81.

41. Carr, *Phenomenology and the Problem of History*, pp. 240-42. For a more extensive development of the multiple meanings of Husserl's concept of the "life-world" — primarily the dual meaning of a perceptually innocent and a culturally concept-laden world — see Carr's essay "Husserl's Problematic Concept of the Life-World," in *Philosophical Quarterly* 7 (1970): 331-39. Reprinted in Frederick A. Ellison and Peter McCormick, *Husserl: Exposition and Appraisals* (Notre Dame: University of Notre Dame Press, 1977), pp. 202-12.

42. Carr, *Phenomenology and the Problem of History*, pp. 195-98.

43. Carr, *Phenomenology and the Problem of History*, pp.231-36.

44. Carr, *Phenomenology and the Problem of History*, p. 242. See Maurice Merleau-Ponty, *Phenomenology of Perception*, trans. by Colin Smith (New York: Humanities Press, 1962), p. xiv.

45. Hans-Georg Gadamer, *Wahrheit und Methode*, 2nd ed. (Tubingen: Mohr,1965), p. 255. For David Carr's thought along these lines, see his essay "Phenomenology and Relativism," in *Phenomenology in Theory and Practice*, ed. by William S. Hamrick (The Hague: Martinus Nijhoff, 1985), pp. 19-34.

46. Carr, *Phenomenology and the Problem of History*, pp. xxii, 181.

47. For Carr's reading of the "positive side" of the historical analyses in *Crisis*, see *Phenomenology and the Problem of History*, pp. 270-77; "Husserl's *Crisis*," pp. 147-48.

48. Carr, *Phenomenology and the Problem of History*, Chs. 6, 7.

49. Bossert, *The Origins and Early Development of Edmund Husserl's Method of Phenomenological Reduction* (St. Louis: Washington University, 1973), pp. 180-93.

50. This debate has been anthologized in Hubert L. Dreyfus, ed., *Husserl, Intentionality and Cognitive Science* (Cambridge: MIT Press, 1982), esp. essays 3-7.

51. For a development of the distinction between "logistic" versus "perceptual" sense in Husserl's thought, see Donn Welton's essays "Structure and Genesis in Husserl's Phenomenology," in *Husserl: Expositions and Appraisals*, ed. by Frederick A. Elliston and Peter McCormick (Notre Dame: University of Notre Dame Press, 1977), pp. 54-69; and "Husserl's Genetic Phenomenology of Perception," in *Husserl and Contemporary Thought*, ed. by John Sallis (New Jersey: Humanities Press, 1983), pp. 59-83. Also, for fuller context and development, see Welton's book *The Origins of Meaning* (The Hague: Martinus Nijhoff, 1983). In response to Welton's first essay see John J. Drummond, "The Phenomenology of Perceptual Sense," *The Southwestern Journal of Philosophy* 10 (1979): 139-46.

52. For a suggestion about the exchange along these lines, see Robert Solomon, "Husserl's Concept of the Noema," contained in *Husserl: Expositions and Appraisals*, ed. by Frederick A. Elliston and Peter McCormick (Notre Dame: University of Notre Dame Press, 1977), pp. 168-81.

53. For a reading of Husserl's mathematical "constructionalism" see Richard Tieszen, "The Notion of Mathematical Intuition and Husserl's Phenomenology," *Nous* 18 (September 1984): 395-421.

54. Harold Bloom, *The Anxiety of Influence* (New York: Oxford University Press, 1973).

55. Welton, loc. cit.

56. For further suggestions along these lines see Jaakko Hintikka and Charles Harvey, "Review of D. W. Smith and R. McIntyre, *Husserl and Intentionality: A Study of Mind, Meaning, and Language*, in *Husserl Studies* 1 (1984), esp. pp. 208-10.

57. See G. E. Moore, *Some Main Problems of Philosophy* (New York: The Macmillan Co., 1953), pp. 29-38; Bertrand Russell, *Our Knowledge of the External World* (London: George Allen & Unwin, Ltd., 1922), pp. 75-88.

58. For a more developed argument along these lines see Gilbert Ryle, *The Concept of Mind* (London: Hutchinson & Co., Ltd., 1949), pp. 213-20.

59. For another form of this argument, see Harmon Chapman, *Sensations and Phenomenology* (Bloomington: Indiana University Press, 1966). It is interesting to note that Chapman's argument against the Husserlian appeal to "sensations" grows from an analysis of the same tradition that we have considered for the development of our reading of Husserl's phenomenology. But we are arguing, further, that it was precisely his growing understanding of this tradition that was leading Husserl away from the "sensation theory."

60. For a very convincing explication, interpretation, and defense of Husserl's notion of "hyletic experience," see Shaun Gallagher, "Hyletic Experience and the Lived Body," *Husserl Studies* 3 (1986): 131-66.

61. For a reading of Husserl's discovery of this "absolute consciousness," see John B. Brough, "The Emergence of an Absolute Consciousness in Husserl's Early Writings on Time-Consciousness," *Man and World* 5 (1972): 298-326. Also contained in *Husserl: Exposition and Appraisals*, ed. by Frederick A. Elliston and Peter McCormick (Notre Dame: University of Notre Dame Press, 1977), pp. 83-100.

5

CONSTITUTIONAL ANALYSES

HUSSERL BELIEVED THAT when the nadir of intentionality is finally reached, the "Heraclitean Flux" of pure experience comes into view (*Time* §§35-39). The critical procedural techniques of epoche and reduction thus reveal the processes of temporal constitution that are normally hidden to the involved consciousness of everyday experience. But this revelation is still a passive viewing. Hence, Husserl writes in the *Crisis*:

> The empty generality of the epoche does not of itself clarify anything; it is only the gate of entry through which one must pass in order to be able to discover the new world of pure subjectivity. The actual discovery is a matter of concrete, extremely subtle and differentiated work. (*C* §71, p.257)

This "subtle and differentiated work" involves another shift of perspective via which Husserl's notion of intentional implication is transformed into that of "constitutive intentionality." Drawing an analogy with the method of analysis and synthesis, we can say that the discovery of intentional implication results from the methods of analysis (i.e., epoche and reduction), while the discovery of constitutive intentionality results from the recognition of the processes of synthesis (i.e., the phenomenological descriptions that portray the coming-to-be and passing-away of intentionally implicated experiences). To the two-step procedure of analysis, a third, synthetic step is now added, namely, phenomenological reflection or description. Well-connected descriptions are the verbal form of phenomenological reflection, which is reflection upon the reduced experiences that follow from the acts of epoche.

If, starting from their nadir, the concrete moments of constitutive intentionality are now described, the constitution of world and Nature would, in theory, be seen to arise in reverse order to the system of grading (of epoche and reduction) developed in section 4.4 of the previous chapter. That is, after epoche$_1$ reduces consciousness to the things themselves, and after epoche$_2$ reduces conscious experience to the purified appearances, well-connected descriptions of the reduced experiences, at the level of reduction$_2$, would reveal the processes of intuitive "building up" — the processes of constitution — of the object-world; when the object-world is thus regained from being held in abeyance to the epoche and seen again as the unified phenomenal manifold (component 2 of Figure 5) this life-world would, in theory, reveal the structures *from* which the natural scientific world is constructed (Domain A of Figure 1), and *to* which this world of natural science must ultimately conform (*C* §§33-34).

Precisely to the extent that these constitutional analyses are successful, Husserl can make good his claim that "nothing is lost" to the epoche (*I* §50, p.140; *PL* 9, 12; *C* §52, p.176). If they are successful, then the entire "world" and "Nature" will be regained, but regained as grounded in transcendental subjectivity rather than as issuing from a physicalistic objectivity. Likewise, the "proof" for Husserl's unique brand of idealism, transcendental phenomenological idealism, can be given only insofar as constitutional analyses convincingly describe the processes by which consciousness constitutes the world.

In concluding the *Cartesian Meditations* Husserl had written, "The delphic motto, 'Know thyself!' has gained a new siglose the world by epoche, in order to regain it by a universal self examination" (§64, p.157). This universal self (and "world") examination is depicted by the phenomenological descriptions that are *of* the processes of constitution. As long as there is consciousness, these constitutional processes are an ongoing affair, and though they can never be completely described (because there are always *more* phenomena), their *sense* can nonetheless be explicated, abstractly and via example.

It is now our task to provide the outlines of some of these explications. In section 5.1 of this chapter we will focus on the constitution of the object-world; in section 5.2 the constitution of natural scientific "Nature" will be considered.

5.1
THE CERTAINTY OF SEEMING AND THE CONSTITUTION OF THE WORLD

While Husserl credits Descartes with the discovery of the transcendental realm achieved via an inchoate form of epoche (*CM* §41, p.83; *C* §17), he credits Hume with the performance of the first proto-phenomenological constitutional descriptions (*EP* I, pp.156-57; *FTL* §100, pp.265-67). Descartes, however, also came close to the performance of phenomenological description, though far more quickly than Hume he was misled by physicalistic prejudices. In this part of Chapter 5 we will attempt to show that where Descartes abandoned the transcendental domain, Husserl maintained, extended, investigated, and described it. This comparison will also help us to explicate the constructive side of Husserl's phenomenology.

(a) Descartes and the Determination of Essences:
The Wax Experience

First, Descartes' description of the wax:

> It has not yet completely lost the sweetness of the honey it contained; it still retains something of the odor of the flowers from which it was collected; its color, shape, and size are apparent; it is hard and cold; it can easily be touched; and, if you knock on it, it will give out some sound. Thus

everything which can make a body distinctly known are found in this example.

But now while I am talking I bring it close to the fire. What remains of the taste evaporates; the odor vanishes; its color changes; its shape is lost; its size increases; it becomes liquid; it grows hot; one can hardly touch it; and although it is knocked upon, it will give out no sound. Does the same wax remain after this change? We must admit that it does; no one denies it, no one judges otherwise.[1]

Descartes' description will suffice for the moment, though it is hardly a well-connected one and certainly not one that reveals the constitutional factors embedded in our knowledge of the wax. Before explicitly developing a phenomenological description of the wax experience, however, let us consider the *reasons* Descartes offers for the claim that in spite of its radical transformations "the same wax is believed to remain; no one would judge otherwise."

His argument follows a familiar Cartesian pattern. He argues that the source of his knowledge cannot stem from his senses, ". . . since everything in the field of taste, smell, sight, touch, and hearing are changed, and since the same wax nevertheless remains."[2] This knowledge cannot stem from imagination, ". . . since I conceive it capable of undergoing an infinity of similar changes, and I could not compass this infinity in imagination."[3] Consequently, Descartes argues, ". . . there is nothing but my understanding alone which does conceive it."[4] Knowledge of this wax in particular, and even more so, of wax in general, is due solely to "an inspection of the mind."[5]

This pattern of reasoning can be found in numerous places in the early and late pages of the *Meditations*, and can be referred to as Descartes' "descending abstractive hierarchy."[6] In arguing for the determination of an essence, that is, an identity statement, Descartes argues that we do not achieve knowledge of an essence through perception because perception can always prove illusory; nor can we determine an essence via imagination, because the possible imaginative variations on any object are infinite; hence, by varying its contents, the mind could never reach the conclusive position needed for the assertion of an identity claim. Consequently, Descartes argues, essences are known via conception alone, via clear and distinct ideas concerning the event, issue, or object in question. These conceptions are attained through the method of analysis that seeks a reduction to simple natures: in the wax experience this process occurs in an abbreviated form as the descending abstractive hierarchy.

However, between perception and imagination on the one hand, and conception on the other, there is a hiatus in Descartes' method for the determination of essences. After the process of eliminative reduction, he tells us that ". . . nothing is left [in our conception of the wax] but something extended, flexible, and movable."[7] Yet soon after he writes that the wax that is known is none other than ". . . the one that I see, that I touch, that I imagine . . . ."[8] But he never tells us *how* our *conception* of the wax can be knowledge of (the essence of) the wax that we *perceive and imagine*. Whereas the essences of material things are claimed to be determined by pure conception alone, these essences are reached only by an *eliminative reduction* through perception and imagination. How, then, can our conception of the wax be *of* the *same* wax as that wax we perceive and imagine?

As J. J. C. Smart has noted, Descartes really is not concerned with what can be known *about* the wax.[9] Indeed, Descartes gives us quite a list of the things he does know about it. The essence with which Descartes is concerned is not the essence of *this* wax, or even wax in general, but the essence of material bodies strictly as material bodies. And, since the essences reached at this level of judgment—the quantifiable essences of natural reductive science[10]—are inexperienceable in principle by perception and imagination, Descartes' wax experiment functions as a red herring if it is read as an attempt to display our manner of determining the essence of particular life-world objects—such as a piece of wax, for example.[11]

The only essences recognized by Descartes were the essential *sine qua non* properties of natural reductive science. He believed that quantifiable relations revealed the essence of the "real" things, the "things" of Nature, and he thereby over-looked the transcendental task of determining the processes by which we know the essence of ordinary things in their manifold appearings. The hiatus that exists between percep-tion and imagination on the one hand, and conception on the other, in Descartes' thought, is paralleled by the hiatus be-tween the world of experience and the "world" of natural reductive science. The "faculties" of perception and imagina-tion are condemned to the world of experience, whereas con-ception, through its mysterious innate powers, intuits the real world (Domain A of Figure 1). Only real things can have essences, and real things are *purely* corporeal. Hence, the only essences are those established by natural science, and these are universal essences concerning the "real" nature of things — their corporeal nature and relations. The essences of the meaningful, experienced things of the life-world are overlooked.

But recall that the descriptions of the wax carried out in *Meditation II* occur within what was earlier termed the "certain-ty of seeming." We now know that the domain of the "certainty of seeming" is experience at the level of the second reduction, the "Cartesian reduction." And indeed, if the appearance transformations undergone by the wax are correctly and thoroughly described (as the experiences of phenomenologically reduced consciousness), then a concrete instance is offered for the observation and description of the "how" of appearances. Such a description is a description of the genesis of the sense-constitution of objects, which even-tually allows for the determination of their essential characteristics.

(b) Excursus: Husserl's Analyses of Internal
    Time Consciousness

In order to provide a phenomenological reconstruction of the wax experience, some notions essential to Husserl's theory of time consciousness must be presented and their im-plications for phenomenology must be drawn out.

The cornerstone of Husserl's theory of time consciousness is his conception of a primal now. He calls this primal
now the "productive point of the now" or the "generative now"
(*Time* §8) because it is the constantly changing moment
wherein all experience occurs as long as experience *is*. The
defining characteristic of this now is its "law of transformation"
(*Time* §11). Each now must constantly pass over into the "just-
past-now" and, from the other direction, each "not-yet-now"
becomes the primal now (*Time* §38, p.102). But within the
limits of the "now-fringe," all of these moments are within the
primal now-consciousness. This range of the now is described
by Husserl as "the threefold limit of [immediate] experience" (*I*
§82). Concerning it he writes that ". . . every *present moment* of
experience has about it a fringe of experiences, which also
share the primordial now-form, and as such constitute the one
primordial fringe of the pure Ego, its total primordial *now-
consciousness*" (*I* §82, p.219). These essentially connected
moments of the now-consciousness are the retentive-now-
protentive structure of all consciousness: the persisting form of
consciousness that remains the same, while its particular contents ceaselessly change and its particular moments constantly
transform.

In *The Phenomenology of Internal Time-Consciousness* Husserl
distinguishes between "primary retention" (*primäre Erinnerung*)
and "secondary remembrance" (*sekundäre Erinnerung*) (§§ 11, 14,
19). "Primary retention" refers to the presently retained immediately past-now (the past-now within the fringe of the primal
now) and is motivated by the constantly ". . . flowing impressional consciousness [which always and necessarily] passes
over into an ever fresh *retentional* consciousness" (§11, p.51). Insofar as this retentive consciousness is within the fringe of the
protean now, it is a "primary retention."

On the other hand, when a retentive moment has passed
beyond the horizon of the now, a special *reproductive act* of consciousness is required in order to bring the impressional moment to "presentification"; this Husserl calls "secondary remembrance." He compares these notions by writing that ". . .
primary remembrance or retention [is] a comet's tail which is

joined to actual perception," while secondary remembrances (i.e., reproductive memories) are ". . . autonomous presentifications [which] appear without being joined to perceptions" (§14, p.57).

As is apparent from these definitions, Husserl believes that presentations must precede retentions because these are what retentions are *of* (§§ 11, 13, 16, 17). Consequently, he writes, "The 'source-point' with which the 'generation' of the enduring object begins is a primal impression" (§11, p.50). The primal impression is an act of direct perception which Husserl calls "originary presentation" (§16).

But not only does every originary presentation of the now have its "comet's tail" (primary retention); likewise, the "comet's" light brightens the region ahead of itself: every originary presentation of the now has its protentive possibilities embedded within itself. About these constantly projective possibilities that are intrinsic to the primal now, Husserl writes, "Every primordial constitutive process is animated by protentions which emptily [*leer*] constitute and intercept [*auffangen*] what is coming . . . in order to bring it to fulfillment" (§24, p.76). These protentive moments of consciousness are Husserl's "motivated possibilities"; they are determined by retentive and reproductive consciousness of what-has-been, while retentive and reproductive consciousness of what-has-been are (of) what they are (of) insofar as past-protentions have been fulfilled, modified, or denied. And just as retentive consciousness, as a moment within the fringe of the primal now, has its external relative in reproductive memory, which snatches the buried past back into the now, so too does protentive consciousness have an ontic correlate: namely, "projective production," which projects possibilities beyond the fringes of the now and assumes about them: "These shall be."

Finally, retentions, protentions, and especially reproductive memory and projective production must be distinguished from "phantasy." Whereas both retention and protention involve a constant "shading-off" of a primal perception, reproduction and production involve a "creative," almost magical, act. Creative consciousness has occurred insofar as a past-now, or now-that-will-sometime-be, is brought into the present-now from beyond the range of the immediate fringe. But, as reproduction and projective production are "free" in relation to primal retention and protention, which is a fixed "sinking-back" determined by its "guiding-now" (§20) or a fixed "rising forward" fixed by the same, so phantasy is free in relation to reproduction and production. Reproductive consciousness (and projective production) ". . . posits what is reproduced [or produced] and gives it a position with regard to the actual now and the sphere of the originary temporal field to which the recollection itself belongs" or to which the production itself may belong (§23, p.74). To the extent that they are confined to their positing theses, however, reproduction and projective production also lack radical freedom.

"In mere phantasy [,however,] there is no positing of the reproduced now and no coincidence of this now with one given in the past" (§23, p.74). Likewise, there is no positing of the projected now, nor is that now necessarily given a place within a fixed temporal manifold. Phantasy consciousness can thus effect a "neutrality modification" in relation to all posited actuality (*I* §111) and thereby attain a freedom unknown by other modes of consciousness. But even phantasy consciousness is ". . . an occurrence of internal consciousness and as such has its actual now, its modes of running-off, etc." (*Time* §20). In phantasy consciousness, however, we ". . . can carry out the presentification more quickly or more slowly, clearly and explicitly or in a confused manner, quick as lightning at a stroke or in articulated steps, and so on" (*Time* §20).

To summarize: the moments of the primordial now-stream flow off an originary presentation given in the constantly streaming primal now. These moments are "fixed" insofar as they are condemned to flow off the originary presentation, though what will be originarily presented can itself often be chosen ahead of time. Slightly more free than the moments within the fringe are reproductive remembrances and projective productions, both of which, and more so the latter, have elements of phantasy in them, though they maintain a positing thesis. These productive modes of consciousness are less determined than the moments within the primal now-fringe because they are acts that leap across the stream of internal temporality to present the past or future. Finally, there is phantasy, which is radically free because it needs no positing thesis — neither temporally, spatially, nor in terms of actuality.

After the 1905 lectures on internal time consciousness, a struggle between the "static" or "structural" method of phenomenological analysis, as developed in the *Logical Investigations*, and the "genetic" method of phenomenological analysis, as eventually introduced in *Formal and Transcendental Logic*, became an inveterate problem for Husserlian phenomenology. Owing to his discoveries in the analyses of time-consciousness, Husserl eventually found it necessary to embrace genetic analysis as the *modus operandi* for phenomenology (*FTL* §85, p.208), even though this sounded the death-knell for some of his original hopes concerning the degrees of certainty of phenomenology's potential achievements. The naive method of static analysis (that is, the method of invoking the division of experienced phenomena into form and content for the analysis of their sense) had made claims to the possibility of apodictic and adequate knowledge of its reduced objects (*LI* 195, 542-43, 745, 747; *I* §34, p.104); but the possibility of adequate, and perhaps even most apodictic knowledge, was lost with the discovery of the need for genetic (i.e., temporally implicative) analysis.[12]

Although Husserl occasionally identifies adequate and apodictic evidence until *Erste Philosophie* (II §31, p.35), the growing awareness of the implications of internal temporality eventually demanded strict recognition of their differences. Ideally, adequate evidence refers to evidence that is so complete, further fulfillment in relation to its object would not be possible (*LI* 195, 542, 745, 763), while apodictic evidence refers to evidence such that all doubt about it is seen as senseless even though just *what* is known about the object of evidence may not be *all* there is to know about it, and so evidence concerning it may be incomplete (*CM* §6, p.15). Adequate evidence, then, seems a sufficient condition for apodictic evidence, while apodictic evidence is necessary though not sufficient for adequate evidence. The discovery of the primal temporal stream demanded the abandonment of at least the claim to adequacy for the following reasons.

If the fundamental layer of objects of consciousness were fixed, e.g., if they were bare static sensations as Husserl tended to believe until 1905 (and continued to suggest long afterwards), then apodictic and adequate knowledge of the fundamental constituents of consciousness was possible. These constituents could be reached through epoche and phenomenological reduction and simply described as they showed themselves. However, with the recognition that the incessantly flowing now-stream lay at the deepest possible level of reduction (*Time* §36; *I* §85, p.226; *CM* §18, p.43), Husserl was forced to abandon the belief in the possibility of adequate knowledge, though he maintained the notion as an ideal possibility (*CM* §22, p.54). Adequate knowledge is not possible at any level of reduction because even the reduced elements of perception incessantly fade from the now-moment while simultaneously pointing to, that is, intentionally implicating, elements of the past moments-that-were or the next moments-to-be. The notion of the incessantly flowing now-stream of consciousness indicates the ceaselessly merging and inextricably layered fabric of the past, present, and future, which lace themselves into the present even when the past and future moments are beyond the fringes of the primal now. Once more we can see why Husserl was "taken aback" in *The Idea of Phenomenology* by the discovery of "hidden transcendencies" within the heart of immanent, reduced experience.

The "hidden transcendencies" are those "objects" which transcend consciousness in its now-moment though they nevertheless remain "in" consciousness (immanence$_2$) a intentionally implicated motivated possibilities. As the deepest layer of consciousness, the retentive-now-protective stream is the transcendental ground for intentional implication and motivated possibilities; it is the basis for the horizon-structure of all consciousness. The moments of this stream permit the transcendence of the world; but, alas, they also makes most of (what was) consciousness transcendent and opaque even to itself. It is along these lines that Husserl and his student Eugen Fink would eventually feel it necessary to speculate about the role of the unconsciousness in phenomenology (*C* 385-87).

The threefold range of the now-moment (its protentive, presentative, and retentive range) is limited. At its fringes the world, or what amounts to the same thing in reduced experience, consciousness of it, blurs and disappears. But since that which has vanished from the range of the experienced temporal stream continues to effect the presentative moments of the stream itself, the possibility of an adequate understanding of the contents of consciousness is lost (*I* §83, p.221). In any given moment there is always more to consciousness than meets the eye of the ego. Again, phenomenology is seen as an infinite project, but this infinity is now seen to make the achievement of adequate evidence impossible.

It has been suggested by Ludwig Landgrebe that this is why Husserl had finally to admit that, "Philosophy as science, as earnest, rigorous, indeed, apodictically rigorous science — the dream is spent" (*C* 389).[13] However one interprets this statement, as Husserl's final confession, or as a comment by him on the beliefs of the philosophers of his age, there are further implications of his analyses of time consciousness that, conjoined with his recognition of the first epoche as developed above, have yet further consequences for phenomenology as originally conceived.

With his recognition that the matter-form schema (the structural-static method of analysis) of his early works was too simple to account for the tacit knowledge-layers of consciousness, Husserl also came to recognize that the constitutional powers effected by these implicit layers of knowledge made suspect the belief in "sensations" and "sense-data." He realized that sense-data theories were physicalistically based prejudices, and realized that he too had been swayed by the "data-sensationalism" of the epistemic psychologies. A manuscript dated in 1932 depicts this realization on Husserl's part. He asks, "Is not my original conception of the immanent sphere with immanent data, which ultimately come to 'apprehension' only through the passive execution of association, still a remnant of the old psychology and its sensualistic empiricism?"[14]

But, as we suggested earlier, the explicit recognition of the first epoche of natural scientific Reality allowed Husserl to suspend the source of such physicalistic prejudices and, via reduction, to see the world as a well-connected manifold consisting of the things themselves. In fact, Husserl's criticisms of the data-sensationalism of the empiricists, in which they were accused of harboring physicalistic prejudices (*FTL* §62; *C* §9, p.30, n. *, §§22-24, §67), can now be understood as also directed against his own early thinking. The explicit epoche of the natural scientific metaphysics helped overcome presuppositions that motivated the belief in such "data."

If Husserl's realization that primal constitution occurs in the primal now-stream (i.e., in the self-constituting stream of consciousness) is conjoined with his gradual, though never complete, rejection of an immanent sphere of sense-data (in the sense of immanence$_1$), then these consequences emerge: The stream of the primal now would no longer be thought to animate the "sensations" of a radically immanent sphere, but rather the intentionally implicative now "animates" (read: "motivates") the "how" of appearances and transforms them, usually without our conscious recognition, into the "what" of the things themselves. It is this ceaselessly changing "how" of appearances, reached in the second reduction, that transforms appearances into things. This deep level of constitution occurs as a series of perspectival temporal syntheses.

Moreover, the realization that the temporal stream of the primal now is, from a phenomenological point of view, "endless on both sides" (*I* §81, p.217) indicates that if ever we did experience "sensations" or "sense-data," the possibility of reducing to them again is virtually null. If, as babes in wool, for instance, we first experienced the booming, buzzing confusion of pure sensations, which were then constituted into sense-data, then into appearances, then into ordinary objects, by the time in life that phenomenological reflection becomes possible, the temporal stream is so long that even its most distant conscious fringes face an insurmountable hiatus between themselves and *nonconstituted*, nonimplicative, appearances. The layers of tacit knowledge built from layers of tacit constitutive intentionality are so far from the primal now that they are usually inaccessible even for phenomenological reduction. All the layers of sedimented constitutive intentionality cannot be excavated, and woe if they were, for then we would no longer be human-beings, no longer "rational animals." The reductions at this level would transform our world into an inarticulate swarm of roaring sensations. But the "mothers" are simply not to be looked upon — at least not by those who would return to the world.

Husserl's recognition of the indefinitely layered now and its equally indefinite constituted layers of meaning, combined with the effects of the explicit application of the first epoche, were leading to the externalization of the phenomenological sphere. Negatively stated, these discoveries were leading to the diminution of significance granted to radical immanence (immanence$_1$), while, however, transcendence$_1$ and immanence$_2$ remain untouched. Ironically, the powers of constitutive understanding are so strong, so persistent, so ubiquitous, they prohibit an unbiased return to the immanent qua immanence$_1$. The domain of radical immanence gains the sense of unforced externalization; "sensations" happen to *me*, to my social-self and to my body. Perhaps this is why, as his thought developed, Husserl came to give more and more consideration to the kinaestheses of the body as providing a uniquely foundational sort of intentional constitution (*C* §28, pp.106-8, §47, p.161, §62, p.217, Apx. III, pp.331-32; *SW* 225-61; esp. 241, 248-50).[15]

Husserl persists, of course, in distinguishing between transcendence and immanence and, somewhat hesitantly, still speaks of sense-data at times. But he struggles with these notions each time he uses them. For instance, in *Formal and Transcendental Logic* he writes: "If . . . we still *separate immanent from transcendent objects*, that can involve a division only *within* this broadest concept of transcendence" (§62, p.166). And yet he goes on to say that this "transcendence" itself *makes its appearance in the purely phenomenological [immanent] sphere of consciousness.*" What this seeming inconsistency amounts to is Husserl's expressed experience of the blending of radical immanence (immanence$_1$ — "sensations") into the appearances of objects (immanence$_2$-transcendence$_1$). In a similar vein the dependence of radical transcendence (transcendence$_2$) on object transcendence (transcendence$_1$) would be recognized in the *Crisis*. The "multiplicities of consciousness," also spoken of in §62 of *Formal and Transcendental Logic*, can be understood to refer to the "how" of appearances that are temporally synthesized by consciousness; and yet (in the case of objects as well as of "idealities") they are "no real part or moment of consciousness, no real psychic Datum" because they are *aspects* of the things that exist "out there." Yet Husserl is still not clear, and probably never was, about the final relation of these kinds of transcendence and immanence, nor about their eventual relation brought about by the epoche, reduction, and the processes of phenomenological constitutive description.

In *Experience and Judgment*, too, Husserl still occasionally speaks of sense-data and calls them "immanent" (§64, p.255), but this is always in relation to the deepest levels of temporal syntheses. However, here too, he has reservations about such notions and provides a footnote by which he attempts to soften any implication of ontological commitment to these "data." Moreover, Husserl refers to these sense-data as "aspects" (p.256), which signifies that they are perspectival adumbrations, that is, appearances, of some thing, and hence also "transcendent" in the sense of transcendence$_1$ and immanence$_2$. He is, then, starting to blend such data with the appearances. But earlier, in *Ideas*, it was precisely the characteristic of "immanent data" that they *were not* "aspectival" (§42).

Finally, in the *Crisis*, Husserl returns to an earlier concern of his (*LI* 852-69) and questions the distinction between "inner" and "outer" experience (§§60-64) and refers to it as a "false parallelism" (§63). He once more explicitly denies that in ordinary experience we encounter sense-data, and argues instead that intentionality goes directly to the "things themselves" (§68, p.234).[16] Along these lines of interpretation, concerning the externalization of the phenomenological sphere, an interesting, though potentially misleading note, appears in the *Crisis*. Husserl writes that:

> The first breakthrough of this universal a priori of correlation between experienced object and manners of givenness (which occurred during work on my *Logical Investigations* around 1898) affected me so deeply that my whole life-work has been dominated by the task of systematically elaborating on this a prior of correlation. (*C* §48, p.166, n. *)

He goes on to comment that this discovery led to the phenomenological reduction, and suggests that the reduction, however, remained *unclear*, at least through *Ideas*, due to hidden naturalistic presuppositions of his own. *But* some of these presuppositions had also enforced a *different* conception of the correlational a priori at the time of these earlier writings — a point that Husserl does not make in the note above.

The universal a priori of correlation as explicated in the *Logical Investigations* is not precisely the same correlational a priori given in the *Crisis*. In his early works Husserl had emphasized a correlation between act and object, or intention and content, where the act or intention animated the sensation-content and only then transformed this content into an object qua object-of-the-world (*LI* 309-10, 356, 573). But in terms of Husserl's later writings, the animation of a "content" by an act would have to be a correlation which allowed *appearances* to appear; a correlation by which *appearance* implicates an object, letting that object manifest itself *in* the appearance. This later implicative mode of consciousness occurs a step higher in the levels of objectifying consciousness than would the animation of a "sensation" into the appearance of some thing. In the *Logical Investigations*, and especially in *Ideas*, the object qua object-of-the-world was suspended and was, even more than the metaphysical "objects" of natural science, a phenomenological problem in the relationship between "Reason and Reality" (*I* pt. IV). In these works it was the animation of "sensation" that was of greatest interest to Husserl. Only gradually, after his investigations of time consciousness, did

Husserl call the correlational a priori primarily a relationship between "appearance" and "that which appears," or, as above from the *Crisis*, a correlation between "experienced objects and manners of givenness." And even in *Ideas*, for example, he still seems to conceive of the a priori of correlation as the relation between act and content (*I* §85). To some extent, then, Husserl probably never did entirely free himself from some form of "data-sensationalism."

It was, then, only with the growing awareness of the implications of his analyses of time consciousness, and with the recognition of the need for a first "preliminary" epoche of the natural scientific world, that Husserl did, though still implicitly, externalize the universal a priori of correlation. The relationship between appearance and that which appears thus becomes a relationship between phenomena "outside" of consciousness, a relationship between that which is transcendent *as* transcendence$_1$ and immanent *as* immanence$_2$. But, with the event of externalization, a difference between these two notions now arises (or rather, what has been understood as two sides of one notion now becomes two notions): transcendence$_1$ becomes the object-of-the-world; immanence$_2$ becomes its appearance or manners of appearing. The correlational a priori still remains, but it is now motivated in terms of an outward-oriented implicative intentionality.

As we must next show, none of this sounds the death-knell for Husserl's phenomenological project as has often been suggested. In fact, we can now, as an example, offer a reconstruction of the wax experience that will show how the externalization of the phenomenological sphere (in the modes of immanence$_2$ and transcendence$_1$) still permits constitutional analyses at the second level of reduction — analyses that reveal the constitutional processes that provide us with the object-world and also, eventually, with all of the higher levels of constituted actuality.

(c) The Constitution of Objects: A Phenomenological
    Reconsideration of the Wax Experience

Constitutional analyses involve a retrogressive-progressive procedure that Husserl sometimes calls the "zig-zag" procedure (*LI* 261; *EJ* §5). Any worldly object that has been bracketed is maintained as an intentionally implicated entity, yet suspended as an ontological or judgmental assumption. In the jargon of *Ideas*, this suspension and simultaneous retention is the noematic modification of the object, which is thereafter spoken of "under a change of signature" indicated by inverted commas around the suspended, yet retained, "object" (*I* §76, p.194; §89, p.240; *CM* §18, p.42). The "object" is retained in reduction yet given in full only as a meaning; in these phenomenologically reduced conditions, the manners of appearance in which the "object" is given emerge. Conversely, these manners of original givenness reveal the predicative and prepredicative processes that had constituted the sense-laden object, now bracketed.

The constitution of an object refers to the accumulation of predicates that, on the basis of past experience, determine that object in its essential definition and sense. Genetic phenomenology is thus the attempt to reveal this series of accumulated senses and thereby to uncover the layers of intentional implications that had been fulfilled in the past and that now become embedded in the object *as* the object's meaning (*FTL* §§85-86). Epoche and reduction are meant to reveal these processes as they originally occurred.

The original event of sense-accumulation occurs in "passive synthesis" (*CM* §§17-18) or "prepredicative experience" (*EJ* §§16-17). Passive synthesis as prepredicative experience is grounded in the intrinsic unity of the temporal stream, which continually produces an identity in difference for ego and objects. In *Experience and Judgment* Husserl refers to the phenomenological field in which passive synthesis is described as "the field of passive data and its associative structures" (§16). This is the field of the "how" of appearances prior to explicit judgmental determination of those appearances *as* predicates of a "thing." Following Robert Sokolowski, we shall refer to this field as the field of "original encounter"[17] — the field in which the "things," as transcendent sets of appearances, are met.

Describing this field in its original givenness is the most difficult, almost inherently paradoxical task, of phenomenological-constitutional analysis. Since ordinary language is presupposed for the description of this field, it is taken into the reduced domain with the reduced consciousness. But this ordinary language is always a language-of-the-world, a language of existence-positing predicative experience. Consequently, descriptions of the "how" of appearances spontaneously and necessarily tend to describe "passive data" as predicated of the things of the world. Suzanne Cunningham has developed this problem as a Wittgensteinian criticism of the phenomenological reductions.[18] It is the problem that an *existence-positing public language* poses for the phenomenological reduction. It is not possible, it seems, to reduce below our public language. And if it were, how could we possibly *describe* the reduced experiences without appeal to our public language and all the presuppositions that go along with it? Again, then, for yet another reason, we see why the reductions can never be complete.

We have, of course, already responded to the general criticism concerning the incompleteness of the reductions in its more particular forms as an object-incompleteness criticism (§4.4b) and as a historical-objective criticism (§4.6b). In both cases we have shown that the incompleteness criticism fails if it is intended as a decisive criticism of the phenomenological reductions. It fails because it criticizes the very possibility of the phenomenological reduction on the basis of its necessary incompletion even while this incompletion is something that the phenomenological reduction recognizes and even *relies on for its possibility*. It is now time to begin to generalize upon this thesis.

Like most criticisms of Husserl's phenomenological reductions (e.g., Heidegger's, Sartre's, Merleau-Ponty's, Gadamer's and Derrida's), the Wittgensteinian criticism is based upon an inadequate understanding of the act of suspension and the event of reduction. Correct, the reductions cannot be made complete, but they can be performed, and they have their clarificatory value quite independently of their completeness. In the reduction the "object" (whatever it may be) is maintained, but it is maintained *as* the noematically modified "nucleus" always intentionally implicated by the reduced experiences; that is, it is maintained as an indeterminate, but (in principle) determinable "x." And this "object" retains its meaning, either as a value-laden tool (Heidegger), an empirical ego (Sartre), the body (Merleau-Ponty), history (Gadamer, Derrida, Carr), or even ordinary language (Wittgenstein, Cunningham, Harrison), even when these "objects" are reduced *from*. In all these cases, the "objects" which are supposedly the bottom layer for reduction can become "objects" of reflection only because we *can* and do reduce "below" them, or at least, below parts of them.

The reasons for the impossibility of a complete reduction are also the reasons that the reductions and constitutional analyses can be *about* the "real" world, the reason transcendental phenomenology can have *significance for* that world. The zig-zag procedure inherent to constitutional analysis is a zig-zag between reduced experience in its processes of constitution and the real (suspended, yet retained; suspended, but not rejected) world. The paradox of describing prepredicative experience is that as soon as we do so it seems to become predicative; and indeed it does to some extent. But these perpetually synthesizing qualities or predicates at the level of the second reduction only *indicate* the "object" or "world" that is still in suspension, still not complete. At this level of reflective description, "object" and "world" are each still determinable in principle, but remain indeterminate "x's" in fact. Only with the completion of constitutional analyses (which never actually occurs), or with the *decision* to remove the brackets, do "object" and "world" once more become what they are in fact. The zig-zag procedure between reduced experience and its "objects," between prepredicative and predicative experience, and between passive synthesis and active predication, can be demonstrated if we return now to the wax experience.

If, in original encounter, or in the attempt at refabricating original encounter via phenomenological reduction, I encounter the "wax," the following may occur: I notice the appearance of the "wax"; it thereby enters the stream of the primal now. In a series of merging actual-nows, I take note of "its" predicates. I am surprised at the sweet honey-like flavor that this "object" contains ("O," s); I note, too, the odor of flowers about it ("O," s, o); it is colored ("O," s, o, c) and bulky ("O," s, o, c, b); when touched it is hard and cold ("O," s, o, c, b, h, c); and when knocked upon it gives forth a sound: it is resonant ("O," s, o, c, b, h, c, r).

In these processes of (what was originally) "passive synthesis" or "prepredicative experience," the sense layers of this indeterminate, but determinable "x" accumulated, and "this self-same thing, the 'x', became enriched" with sense-predicates (I §149, p.382). The sense-predicates of the "object" underwent a steady and constant, and thereby *unnoticed*, synthesis of perspectives that, when condensed, provide the rudiments of the essential sense of "wax." From this time on (say, t_1) I cannot encounter wax (freshly taken from the hive) without these embedded, and usually unnoticed, senses.

But now I will bring the "wax" close to the fire. Suddenly its sweetness begins to evaporate ("W," $\sim$s); its odor vanishes ("W," $\sim$s, $\sim$o); its color changes ("W," $\sim$s, $\sim$o, $\sim$c); its bulky shape is lost and its size increases ("W," $\sim$s, $\sim$o, $\sim$c, $\sim$b); it becomes liquid and grows hot ("W," $\sim$s, $\sim$o, $\sim$c, $\sim$b, l, h); and when knocked upon it gives forth no sound, it has no resonance ("W," $\sim$s, $\sim$o, $\sim$c, $\sim$b, l, h, $\sim$r). Does the same wax remain after these changes? We must admit that it does; no one judges otherwise. But *why*?

In the tightly knit fabric of appearances, the "wax" never lost its identity. It simply acquired a number of radically new predicates. It is flammable, and susceptible to inteneration and its "new" predicates cannot exist *simultaneously* with some of the predicates originally encountered. But *if* there is doubt about the nature and identity of the "wax," the experience can be repeated, and repetition will eventually nullify such doubt by transforming it into doxic certainty through repeated confirmation of one's doxic expectations. Consider the wax experience again, now after some number of similar experiences (t_n).

When I bring the "wax" close to the fire, the process of

passive synthesis occurring in the primal now has as its protentive fringe the possible transformation of the "wax." (If this experience has been had often enough, and is not the object of phenomenological scrutiny, passive synthesis will be unnoticed; sedimented, tacit knowledge will conceal the "how" of appearing and consciousness will note only the "what" of the thing.) If I focus upon the appearances of the "wax," passive syntheses of consciousness begin actively to "modalize." Because of the past experience with wax, I leap beyond the fringes of the now-stream and reproductively reproduce past experiences with wax brought close to a fire, at t_1 for example. I recall from the past that part of the essence of wax is its susceptibility to heat and its ensuing transformation of predicates. Upon the basis of this secondary remembrance, I project into the future (again, beyond the fringes of the now-stream) and projectivity produce the fate of the wax. Finally, I imaginatively predelineate its scope for further possible transformations, refocussing my knowledge of its essential nature.

There is no mystery surrounding my knowledge that the "same wax remains"; it is part of the essence of wax to maintain its identity in radical difference. Its great span of possible predicates *is* a major part of its identity. Most entities cannot endure such radical change and yet remain the same or even keep the same *name*. In fact, at $time_n$, the time of our repeated experience, my tacit knowledge concerning the wax was an understanding that the wax was an entity with the qualities of sweetness, odoriferousness, color, bulk, hardness, coldness, and resonance, and with the *possible qualities* of expansiveness, softness, and hotness, and the absence of sweetness, odoriferousness, color, bulk, and resonance. In all my past experiences with objects of this sort—the sort I call "wax"—such objects had shown themselves to be constituted as the kind of entity with just these *actual and possible* predicates.

The modalization of appearances on the part of the wax led to no modalization of judgment about it. None of my noemata "exploded" as Husserl might have said in *Ideas* (§§ 138, 151).[19] And indeed, because of the sedimented layers of meaning that constitute the idea of "wax," if the wax *had not been transformed*, if it did not change most of its qualities when put near the flame, *then* my beliefs would have modalized, and perhaps my belief in *this object as "wax"* would have canceled itself.

When Merleau-Ponty makes the cryptic statement that ". . . consciousness can forget phenomena only because it can recall them . . ."[20] he probably means that the synthetic function of time consciousness is so potent that in recall, and in ordinary seeing, we notice the "what" of the thing and forget the "how" of its givenness. But the "how" of appearing constitutes the object as a sense-full thing of the world by synthesizing the perspectival predicates, which merge in the understanding and thus become the thing that we know. Object-constitution is thus the continued attribution of predicates to an object, which makes this object become what it is.

Constitutional analysis of objects is the description of this process of "building up," a process that becomes visible by way of epoche and reduction. The object itself as an indeterminate but determinable "x" is not hopelessly undetermined as an entity *known* just because it is indeterminate in terms of the totality of its predicates and relations; in fact, it is usually known *as* "wax," as "mother," as "Venus," and many things are known *about* it; but it is indeterminate insofar as further constitutive predicates can be found for it or are uncovered as already part of it. Its complete nature, then, is always undetermined *in fact* because the constitutive stream always runs deeper back into the past and is always open-ended with respect to the future; but the thing is in principle determined and determinable insofar as it has been predicatively constituted *as* sweet, *as* odoriferous, *as* cold, etc.; and, insofar as an object is an object, it has been constituted by some significant sense-predicates.

An object, insofar as it is an "object," is "its" totality of meanings, the most primitive of which are its sensory predicates. Its causal, "purely corporeal" aspects and relations are also *part* of its meaning, but taken as *qualities in themselves*—the qualities of natural reductive science—these sense-predicates come late in the processes of constitution. Just as the appearances provide the constitutive content for the thing of the world, so the object qua thing-of-the-world provides the constitutive content for the higher level predicates of natural science. Hence, these natural scientific senses do not depict the only sort of cause of the thing. On its part, consciousness can be considered the epistemic "cause" of the thing as known, that is, of the thing's sense as a unification of significant predicates, which include its natural scientific, causal predicates. In short, consciousness is the constitutive cause or epistemic source of the thing as we know it; an organizational or articulative cause, we might say.

This is the result of the first layer of constitutional analysis in Husserl's epistemological reversal. Beyond the thing as we know it, beneath its predicative sense-layers or outside of the brackets, is an infinitely distant idea of the thing still being, and forever to be, constituted.

(d) The Constitution of the "World"

Just as the intentional implications embedded in every appearance pointed beyond the appearance to that which appears—the thing itself—correlatively, every *thing* intentionally implicates further appearances of itself and points to that *in* which it appears, namely, the world (*C* §47, p.162). Insofar as the object implicates further appearances of itself, it points to its "inner horizon"; insofar as it points beyond itself, to its thingly context, it points to its "external horizon" (*C* §74, p.162; *EJ* §8, p.33). Every object has both an internal and external horizon. The horizon of all horizons, the ultimate external horizon, is called the "world" (*C* §37; *EJ* §§7-9). Like the thing, the world is a regulative idea in the Kantian sense (*EP* I, pp.274, 276). As with the constitution of objects, the constitution of the world is motivated by the genesis of sense-predicates. The nadir of this constitutional feat is found in the primal Here of *oriented space*.

The primal Here of spatiality is the spatial correlate to the primal now of the temporal stream. This primal Here is the zero-point, the orientational center, in the genealogy of the external horizon and the concept of "world" (*C* §47; *WLP* 249-50). The primal Here has its locus in the body, and the incarnate ego is thereby essentially a being of distances (*C* §62, p.217, Apx. III, pp.331-32; *WLP* 248-50). The world, Husserl writes, ". . . exhibits itself to me . . . through its internal and external horizon-validities" (*C* §47, p.162). The original presence is the presence of the thing, and the thing always appears as a "there" in relation to the primal Here where I am. The "there" varies as the "near," the "far," the "right," the "left," "above" or "below." These are the original values for the concept of "space."

The fringes of the primal Here implicate the region of regions we call the world. The first sense-predicates involved in the constitution of the world (beyond the internal predicates of the objects themselves) are, thereby, *relational predicates*, in short, relations. The near and the far, the right and the left, the above and below, are the primordial relational predicates ("senses") in the constitution of the spatial world.

But even the constitution of objects involves much more than mentioned thus far, much more than the accumulation of strictly sensory predicates. It also involves the accumulation of *values* — meanings in the most profound sense — which are almost inextricably interwoven with the sensory and relational predicates (*I* §139). In fact, it is not only the indivisible stream of temporality and historicity, or the inalienable Here of any particular consciousness, that nullifies the possibility of a complete reduction; *the ubiquity of values* is another phenomenon that makes a complete reduction impossible. As Jean-Paul Sartre and Merleau-Ponty suggest, one cannot even see the red of the carpet without seeing it as the "woolly red" that might be comfortable to lie upon.[21] And, as Heidegger has shown, the world of everyday life, the world that Husserl suspends with the epoche, is a manifold of significance, "significance" so thickly layered that we cannot even see entities as Things (*Dinge*) until they fall apart as tools (*Werkzeuge*).[22]

Inherent to the relation-senses of the near and the far, then, are values such as "the familiar and comfortable" or "the foreign and the strange." As with the accumulation of strictly sensory predicates, these value predicates are varied, layered, and sedimented, with changing experience. For example, the "near," which is always a "near" in relation to my "primitive home" (*SW* 228), varies and expands with the accumulation of years. The one-time foreignness and strangeness of the philosophers of the distant university no longer seems foreign or strange. The "here" of the home-world, if not entirely transferred, has at least been extended. What was only a horizon of the world has thus become the world in primal presence. The "here" of the original home-world has moved to the "there" of a one-time horizon, and the "there" of that horizon has proven intrinsically capable of becoming a "here." This is the kind of confirmatory basis that, encountered again and again, and fulfilled again and again, is finally projected in the form of the "and so forth" (*und so weiter*; *EJ* §51, pp.217-18). The "*und so weiter*," taken in its broadest signification, is the linguistic ex-experience (*EJ* §7), while this experience itself constantly "fills in" the projected horizon that we designate "world." Like the tion, of every culture, at any time, is in the process of being constituted. In fact, for the phenomenologist who has bracketed God as well as pure corporeality (*I* §58), "constant constitution" must replace the position once reserved for "constant creation."

But the notion of "the constitution of the world" may still sound like a metaphysically loaded one. Yet it only refers to our belief in the world as the ultimate horizon for all possible experience (*EJ* §7), while this experience itself constantly "fills-in" the projected horizon which we designate "world." Like the "object" ultimately implicated within the second reduction, the notion of "world" is noematically modified. Within the epoche it has undergone a "change of signature" (*I* §76, p.194, §89, p.240). But nonetheless, "world" is an actual meaning, signifying something believed to be real, and like the "object" it is constituted by a multitude of means. We will consider only one of those means here.

In a manuscript now entitled "The World of the Living Present and the Constitution of the Surrounding World External to the Organism," Husserl considers the constitutive processes that occur with the act of *walking* (*WLP* 248-50). Walking is the ground possibility for the intentional-constitutive transformation of the "there" into a "here," of a "that" into a "this," and of an appearance into a thing. "Walking" as the phenomenological ground-phenomenon (of course there are vehicles that might quicken the process) permits the idea of "my place," as an idea of my immediately lived-world, to be "apperceptively transferred" into the idea that "my place" is ultimately "the world" and "the cosmos."

Husserl argues that, "The 'I rest' precedes the 'I move myself' insofar as the latter must be conceived of as a continuum of possible resting-points" (*WLP* 248). But the a priori possibility of changing the resting-point gives things their predicative sense as "close" or "distant." My "core-world" is a world within the immediate reach of my kinaesthetic activity, and this core sphere is the optimal range for constitutive syntheses because here I can see the things clearly, handle them, even change their place by thrusting and pushing with my body. But this core-world can be radically extended by walking. What is distant can become close, what is vague can become clear, what is indeterminate can be "determined." "From the beginning the animate organism has constitutively an exceptional position" (*WLP* 249). It can bring the "world" within range of itself, and constitutive understanding can thus become constituted knowledge. In walking, the subjective manifestation, of appearances of my surrounding world (the "how" of appearances) are synthesized. Owing to the synthetic activity of memory, the oriented space of appearances can be cognized as an objective space, and the appearing sides of things can be synthetically constituted into the self-same identical thing. Indeed, every "kinaesthetic activity functions as sense-bestowing . . ." (*WLP* 250).

Kinaesthetic activities are even the source of the "primary" predicates such as weight, shape, size, relation, etc. So-called primary qualities do not reach us through the screen of appearances, they are *in* the appearances and *of* the appearances; they are constituted as the primary predicates encountered in my kinaesthetic encounter with the things of the world. Primary qualities *are* primary predicates, and only because of this have they become the primary senses for natural reductive science. They became these primary senses precisely because they are the primary (and usually *prepredicative*) predicates of life-world experience. Here, Husserl takes the side of Locke, as opposed to Descartes, in emphasizing the *solidity* of matter in contrast to its mere "extensiveness." *Res extensa* is here recognized as an abstracted sense-stratum *derived from* the bodily corporeal (*I* §§149-50).[23] As inherent to the deepest level of kinaesthetic constitutionality, primary qualities are a constitutive source of *corporeal experience*, which is not a metaphysical pure corporeality, but a body-physical lived corporeality. The corporeal centeredness of the body is itself constituted by a synthesis of primary encounters with other corporeal beings.

Upon the basis of walking (and travel in general) "the openness of the surrounding world" becomes territorial openness (*SW* 222). If I have not crossed the borders of my nation or country, I know others who have. In this mode of intercommunication, Husserl writes:

> The idea of the earth comes about as a synthetic unity in a manner analogous to the way in which the experiential fields of a single person are unified in continuous and combined experience. Except that, analogously, I appropriate to myself the reports of others, their descriptions and ascertainments, and frame all-inclusive ideas. (*SW* 222)

This latter point is Husserl's version of Russell's "knowledge by description,"[24] and through it my place among things becomes a place in the space of the world. And even the space of the world is eventually realized as the *place* of the world in the *space* of the Cosmos. But it is not the purely corporeal Nature of natural science into which we are born. The nature into which we are born, in which we walk, is the nature composed of things and of forces as seen and *felt* by the conscious body. Through intentional implication as constitutive intentionality "Nature" emerges. And, as we will see, "Nature" emerges only upon the basis of nature.

(e) The Determination of Essences: A Variation of the Wax Experience

The constitution of objects and world is a perpetual event; consequently, so is the need for constitutional analyses. But in spite of the open-endedness of the "what" of any given thing and hence, of the phenomenological project, Husserl believed that the essences of objects and world could still be determined. Constant constitution does not eliminate the possibility for the determination of essences, though it does always leave open the possibility that (what we know as) an essence may change.

The act of epoche$_2$ was a conscious suspension of belief in, and judgment-dependence upon, the world's existence. But the need to suspend this belief and judgment-dependence indicates that belief in the world was already a fact, and that judgments were already dependent upon that belief. Even in epoche$_2$, some degree of belief in this "world" and its "objects" was retained because of the intentionally implicated horizon of reduced experience. So the world cannot be *fully* reduced, the natural attitude is simply too strong. Hence, "world" and "objects" are suspended, yet simultaneously and necessarily retained as meaningful horizons.

Indeed, the epoche and reduction were originally needed to help us see the world in the "how" of its constitution, rather than to see it in the "what" of its being. Hence, we have always already known the world and its objects; what was not known was *how* we know them or *how* they came to be what they are in our knowledge of them. So even though constitutional analyses are never complete, our actual knowledge of the objects being described usually surpasses the point reached in the constitutional analyses of them.

To determine the essence of the world or its objects is to make explicit what we already know implicitly about these phenomena by making that knowledge explicit in terms of the essential forms via which we *recognize* and *identify* such objects. Essences are something we already know, though we do not know how we know them or *precisely what* they are for any given subject matter. But to ask the questions we asked earlier, "How is this object or object-type constituted?" implied and depended upon knowledge of essences because these questions implied knowledge of identities. At that time the identities were bracketed. But the identities can be made explicit by giving an account of the invariant structures inherent to our knowledge of entities or entity types. "Free imaginative variation" is the method for providing this account.

Whereas Descartes found the essences for the things of the world in the things *in* themselves, *res extensae*, Husserl finds these essences in the things themselves—themselves! This difference between the essence of a theoretical posit and the essence of the things that appear allows us to understand Descartes' procedure for the determination of essences as an *eliminative reductive procedure*, while Husserl's can be understood as a *reduction through continuity*. Descartes, as we have shown, eliminates perception and imagination as the possible sources for our knowledge of essences and lights upon "conception"— the possibility for which is an innate idea causally activated by that which it knows.[25] On the other hand, Husserl's method for the determination of essences *motivates* perception beyond itself, to imagination, and through imagination it attempts to articulate the pure concepts or essences of the world (*I* §70; *PP* §9; *EJ* §87). In this sense our knowledge of an essence can never transcend our knowledge of the *type* of factual being that the essence is an essence of.

Imaginative determination of essences is possible because the world and its objects are already known; and to the extent that they are known we can also know when we violate their essential characteristics in free imaginative variation of them. This is because the determination of the essences of world and objects is simultaneously the delineation of the limits of our knowledge of the world and its objects as that knowledge exists in our everyday understanding. Once again, then, the world and its objects are presupposed for the initial possibility of phenomenological method; and, once again, the universal a priori of correlation is intrinsic to Husserl's method, and his ultimate subject matter is, again, the world as experienced and known in the natural attitude.

Free imaginative variation, as the method for the determination and acquisition of pure concepts or concepts of essences:

> . . . is based on the modification of an experienced or imagined objectivity, turning it into an arbitrary example which, at the same time, receives the character of a guiding "model," a point of departure for the production of an infinitely open multiplicity of variants. It is based, therefore, on a *variation*. (*EJ* §87, p.340)

Within this variation:

> It then becomes evident that a unity runs through this multiplicity of successive figures, that in such free variation of an original image, e.g., of a thing, an *invariant* is necessarily retained as the *necessary general form*, without which an object such as this thing, as an example of its kind, would not be thinkable at all. (*EJ* §87, p.341.)

When we direct our conscious regard to this invariant structure, we see that it prescribes the limits to which all variation must be confined if the model we have started with is to remain a thing of its kind or type: "The essence proves to be that without which an object of a particular kind cannot be thought, i.e., without which the object cannot be intuitively imagined as such" (*EJ* §87, p.341). Let us once more reconsider the experience of the wax.

While the method for the determination of essences must ultimately free itself from straightforward perception, it can take its start from there, though this is not required (*PP* §9e; *EJ* §93, p.361). For instance, if I see the wax, freshly taken from the hive, I can imagine it in a manifold of possible appearances. Even prior to placing it near the fire, I can vary its size: it might be larger or smaller than it is and still be the same wax ("W," l v s); I can vary its shape: it might be square, oblong or rectilinear in shape and still be the same wax ("W," s v o v r); its color may darken or lighten ("W," d v l); its flavor may prove bitter or sweet ("W," b v s); its odor may be thought to vary from pungent to fragrant ("W," p v f); nevertheless it remains "wax" freshly taken from the hive.

I can imagine the wax put close to a flame and again all of its qualities may change, yet the same wax remains. But if I should imagine a flower budding forth from the melted pool ("W," f), or an expanse of grass starting to grow from it ("W," g), I would know that in my imaginative variations I had violated the identity of "wax." I have exploded its essence, I have made "it" what it is not, a counterfactual situation has been imagined that violates the essence of (the meaning of) "wax."

Just as the constitution of objects occurs as the accumulation of predicates, and constitutional analysis is the attempt to unearth these accumulative processes, so the determination of essences occurs as the *variation of predicates*, which would delimit the essence of an object in terms of that object's possible predicates, that is, in terms of its full range of predicate-senses. Note, for example, that if we had originally varied (or melted) a *candle*, a species of the genus "wax," after its total inteneration we would not say that "the same candle remains" as we said "the same wax remains." We would not say this because the essence of "candle," as a species of wax, has a much narrower essence than does the genus wax. A pool of wax without noticeable wick would hardly count as a candle. The invariant features of this species, "candle," vanish with the transformation of certain predicates. Wax without wick and without definite form is not a candle. The essence of a candle, then, involves a wick and some definite solidified form.

In the attempt to determine essences, certain rules for variation must be adhered to. Although the formation of variants can be radically arbitrary (*EJ* §87, p.342), the model or example used as the starting point for variation must be "retained in grasp" and *maintained* as the same. If this commitment to the self-same model were forsaken, then there would be no actuality-basis for variation to stand in relation to. Wax could be transformed into flowers and flowers into dung without any violation of predicates, because the individual-type, or predicate-substrate would itself have changed. The example must be retained in the grasp of memory, as the self-same example, if the determination of essences, via the possible violation of predicates, is to have an effect. A violation of predicate-sense can only occur as a relation to an object already known and maintained as "itself."

The phenomenological determination of essences is thus an attempt to clarify what we already know. It attempts to provide an account of epistemic identity claims in terms of "knowing that," where previously we only "knew how" (to identify such and such things). Free imaginative variation, as the phenomenological method of playing with predicates or counterfactual possibilities, allows us to provide *an account* of our "knowing how" to identify entities and states of affairs in our everyday life. A well-connected description of the variation of predicates, a location of the limits where their variation would make an entity or entity-type other than it is, depicts the essence of the entity or entity-type in question.

Husserl expresses one aspect of the nature of essence-determination particularly well when he writes that ". . . phenomenological explication does nothing but *explicate the sense this world has for us all prior to any philosophizing*, and obviously gets solely from our experience — *a sense which philosophy can uncover but never alter . . .*" (*CM* §62, p.151). Husserl's point is that the essences of the world are always already there; we know them, though we don't know *how* we know them, nor can we always articulate them. Husserl would argue that they are what they are because of the processes of constitution that have given them their sense, and we can come to know them explicitly by freely varying this sense and thus discovering its limits.

As sense is built upon sense, so too is essence built upon essence. The *relational essences* of the world are some of the higher-level essences; these are depicted by the regulated a priori typology of life-world experience, and this life-world typology, Husserl believes, provides the structural basis for the constitution of "Nature." But notice that even these structural types and styles can be determined by variation, and this means that, whereas Descartes was forced to leap beyond the things and essences of this world in order to reach the essences of "Nature," Husserl's method for the determination of pure concepts, i.e., essences, demands no such leap; we achieve conceptions via an imagination that ultimately refers back to the Urdoxic certainty of perception (C §9, p.31; EJ §87b).

Husserl thus rejects Descartes' belief that the infinity of imaginative possibilities disqualifies imagination as the source of conception. He seems to be thinking of Descartes when he writes that ". . . this open infinity [of imaginative possibilities] does not signify an actual continuation in infinity, the nonsensical demand *actually* to produce all possible variants — as if we could only then be sure that the eidos which subsequently becomes grasped actually accords with all possibilities" (PP §9, p.57). By Husserl's lights, if the possible process to infinity disqualifies imaginative variation as a method for the determination of essences, it would likewise disqualify perception as a possible means for the ascertainment of evidence because perception, too, is a potentially infinite process, even in relation to any single thing — but surely *it* must be admitted as the primary, first source of knowledge. On this point, of course, Husserl and Descartes are simply at loggerheads. For Husserl the "principle of all principles" is perceptual intuition (I §24); for Descartes it is something called "mind." But whereas Descartes' methodological loyalty to his principle results in a world buried by a metaphysical Nature, Husserl's methodological procedure will provide a conception of Nature that can still be epistemically and ontologically connected to "world."

5.2
The Certainty of the World and the Constitution of Nature

The certainty of seeming, in which appearances are taken as they are given, becomes a certainty of the world. This "world" transcends the range of immediate givenness, though it is always implied by whatever is given. After steadily accumulating fulfillments and occasional cancellations of the "this will come next," the doxic-certainty of appearances becomes the doxic-certainty of the world. The lived-world, which was put in abeyance with epoche$_2$, is reattained in its original givenness: now founded, however, in the doxic-certainty of seeming. Insofar as constitutional analyses at the level of the second reduction have been successful, the world, which had to be bracketed in order to be understood, has been made comprehensible, and the urdoxa that accrues to it now, as before, is the basis for the constitution of natural scientific Nature; and, somewhat ironically, for its reificationistic tendencies as well.

(a) The World as Universal Ground of Belief and the Life-World Typology

"To live is always to live-in-certainty-of-the-world" (*C* §37, p.142). This is true for the natural attitude in its naïveté prior to any phenomenological reduction, and it is true after the constitutional analyses carried out at the level of reduction$_2$, after the appearances have been re-cognized as "world." The consciousness of the natural attitude as consciousness of a world, and as the subject matter of phenomenology, has the certainty of being (*Seinsgewissheit*) as its most persisting everyday trait. Every imaginative modification of experience is a modification of this world-certainty, just as all forms of modalized certainty such as conjecture, doubt, and negation are modalizations of the simple believing consciousness. This mode of consciousness, Husserl writes, "is the medium in which all existents as objects of experience are at first simply pregiven for us . . ." (*EJ* §7, p.29). To be conscious means to presume this world in the certainty of its being and to have this certainty as a certainty of belief. "Everything which,as an existing object, is a goal of cognition is an existent on the ground of the world, which is taken as existing as a matter of course" (*EJ* §7, p.30). No perceptual error nor higher-level predicative mistake can cancel this certainty of the world; it is always presupposed as the ever-present background for explaining perceptual error and predicative confusion. All judgmental modification occurs with this world as its guiding presupposition.

The horizon-structure of all experience points ultimately to this world-totality. But the predelineated possibilities sketched within the horizon range from particular expectations to universal themes, which then govern the expectation of other particular "showings." The universal guiding themes are generated by the type-structure of the world, which was itself originally manufactured by the similarities or family resemblances inherent in the manifold of particular showings. In fact, these universal themes, which govern our expectations concerning the world, are referred to by Husserl as the world's "typology" (*PP* §7; *C* §34, p.124, §36, p.139, §51, p.173, §62, p.218, n. *; *EJ* §§ 8, 26, 83). The world's typology is the hierarchy of types, styles, and "habits," often called "universals" in their ossified form, that allow us to navigate the world, to understand it, even when none of its *particulars* are familiar. When J. N. Findlay wrote that "I . . . am at times inclined to doubt whether I have ever encountered any individuals at all . . .",[26] he was probably referring to the density of this typological garb of ideas (*Ideenkleid*). The type-structure of the world—another product of the processes of sense-constitution—is embedded in the act and object horizons; these type-horizons inform us about the world's most general structural possibilities before these possibilities emerge in particular form (though, of course, they have emerged in particular form time and again in the past).

This *Ideenkleid* of the life-world, which was earlier suspended by epoche$_2$ and reduction$_2$, is made articulate through well-connected descriptions, or, in Husserl's language, constitutional analyses. The garbs of ideas casting their conceptual cloaks over the world are not rejected by phenomenology and its attempts at reduction: reduction is meant to *highlight* these conceptual cloaks in their processes of plaiting. In order to understand the constitution of natural scientific Nature, the life-world's typological cloak must now be considered.

The life-world is both the *terminus a quo* and the *terminus ad quem* of scientific-theoretical research. Its beings, its structures, its relations, and its types are the presupposed givens for scientific investigation, and these givens are ultimately the materials that science hopes to explain (*C* §33, p.121). Most important, the constant role played by the world of ordinary experience is that it is "the ground of validity, and every available source of what is taken for granted . . ." (*C* §33, p.122). It can function as the ground in this manner, Husserl believes, because of *its grounding* in the transcendental processes of constitution (*C* §33, p.122).

Husserl recognized, as did Dewey and Heidegger, that in life-world experience we have the first natural domain of verification. "In prescientific life," Husserl writes, ". . . there is a realm of good verification" (*C* §34, p.125). Indeed, in ordinary life-world experience, because of its grounding in the temporal stream and our understanding of types and typological relations, we have the first predictive hypotheses that are based upon a proto-induction that is self-correcting. The methods of natural science grow from these proto-methodologies intrinsic to the possibilities for having a world.

As we have noted, the retaining-in-grasp and expectations of the now-consciousness are inseparable components of all experience; they make experience possible. Experience cannot be separated from the horizon structure nor the horizon structure from experience. More important, the horizon structure of consciousness, which is always a relationship to the world, is "proto-induction" (*C* §9, pp.50-51, §34, p.127, n. *; *EJ* §8, pp.32-33). This accounts for the inveteracy of intentional implication even at the level of the first reduction. Since the temporally based horizon structure is intrinsic to experience itself, induction, too, is inherent to experience. One might even define experience as a unified act of proto-induction, where future and past are laced into the present and experiential possibilities are predelineated in terms of that past and present. It is in this sense that the so-called problem of induction would be seen as a pseudo-problem and dissolved by phenomenological analysis. There is simply no world without induction.

Owing to the proto-inductive ground inherent to the very possibility of experience, experience at its everyday level is already a "methodology" for understanding. As experience, it constantly and necessarily projects possibilities (that is, it makes hypotheses), corrects and modifies these hypotheses if something does not turn out, and verifies or falsifies these hypotheses as experience dictates. All these achievements are normally unnoticed; they are the hidden processes of constitutive intentionality (C §29, §52, pp.175-76, §59). As Alain once suggested, for Husserl too, perception is an incipient science,[27] and the methodology of science is the articulate condensation and application of the proto-methods of cognition that make meaningful experience possible. By systematizing these methods and reapplying them to the world, experience constitutes "Nature"; or, stated otherwise, Nature, as constituted in natural science, is systematically woven out of nature as encountered in the everyday world.

The general conclusion Husserl derives from the recognition of these proto-methodologies of life-world experience is that:

> The contrast between the subjectivity of the life-world and the "objective" the "true" world, lies in the fact that the latter is a theoretical-logical substruction, the substruction of something that is in principle not perceivable, in principle not experienceable in its own proper being, whereas the subjective, in the life-world, is distinguished in all respects precisely by its being actually experienceable. (C §34, p.127)

Husserl's epistemological reversal of the ontological reversal of the natural scientific tradition in philosophy is thus given expression. The lived-world and our consciousness of it is understood as the ground of Nature and our knowledge of it, not vice versa. The demonstration of this reversal of perspectives must now be grounded in a phenomenological description of the proto-methodology of experience, of its development into natural scientific methodology, and finally, of its constitution of natural scientific Nature out of these methods. On the basis of such phenomenological descriptive analyses, Husserl would hope to show how "Nature" is grounded in "nature."

(b) World, nature and Nature: The Processes of
      Idealization and the Restoration of Meaning

In his Galileo analysis Husserl attempts to disclose the methods by which Galileo and his successors were able to transform the world and its experienced nature into the mathematical "Nature" of natural reductive science. As with the constitution of the world, there is an indefinite number of steps in this process. Only a few of these transformational occurrences will be considered here. They are the geometrization of the life-world, the algebraization of geometry, and the "physicalization" of algebraic formulae via the idealizing processes of experimentation. As was noted earlier, the misguided belief that the result of these idealizing processes, the belief that the purely physicalistic notion of Nature was the only real nature, led to the depletion of meaning in natural scientific formulae and threatened these formulae with absurdity. By providing constitutional analyses that ground the meaning of these formulae in the life-world, Husserl hopes to restore meaning to the natural scientific interpretations of the world, and thereby to reveal the actual foundations of the natural sciences.

Everyday experience is experience with and within the vague typicalities and "habits" of the world. The experience of bodies and our fore-knowledge ". . . that they are restricted by the [type of] changeability that is essential to them . . ." (C §9, p.30), is probably the lowest common denominator of this typicality. Bodies are experienced as depending upon one another in their being and their behavior and as belonging together simultaneously and successively. In short, the world is known in terms of its "habits." As Husserl writes, ". . . our empirically intuited surrounding world has an *empirical over-all style*, (C §9, p.31). Even when we vary the world in imagination ". . . we necessarily represent it according to the style in which we have, and up to now have had, the world . . ." (C §9, p.31). And this "universal causal style of the intuitively given surrounding world makes possible hypotheses, inductions, predictions about the unknowns of its present, its past, and its future" (C §9, p.31). As we have noted, these possibilities and the structures of the world itself are themselves grounded in the transcendental act-structures of consciousness disclosed at the level of reduction$_2$ (C §51, p.174). Growing from these structures, the inalterable style of the world "gives to the word 'world' its sole original sense . . ." (C 344), and from this inalterable style all higher-level senses are derived. But *how*, from this domain of *doxa*, in which all particularities constantly change even within the overall invariant style, do the higher-level sense-significations such as "Nature" arise?

The transformation and idealization of sense probably had its start in the *measurement* of the ordinary things of the world, and indeed, of the earth itself, as the etymology of the word "geometry" suggests. Husserl's mythical "Thales of geometry" (*OG* 369) was probably a farmer-become-surveyor, with need to demarcate his part of the world. As Husserl notes:

> Measuring belongs to every culture, varying only according to stages from primitive to higher perfections. We can always presuppose some measuring technique, whether of a lower or higher type, in the essential forward development of culture, [as well as] the growth of such a technique, thus also including the art of design for buildings, or surveying fields, pathways, etc. (*OG* 376)

This need to measure the world, and the measurement itself, carries its meanings with it. There is no threat of meaning-depletion here because the act of measuring—an act of manipulative and cognitive intentionality, literally, *constitutive* intentionality—is, simultaneously, an obvious sense-bestowing act. As directed towards "something to be measured," and then, as measured and of "such and such proportions," the measurement is sense-bestowing and sense-full because its significance is immediately tied to life-world experience.

As Husserl notes, however, there were certain shapes and forms that emerged as particularly useful for our everyday practical needs. Hence, various forms of technical praxis emerged that were oriented towards the construction of such preferred shapes (*OG* 375). This tendency towards preferred shapes was probably motivated by the drive towards "practical perfection" and the phenomenological-psychological tendency towards "good form." The need for better tools conjoined with the phenomenological-gestalt principle of *Prägnanz* may themselves account for the "origin of geometry." Husserl speculates on the genesis of the geometrical sciences in the following way:

> First to be singled out from the thing-shapes are surfaces — more or less "smooth," more or less perfect surfaces; edges, more or less rough or fairly "even"; in other words, more or less pure lines, angles, more or less perfect points; then, again, among the lines, for example, straight lines are especially preferred, and among the surfaces the even surfaces; for example, for practical purposes boards limited by even surfaces, straight lines, and points are preferred, whereas totally or partially curved surfaces are undesirable for many kinds of practical interests. Thus the production of even surfaces and their perfection (polishing) always plays its role in praxis. (*OG* 367)

Examples of this polishing process occur with the need to make wheels into more perfect "circles," buildings into more perfect "squares," roads and borders into more perfect "lines." With the determination of borders and life-spaces in general, objectivity as intersubjective agreement also has its start. Neighbors must be the first to agree about the objective validity of imaginary lines, and thus, intersubjective agreement spawns the objective as what is "true for one and all." From this praxis in the life-world, which constantly perfects the vague invariant structures of the life-world itself, the processes of objectification and idealization begin.

First, "the art of measuring discovers *practically* the basic empirical shapes, concretely fixed on empirical rigid bodies . . ." (*C* §9, p.28). The standard ideal shapes, however, are not actually in the bodies as experienced, but they are *manufactured from* the typically vague invariance of these empirical bodies through further acts of sense-perfecting. Measuring gives rise to numbers on a scale and the art of measuring becomes:

> the art of pushing the exactness of measuring further and further in the direction of growing perfection. It is an art not [only] in the sense of a finished method for completing something; it is at the same time a method for improving [this very] method, again and again, through the inven-

> tion of ever newer technical means, e.g., instruments. Through the relatedness of the world, as field of application, to pure mathematics, this "again and again" acquires the mathematical sense of the *in infinitum*,and thus every measurement acquires the sense of an approximation to an unattainable but ideally identical pole, namely, one of the definite mathematical idealities or, rather, one of the numerical constructions belonging to them. (*C* §9, pp.40-41)

These mathematical poles of identity are, at first, the "ideal limit-shapes" constructed from the empirically familiar invariants and projected as the *eidos*, as the ideal, perfected, and usually reified horizons, in which all empirical entities participate.

Though these ideal limiting-shapes are never actually given in perceptual intuition, they are, Husserl believes,given in "idea-intuition." For example, a right triangle defined as "a polygon having three sides whose internal angles equal 180 degrees with one of these angles equal to 90 degrees" is a perfected idea-intuition that, as idea, functions as the ideal idea-horizon (the ideal limiting-shape) for the subsumption of vague empirical variations under the idea. The idea itself, however, is a sense-constituted ideality originally emergent from acts of sense-bestowing (manipulative and cognitive) intentionality. Through conscious acts of intentional implication, the ideal is then projected as an ideal limiting-shape. This ideal becomes the eidos-horizon for all empirical variants of the shape, and they become approximations of the eidos. The idea-ideality can thus have efficacy in relation to the world because it came from the world, and the things of the world can "participate" in the idea for the same reason. The conscious acts that originally constitute the world constitute pure limiting-shapes upon the basis of that world.

In the constant push towards exactness, the things of the world as *res extensae* are always presupposed. But as presupposed they are given in their plenum-form; that is, their shapes are always filled in by sensory content. Hence, they are not initially pure *res extensae*, "pure corporeality," or ideal identity-shapes. However, through the process of rendering the shapes of the object exact (and the "object" has many shapes in its vague typicality and adumbrational showings), the ideal-shape, as spatiotemporal skeleton of the qualities, emerges. This identity of shape, the ideal limit-shape of the object, emerges as the synthesis, idealization, and objectification of the identities of the shape distributions given in conscious, communal time. Given along with the identity of shape distributions in their temporal sequences are the causal relations in the form of continuity, succession, and constant conjunction between the corresponding shape-configurations as they emerge in connection with one another (C 306-7). As the shapes of the "object" merge towards the exact identity of a limit-shape, the causal relations of the object with itself and with other objects also become idealized and objectified. Causal relations become relations of functional dependency between the ideal qualities of the objects.

Consider, for instance, the idea of a triangle. A triangle in its ideal form never appears in the world, but through the process of imaginary perfecting, we can abstract an *image* of a triangle from the things of the world. The result is obvious to all of us.

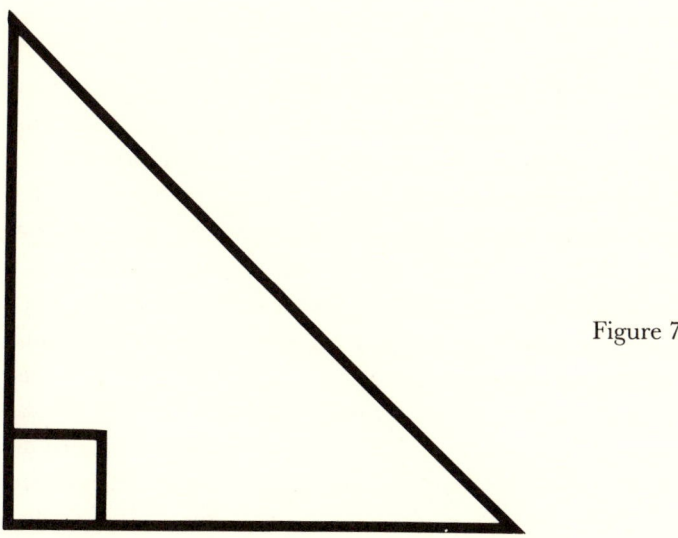

Figure 7

An ideal is already attained in this image because no *natural* object of the world attains to this degree of perfected angularity. If we further assert that the internal angles of this (or any) triangle equal 180 degrees, and that Figure 7 is a right triangle, then we establish, through another act of cognitive perfecting, *an ideal that cannot even be perceptually intuited*; we establish an ideal limiting-shape, the *idea* which we call a "right triangle."[28]

The vague invariant structure of "belonging-together," which first binds the being of certain appearances to certain things, and the being of certain things to certain aspects of the world, is made an absolute invariance in the case of such ideal limiting-shapes. Whenever three lines are connected to form an enclosed space, the internal angles of these lines will, ideally, equal 180 degrees. This invariant relation of necessary interdependency is an abstract and idealized analogue to the invariant relations of the things of the world with themselves and other things. In fact, because of the derivation of exact ideal limit-shapes from the things of the world, the reapplication of these ideal shapes to the world is an ever-present possibility. But this reapplication inundates the world with an exactness (of spatial relations) not previously recognized. Even the vague invariance of the "belonging-together" of certain things and events in the life-world now seem to harbor sets of necessary causal relations determinable with exactness. The "zig-zag" procedure of natural science (*FTL* §44, p.125) is now fully underway: the vague invariant structures and relations of the life-world generate (with the aid of intentional consciousness) the exact idealities and exact identities that inundate the vague invariance with quantitative exactness. This process of "idealizing reciprocation" (the way "up" and the way "down") is extended with the advent of Cartesian analytic geometry, and extended still further into purely symbolic algebra. This new act of idealization, as an act of method transformation, takes us a step further from the original *Sinnesfundament*.

Husserl summarizes the foregoing account of the derivation of eidé from their sense-basis as "the advent of the *mathesis universalis*": Measurements give rise to numbers on a scale, and, in general propositions about functional dependencies of measured quantities, they result not in determined numbers but in numbers in general, stated in general propositions which express laws of functional dependencies" (*C* §9, p.44). These laws of functional dependency signify the mathematical functions or equations that, with the advent of symbolic algebra, replace geometrical proportion for representing shape.[29] When Descartes claimed that "Any problem in geometry can easily be reduced to such terms that a knowledge of the lengths of certain straight lines is sufficient for its construction,"[30] and proceeded to show how this could be done,[31] he provided a method of idealization that could bypass reference to idealizing *representations* such as *drawn* triangles, squares, etc.

Descartes reduced geometry to relations between lines, identified lines with symbols via the discovery of analytic geometry, and then showed how operations with symbols may replace operations with lines. This, in short form, is the algebraization of geometry in which pure relations with symbols (functional relations) take the place of visually representational line-relations. The ideal limiting-shapes that were previously *represented*, come to be expressed as relations between ordered pairs and ultimately as relations between pure numbers. Ideal limiting-shapes no longer need to be directly conceived of *as* shapes; they become purely symbolic relations, and these symbolic relations often seem to refer to themselves alone, or to some ideal world, rather than to the world which spawned them and to which they always ultimately refer. Husserl states his case in the following way:

> This thinking [concerning the transformation of geometrical shapes into general propositions concerning functional dependency] is soon applied in all its extensions — in geometry, in the whole pure mathematics of spatio-temporal shapes — and the latter are thoroughly formalized algebraically for methodical purposes. Thus an "arithmetization of geometry" develops, and arithmetization of the whole realm of pure shapes (ideal straight lines, circles, triangles, motions, relations of position, etc.). They are

> conceived in their ideal exactness as measurable; the units of measurement, themselves ideal, simply have the meaning of spatiotemporal magnitudes.
>
> This arithmetization of geometry leads almost automatically, in a certain way, to the emptying of its meaning. The actually spatiotemporal idealities, as they are presented firsthand [*originär*] in geometrical thinking under the common rubric of "pure intuitions," are transformed, to to speak, into pure numerical configurations, into algebraic structures. In algebraic calculation, one lets the geometric signification recede into the background as a matter of course, indeed drops it altogether; one calculates, remembering only at the end that the numbers signify magnitudes. (*C* §9, p.44)

It was, in this way, that the sense-idealization and articulation of the lived world ". . . acquired, unnoticed, a displaced 'symbolic' meaning" (*C* §9, p.45). This symbolic meaning was then correlated with a world in itself, a pure "formulae world" (*C* §9, p.48).

But even the *mathesis universalis*, "the science of the forms of meaning of the 'something-in-general' " (*C* §9, p.45), the science of the thing as *res extensa*, as pure corporeality, must refer back to the life-world. Even "pure" proportions must be proportions of something; if they are not, they have no meaning. This is why, even in its most abstract forms, the *mathesis universalis* is still, *necessarily*, the science of the "some-*thing* in general." The idealized abstractive figures that represent ideal limiting-shapes, and the possibility of ideal equations that grow from the ideal shape-relations, are, in this sense, dependent upon the world for their foundational meaning. Moreover, insofar as they are constituted or constructed in a systematically connected order of ascending intuitions (*C* §9, p.43), the possibility of applying these higher-level idea-intuitions to the life-world is a possibility that *can* be actualized. This is especially the case when, in order to give support to its abstractive tendencies, mathematics "descends again" (*C* §9, p.32) into the world of doxa. However, by *exporting mathematical idealities into the world*, the world, too, is idealized. As such, it is soon forgotten *to be* the fountain of sense.

It was for these reasons that Husserl found it necessary to *suspend* our belief in reified idealities and things in themselves and *reduce back* to the life-world, in order to re-discover that world as originally given. The acts of revealing and describing the processes of idealization that stem from this life-world and that are usually taken for granted, are the constitutional analyses that provide the *restoration of meaning* to the natural scientific formulae. In fact, where the ontological reversal promoted the depletion of meaning and threatened to negate that meaning altogether, Husserl's epistemological reversal strives for the *restoration of meaning* by showing *how* the "formulae world" is built up from the life-world and is not a magical intentional reference to a world-in-itself.

The next step in the idealization of the world is the projection of a universal, idealized, and *exact* causality.

The ideal limiting-shapes are exact *spatial* relations between lines. When the lines disappear and analytical geometry replaces them with x and y axis coordinates and when all direct references to the analytical coordinates vanish and are replaced by purely numerical equations, these hidden spatial relations remain exact. Yet, in all these cases, reference to the space of the world bestows the fundamental sense to these relations. In idealization$_1$ — the geometrization of Nature — causal interdependency between bodies corresponds to the necessary interdependency between the geometrical magnitudes of ideal shapes. For instance, while the imaginary lines xy, yz, and xz do not *necessarily* belong together, if they are defined as a "triangle" (= ideal limiting-shape), then it does necessarily follow that the internal angles of the shape equal 180 degrees. In idealization$_2$ — the arithmetization of geometry — causal interdependency corresponds to the relations of "numbers on a scale," that is, the relations between the numbers on the x and y coordinate axes, and these relations are abbreviated as the functional relations between the ordered pairs (x,y), (y,z), and (x,z). Again, the spatial relations these coordinates indicate is enclosed within an ideal space of 180 degrees. Finally, causal interdependency becomes a set of exact equations in idealization$_3$ — the algebraization of geometry — signified by pure functional relations, that is, symbolic relations, such as $H^2 = x^2 + y^2$. And again, these relations are meant to refer to a set of spatial relations equal to 180 degrees. These functional relations help effect the ultimate transformation of world into Nature by the correlation of numbers obtained by measuring physical magnitudes with pure geometrical magnitudes. The geometrico-physical magnitudes are then transformed into pure functional relations, thus idealizing the relations of lived space.

Because these spatial relations can be applied to *any* space and the relations between objects in that space, the relations between objects can be made exact within the coordinate/equation system, and they can still be called "causal" relations. By casting this garb of ideal relations over the relations between entities in the object-world, the world and nature ("nature" as the *felt tension* of causal relations) are, for the first time, transformed into abstract mathematical "nature," a "Nature" that has analytic necessity embedded in it *because it is an idea produced in terms of analytical necessity*. Experience and the horizon for all possible experiences is thus charged with an a priori possibility for mathematization. General causal concepts can be developed that correspond with any particular type of mathematizing act to help reify that act and its achievement. For instance, the idea of "gravity" can be developed as a universal eidetic concept. Everything from an apple falling from a tree to the physical relations between interstellar bodies can be subsumed under this concept; and particular mathematical "laws," *mathematical causal laws*, can articulate the necessary spatiotemporal sequences of these particular occurrences. The possibility for an exact universal causality and an exact universal inductivity is thus achieved. Husserl makes these points rather generally when he writes that:

> All the things of the empirically intuitable world have, in accord with the world-style, a bodily character, are *res extensae*, are experienced in changeable collocations which, taken as a whole, have their total collocation; in these, particular bodies have their relative positions, etc. By means of pure mathematics and the practical art of measuring, one can produce, for everything in the world of bodies

which is extended in this way, a completely new kind of inductive prediction; namely, one can "calculate" with compelling necessity, on the basis of given and measured events involving shapes, events which are unknown and were never accessible to direct measurement. Thus ideal geometry, estranged from the world, becomes "applied" geometry and thus becomes in a certain respect a general method of knowing the real. (*C* §9, pp.32-33)

This applied method for knowing the real, however, has another idealizing element to which Husserl pays only little attention. This element is "experimentation."

Husserl does, however, hint at the role of idealizing experimentation in the constitution of Nature when he writes that:

All knowledge of laws could be knowledge only of predictions, grasped as lawful, about occurrences of actual or possible experiential phenomena, predictions which are indicated when experience is broadened through observations and experiments penetrating systematically into unknown horizons, and which are verified in the manner of inductions. (*C* §9, p.50)

This notion of "broadened experience," brought about through experiments, suggests another kind of ideal limit, the ideal limiting-*case*. Experimentation, combined with a mathematized ideal-limiting case, further promotes the physicalization of natural scientific mathematical formulae.

For the natural philosopher at work, the world of experience is the world of experiments. Through mathematizing and idealizing experimentation, that is, through rigorously controlled experience, the world of ordinary experience is transformed into the purely physicalistic mathematical manifold. "Causal" connections, *as* relations between purely quantifiable magnitudes, are achieved when experiments measure physical magnitudes and articulate the interdependencies between these magnitudes. Experiments allow for the instantiation of mathematical functions, much as a geometrical figure is the instantiation of a geometrical theorem or proposition.

Indeed, similar to ideal shapes and formulae in general, experimentation has an inveterate "up-down" movement in relation to world and "Nature." It often postulates ideal limiting-*cases,* which are drawn from observations in the life-world, and then "idealizes" the life-world itself by placing it under the eidos of the ideal limiting-case, that is, by placing it under an eidos for pure physicality and total lawfulness. An example of this kind kind of idealization is found in Galileo's analysis of freefall.[32]

Observing certain invariant structures of life-world experience, Galileo argued that objects of the same weight ("specific gravity") do not fall with a common ratio of movement in mediums of different degrees of resistance, nor do objects of different weights ("specific gravities") fall with a common ratio of movement in mediums of the same resistance. (This claim, of course, was directed against the Aristotelians, who held the common-sense belief that the velocity of freefall was determined by the ratio of the heaviness of the falling object to the resistance of the medium.) Furthermore, Galileo claimed, ". . . I found that the inequality of speeds is always greater in the more resistant mediums, as compared with those more yielding."[33] Thus, on the basis of this second observation, he asserted, "I came to the opinion that if one were to remove entirely the resistance of the medium, all materials would descend with equal speed."[34] On the basis of these two observations of (not so obvious) life-world typology, Galileo postulated an ideal limiting-case for free fall — a purely physicalistic case beyond all possible life-world experience. The ideal limit-case is the "case" of free fall with *no* resistance and hence, in *no* medium — the "case" of free fall in a *void* or *vacuum.*

Like the ideal limiting-shapes, the ideal limiting-case is an idea-intuition, never a perceptual one. And, as an idea-intuition, the ideal case can render exactness to the physical world because its nature is made articulate only via ideal shapes and/or equations. In fact, the ideal limiting-case *is* the idealized physicalistic concomitant of mathematical idealities. Consider, for instance, the following graphical representation of the ideal case for freefall.[35]

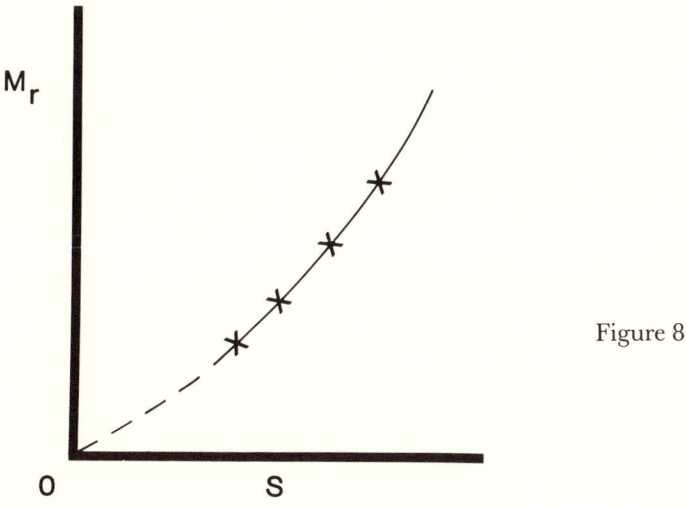

Figure 8

In figure 8 "M_r" equals the resistance of the medium, "S" equals the difference in the speed of fall for objects of two different specific gravities in that medium, and "O" equals the ideal limiting-case for free fall in a void; that is, where "M_r" equals "O," "S" also equals "O." The crosses indicate some random empirical measurements of an object in descent, and the dashes indicate the extrapolation of the geometrical curve towards the void as an infinite ideal. Since this void is an ideal never encountered in nature "M_r" never actually equals "O" (though, as an ideal, "M_r = O" is essential to the constitution of "Nature"). Even so, the ideal case can still function as the *guiding* limit-case.

Each measurement of a body falling is now viewed as an *empirical modification* of free fall in a void. Hence, Galileo must introduce the "buoyancy effect" and the "friction effect"[36]—effects of the empirical world, and these must be taken into consideration for *every actual case* of free fall as such cases *actually occur* in the world. Consequently, the *Ideenkleid* once more covers the world and nature with an idealized "Nature," but with a necessary concession to empirical contingencies and variants such as weight, length of fall, friction, and buoyancy. The ideal limiting-case also manages to describe and explain the world by reference to the purely idealistic mathematical formulae that cover it—here, in relation to bodies falling.

But as we have now seen in a number of selected instances, both the mathematical and physicalistic idealities are themselves constituted from conscious acts in relationship to the life-world. In short, the highly complicated meaning content of these idealities is achieved as the result of the processes constituting them *and* the processes of their reapplication to the world. These processes are acts of both cognitive and manipulative intentionality—an intentionality that, literally, constitutes (the meaning of) "Nature."

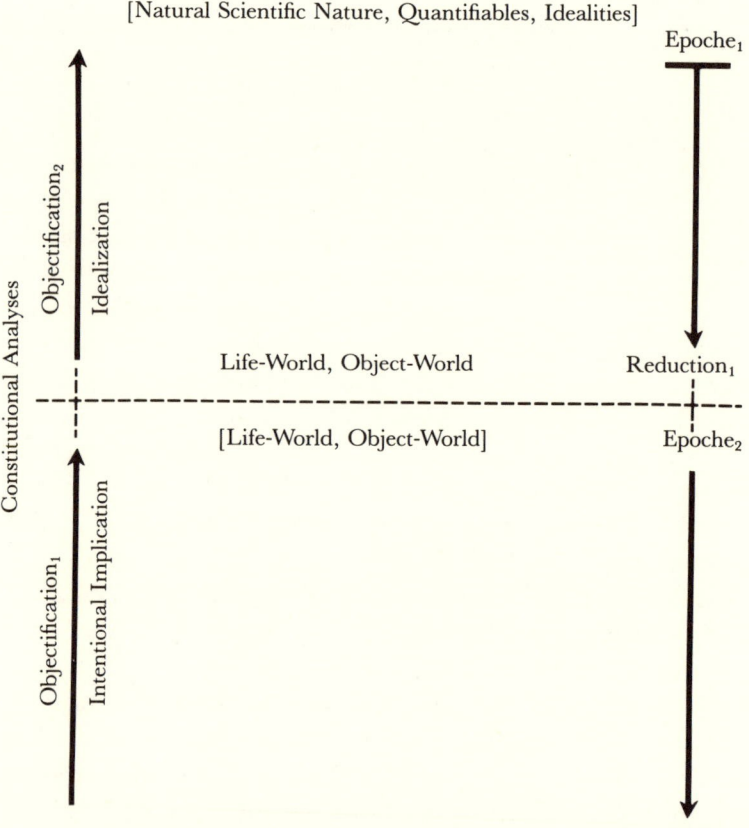

[Natural Scientific Nature, Quantifiables, Idealities]

Epoche₁

Constitutional Analyses

Objectification₂

Idealization

Life-World, Object-World

Reduction₁

[Life-World, Object-World]

Epoche₂

Objectification₁

Intentional Implication

Transcendental Consciousness Reduction
Temporal Stream, The Primal Here and Now, Pure Appearance[2]

On the basis of our (necessarily partial) constitutional analyses, Husserl's epistemological reversal, and more generally, the architectonic structure of his phenomenological program now can be displayed. Figure 9, at left, depicts the completed set of relations between $epoche_{1-2}$, $reduction_{1-2}$, and constitutional $analyses_{1-2}$. Also, starting from the notions of "Natural Scientific Nature" and "$epoche_1$," it displays the broad structure of the arguments and descriptions developed in this text.

(c) Doxic Certainty and Ontological Genesis in the Positing Theses of Natural Science

As we have seen, the problem of an ontological reversal is reinforced by the sedimentation of higher-level idealities, which, because they are sedimented and reified, seem to exist disconnected over and above the manifold experiences of life-world becoming. There is another tendency, however, as inveterate to consciousness as is sedimentation, that also leads, almost inexorably, to the reification of higher-level, ideal meaning-systems. This tendency, too, is inveterate to the natural attitude; it stems from the doxic-ontic certainty, the belief in being inherent to our knowing acts. And this belief in being infiltrates all levels of phenomenological-epistemic constitution; it "flows-up" from the life-world into the higher-level idealities, and thus promotes their reification as a sort of being.

The reification of ideal relations as radically transcendent beings ($transcendence_2$) occurs as a process of *ontological genesis* that is motivated by consciousness itself. Ontological genesis, as the reification of idealities, is an intentionally implicated motivated possibility inherent to the belief in being inherent to almost all ordinary acts of consciousness. "Being" is the (believed in) correlate to all such acts. And, since the ideal kinds of being ("$transcendence_2$") function to explain beings-in-becoming, these idealities have often been believed to be *Being itself*. Husserl suggests that certain facets of intentional implication or motivation, as well as the use of models in natural science, promote this tendency towards the ontological reification of idealities.

In many different ways we have heard Husserl argue that ". . . in physical method the *perceived thing itself* is always and in principle *precisely the thing which the physicist studies and scientifically determines*" (*I* §52, p.145). This thing may be any given thing as encounterable in life-world experience; for example, a stone, a swamp, an animal, a star. Though the natural scientist may argue *at the end of his investigations* that the sensory *thing itself* is a mere sign for the true, scientifically determined "thing *in* itself," observation of his actual activities in the scientific determination of this so-called thing *in* itself discourages acceptance of this claim. Thus, the "thing of physics," Husserl argues, is not behind the sensory thing, and the sensory thing is not a copy or sign of the purely physical thing. Instead, ". . . the physical thing is nothing foreign to that which appears in a sensory body, but something that manifests itself in it and in it *alone* . . ." (*I* §52, p.145).

Like the thing itself, the would-be "thing *in* itself" must be made comprehensible through its series of manifestations. Thus Husserl writes:

> . . . even the sensory determining-content of the *x* which functions as bearer of the physical determinations does not clothe the latter in an alien dress that conceals them: rather it is only in so far as the *x* is the subject of the sensory determinations that it is also subject of the physical, which on its side *announces itself in* the sensory. (*I* §52, pp.145-46)

The "thing" as determined and ideally constructed by natural science is grounded in the thing as given in life-world experience—even when this experience is the micro-experience (the experiment) of the physicist:

> The thing which he observes, with which he experiments, which he sees continually, handles, places on the scales, "brings to the fusing-furnace," this and no other thing is the subject of physical predicates, since it is it that has the weight, mass, temperature, electrical resistance, and so forth. So too it is the perceived processes and connections themselves which are defined through [and in turn structure] concepts such as force, acceleration, energy, atom, ion, and so forth. (*I* §52, p.146)

However, since the scientist, almost always in a condition of *Selbstverstandlichkeit*, experiences the thing with which he experiments as laced through by the historically inherited *Ideenkleid* of his science, this experienced thing, even prior to its full scientific determination, is *predetermined* by transcendent idealities.

This predetermined scientific determination is the effect of constantly active, yet unnoticed, sedimented meanings. Because of these sedimented, inherited meanings, the physicist has always already *predetermined* the physical qualities and relations of the thing in terms of signs and symbols. This is the process that we noted when we considered the geometrization and then the algebraization of the physical experiment. The predetermining signs and symbols therein *stand for* the wealth of causal properties intrinsic to the experienced manifold within which the thing appears and has its being (*I* §52, p.146). However, Husserl argues, on the basis of the physicist's cognitive and manipulative intentional operations with the thing, it is clear ". . . that *even the higher transcendence of the physical thing does not imply any reaching out beyond the world . . .*" (*I* §52, p.146). Conjoined with the previous analyses we have made, this means that Husserl intends to draw transcendence$_2$ — the domain of "Nature" — back into nature, because "Nature" is now recognized as a structured set of ideal relations that are logical constructs stemming from and belonging to the full concreteness of life-world experience (*C* §34e). But neither these nor any other idealities change ". . . in the least the fact that these are human formations, . . . and thus belong to this concrete unity of the life-world, whose concreteness thus extends farther than that of 'things' " (*C* §34, p.130). Indeed, it is precisely because ". . . physical thought builds itself up on the basis of natural experience . . . *[f]ollowing [out] the rational motives* which the connexions of experience suggest . . ." (*I* §52, p.146), and because the concrete unity of the life-world does extend further than the unity of mere things, that ontological genesis and the reification of idealities occurs.

As early as the *Logical Investigations* Husserl's comments about the concept of "motivation" recognized the potential for occurrences such as "ontological genesis." Describing the phenomenological process of motivation, he there described:

> . . . as a common circumstance the fact that certain objects or states of affairs *of whose reality someone has actual knowledge* indicates to him *the reality of certain other objects or states of affairs*, in the *sense that his belief in the reality of the one is experienced* (though not at all evidently) *as motivating a belief or surmise in the reality of the other*. This relation of 'motivation' represents a *descriptive unity* among our acts of judgment in which indicating and indicated states of affairs become constituted for the thinker . . . . Plainly such a state of affairs amounts to just this: that certain things *may* or *must* exist, *since* other things have been given. (p.270)

Given the things of the natural scientific experiment, then, and the events occurring in relation to it, other things "may or must exist." These "other things" are sometimes what we call "theoretical entities," and, owing to the force of motivation, or, in our earlier terminology, the force of intentional implication, we *posit* them, that is, we give them existential status. Moreover, since certainty and all of its modalities are grounded in the doxic-ontic certainty of life-world intuition (*EJ* §7), the *lack* of intuitive correlates for the higher-level idealities that are spawned from our relations with everyday things and that seem to provide certainty in relation to those things generates an uneasy feeling in the human subject. This uneasy feeling is probably what in turn motivates the construction of pictures and models "of" those categorial unities (i.e., pure idea-intuitions, or pure thought-unities) that themselves cannot be perceptually intuited.

Suspicious of the effects of such "pictures," Husserl argues that:

> What is unintuitable to sense has been taken as *symbolically representing* a concealed entity which could be made simply sense-intuitable through improvements in the organization of our ideas, and the models have served as intuitable schematic pictures of this hidden thing . . . . The *transparent* meaning of the constructive forms of thought *as such* is disregarded, as is also the fact that the hypothetical element is bound up with the work of synthetic thinking. (*I* §52, p.148)

The concealed "transparent meaning" is the fact that categorial and idealized determinations of the world *cannot* be presented because they are not things; they are *ideas* which have gained their meaning from conscious acts in relation to things and thing-relations. The "hypothetical element" bound up with synthetic idealizing thinking is found in the fact that *ideas* function as infinite poles allowing us to effect the synthesis and building up of appearances and of meanings. But ideas can do this precisely because they are ideas and not things.

Hence, Husserl is quite right when he writes that, "Even a divine physics cannot make categorial [i.e., symbolic] thought determinations of realities intuitable in the plain, ordinary way, as little as divine omnipotence can bring it about that elliptic functions should be painted or played on the fiddle" (*I* §52, p.148). But the doxic-certainty inveterate to our perceptual faith, and the desire to ground all knowledge *immediately* in perception, would like to paint these elliptic functions and hear them played on a fiddle. Our models of nonintuitable "entities," that is, our models of the would-be *reversed ontology*, are a symptom of the continuing attempt to achieve something just like the presentative portrayal of functions—the misguided attempt to generate "onta" out of ideas.

(d) Epoche, Constitution, and Ontological Status

The epoche was originally needed to counteract the tendencies towards ontological genesis, reification, and reversal. By suspending the existence of reified transcendencies, normally used as premises for natural judgment, it became possible to see the phenomena anew. Well-connected descriptions of these phenomena in their modes of synthesis then provided constitutional analyses of "nature" and "Nature." But if natural judgment has been outlawed, what kinds of judgments do these analyses eventually allow us to make?

Husserl had concluded *Ideas* by writing that, "*Phenomenology does not judge ontologically . . .*" (§153, p.394). This statement can lead to the suspicion that the possible positive results of phenomenological analysis are null, because if phenomenology does not make judgments about "onta," then it is inevitably alienated from the world as normally lived. However, Husserl's all-too-elliptical statement here must be thought through in conjunction with an earlier statement made in *Ideas*, namely, that "As applied, phenomenology supplies the definitive criticism of every fundamentally distinct science, and especially, thereby, the final determination of the sense in which their objects can be said to 'be' " (§62, p.166; with trans. changes). And here the question becomes this: How can phenomenology propose to provide the definitive criticism of the sense in which objects can be said to "be," yet not judge ontologically?

The distinction we must make is this. When Husserl claims that "phenomenology does not judge ontologically," he means that phenomenology does not *base* its judgments on presupposed "onta," "objectivities," or "transcendencies," because the existence of such has been suspended from the beginning of phenomenological investigation. On the other hand, phenomenology can provide the definitive criticism of the way in which objects can be said to "be," because constitutional analyses, grounded in the purified experience of phenomena, reveal the manner in which the sense of onta, objectivities, and transcendencies comes-to-be, and hence, the sense in which they "are." Whereas natural thinking necessarily judges ontologically because all its judgments are based upon the belief in being, phenomenology, as a critical, transcendental philosophy, passes judgment on the *premises* of natural thinking by determining the sense and validity of the claims to ontological status attributed to the objects on which those premises are based. In fine, the premises of naturalistic thinking are the "conclusions" for phenomenological thinking. In this sense phenomenological procedure resembles certain methods of geometrical or logical proof, where the conclusions are had from the start and the "proof" is the establishment of the proper procedures that are (or were) necessary for the achievement of the conclusion.

The presupposed existence-positing premises of natural thinking, in its condition of *Selbstverstandlichkeit*, sometimes concern radically transcendent beings (transcendence$_2$, which fell to epoche$_1$), and sometimes concern ordinary objects (transcendence$_1$, which fell to epoche$_2$). But as a philosophy *of* the natural and natural scientific attitudes, phenomenology (if its methods are successful) can pass judgment *about* the ontologies of these domains of thinking. It can describe the way in which their objects can be said to "be," though it cannot *judge ontologically* insofar as this means making judgments *based upon* the ontologies of natural modes of thinking. To make such judgments would be to commit the *petitio principii* which phenomenology, as an attempt at radically presuppositionless epistemology, set out to avoid from the beginning.

But "bracketing ontology" in order to regain it aright has some strange consequences. If phenomenological constitutional analysis could be completed, Husserl's claims that "nothing is lost to epoche" (*I* §49, p.139; *C* §52, p.176) would, we suspect, prove to be a tautology — albeit a gargantuan one, and anything but empty. Once natural scientific Nature is bracketed as ontologically primary, reduction, and then constitutional analyses, would presumably regain all that had been suspended. But what is regained is not necessarily conceived of as it had been conceived of *prior to* suspension, reduction, and reattainment. For instance, after the suspension of and reduction from the domain of pure corporeality, and the ensuing constitutional analyses that bring us back to its actual sense, the domain of "Nature" is regained, but it is regained as a constituted set of ideal relations. It is still the natural scientific Nature that helps to explain the world of experience, but it is now understood to be, in large part, a set of ideal relations, ideal relations not ontologically determinate of the experienced world, but ideal relations epistemically determined and epistemically motivated by that experienced world and the conscious acts intrinsic to it. Nothing is lost, then, that was actually there to be bracketed, and what is regained with an existential index is, by definition, all that was actually there to begin with. What is regained, however, may not be what was *thought* to have been initially suspended. The "signature" on its ontological status may have changed.

We have no wish here to make of Husserl a Wittgensteinian by making a "ladder trick" of epoche, reduction, and constitutional analysis. They are not ladder tricks in the early Wittgensteinian manner because constitutional analyses are not thrown away once the world and Nature are regained; indeed, they are retained as the epistemic ground of world and Nature *as* regained. But as with the Wittgensteinian ladder, when constitutional analyses are successful, the epoche should dissolve; nothing understood to be constituted as "real" will have changed, but the world will appear aright because it will now be understood in terms of its constitutional development, and in that sense it will be understood anew.

Hence, when Husserl says that "nothing is lost to the epoche," he presupposes and projects the ultimate validity and fulfillment of the phenomenological method. Everything that was really there will eventually be regained, but it will then be understood aright. What is not regained with an existential index — for instance, a *purely* corporeal, causally efficacious, world in itself — cannot be lost because it was never there to begin with. As constitutional analyses progress, the brackets will gradually dissolve,[37] but what is revealed with the dissolution of epoche is not necessarily that which was (believed to be) suspended by epoche. What is regained is what is really there, but now understood in the actual way in which it can be said to "be."

If the phenomenological method of epoche, reduction, and constitution is successful, then Husserl's tautology is not a question-begging vicious circle, but a "phenomenological circle"; that is, it is a relation between the transcendental and the transcendent, because whatever is regained is regained from the primordially given (in reduction) without conscious appeal to, or even conscious rejection of, "that" which was bracketed (though still intentionally implicated) due to transcendence. And if that which was (thought to be) suspended is not regained with the same existential signature, then it simply never was what it was *pre-scribed* to be in the first place.

One of Husserl's famous, but (in some contexts) unfortunate, assertions can help us to develop a brief defense of these statements. The assertion is made in *Cartesian Meditations,* where Husserl writes that ". . . phenomenological explication does nothing but *explicate the sense this world has for us all, prior to any philosophizing,* and obviously gets solely from our experience — *a sense which philosophy can uncover but never alter . . .*" (§62, p.151). The reason this Husserlian phrase, so contrary to the famous Marxian slogan, is unfortunate, is that with it Husserl disregards the critical-reconstructive facets of his own phenomenological methods. This can best be seen, in light of what we have done thus far, by focusing on problems internal to the statement just quoted. Owing to the infiltration of the natural scientific metaphysics into the everyday world — a metaphysics developed and sanctioned by early modern *philosophy* — the sense of the world "prior to any philosophizing" is a sense unknown and unhad *by any of us* while still wearing our everyday, naturalistic hats, prior to phenomenological epoche and reduction. Insofar as the sense-infiltration of this natural scientific metaphysics into the life-world has occurred, and insofar as it has then been shown by phenomenological analysis to promote absurdity and countersensicality, then to just this extent the constitutional analyses that replace this metaphysics *must alter the sense* that the world has for us. If they do not, then the epistemic uses of phenomenological analysis are null and the critical-reconstructive facts of phenomenology are lost.[38] Let us conclude this chapter by showing how this process of "metaphysical dissolution" and ontological revaluation proceeds in relation to one of our guiding problems, namely, the problem of the ontological status of unobservables in the natural sciences.[39]

If the nature of the "thing of physics" is to be understood, attention must be paid to what scientists *do* and not only to what they *say* about what they do (*I* §52, p.143). When Husserl makes this suggestion he means to direct attention to the life-world objects that are determined as natural science understands them. These objects, which are "handled, placed on the scales and brought to the fusing furnace," are the objects of the everyday world. These objects are, by definition, perceivable in principle, though, as scientifically determined, they are *represented* as a set of sign or symbol relations determinable with a relatively high degree of exactness. These exact sign/symbol relations are "categorial unities" and as such are purely intentional thought unities manifest in symbolic form alone, and sometimes manifest only in that form. Here again, Husserl's epistemic reversal literally reverses the ontological reversal, which would have made the perceived thing the sign or symbol of the would-be thing in itself of the metaphysical physics.

If, as Husserl claims, the idea of the purely physical "thing" is built up by following out "the *rational motives* which the connexions of experience suggest," then the "purely physical 'thing' " that was suspended by epoche$_1$ is generated from and motivated by the things of the world as those things are determined through the cognitive and manipulative intentionality of the natural scientist. The connection between the thing of physics and the thing of the world is not achieved by a "mythical bond" between "real" push-pull causality and conscious subjectivity; it is not effected by a radically transcendent "thing" (transcendence$_2$) that causally constitutes the thing of the world. Rather, the thing of physics is constituted as an idealized pole of exact mathematical relations, an *idea* in the Kantian sense, which, as such, is a constituted intentional unity generated by conscious acts, just as the "thing," as thing of the world, was generated from the synthesis of appearances at the level of reduction$_2$. The conscious acts that motivate the thing of physics, however, are higher-level categorial acts — symbolically "encapsulated" acts — which, because of their ideal interconnections, allow for the constitution of "secondary worlds," that is, insulated semitotalities of symbolic relations such as the "Nature" of natural science.

Showing that the formulae of mathematical natural science are exact intentionally constituted sign-systems, however, does not totally resolve the question concerning the ontological status of unobservables. Not *all* the unobservables postulated by natural science are sign/symbol relations for the real intuitable world; nor are they all unobservable *in principle* as are categorial unities of thought (*I* §52, p.148). Husserl seems to recognize that a sharp distinction must be drawn between (1) purely symbolic relations (that is, categorial thought unities), (2) would-be "entities" unobservable *in principle*, and (3) entities unobservable *in fact*, but not unobservable in principle. For instance, he writes:

> . . . an explanation of the perceptually given events through causal realities hypothetically assumed, through unknown entities of the nature of a thing (as, for instance, the explanation of certain planetary disturbances through the assumption of a still unknown planet, Neptune), is something that differs in principle from explanation in the sense of a physical determination of experienced things and through physical means of explanation after the style of atoms, ions, and the like. (*I* §52, p.144)

Husserl is here suggesting that the postulation of an unknown and, as yet, unperceived *but perceivable* entity, is a legitimate mode of existence-positing hypothetical explanation. The planet Neptune is perceivable *in principle*, even though it may not be perceived *in fact*. This manner of hypothetical explanation still bases itself upon existential realities, that is, upon things of the world. On the other hand, Husserl argues, the explanation of experienced things and events through the purely physicalistic existence-positing of entities *not experienceable in principle*, such as atoms, ions, energy, and force, is a misguided interpretation of natural scientific explanation that leads to, and is then based upon, the ontological reversal. In turn, this reversal, as has been seen, leads to (and is motivated by) the depletion of the meaning of natural scientific formulae. This is why Husserl argues that ". . . if the unknown cause we have assumed *exists* [ist] at all, it must be *in principle* perceivable and experienceable, if not by us, at least for other Egos who see better and farther than we do" (*I* §52, p.144). With the constant improvement of scientific instruments, however, "egos" are, in fact, learning to see "better and farther" than ever before; and while this fact makes some of the factual claims in Husserl's previous argument problematic, the logic of his argument remains sound.

Husserl's example of an "atom" as a postulated entity unperceivable *in principle*, that is, unperceivable by any ego, is misleading precisely because "egos" have learned to see "better and farther" than was possible in Husserl's own day. The intuitive evidence for the real existence of "atoms" suggests that they are perceivable in principle, even though still not directly perceivable in fact. However, as things of the world (though not of the *everyday* life-world), "atoms" are, with a very high degree of probability, intentionally implicated as real existents. For example, traces in a cloud chamber and atomic explosions intentionally implicate the actual physical reality of atoms. It would be a difficult task, no doubt, to convince an August 6th, 1945, resident of Hiroshima that "atoms" were mere theoretical entities, mere categorial unities of thought.

Nevertheless, though factual circumstances have changed, the general purport of Husserl's argument remains untouched. Some unobservables of natural science are categorial unities and symbolic forms by their very nature, and must remain so forever. For instance, the notions of "force," "energy," and "gravity" seem to be categorial ideas by virtue of their eidetic essences alone; they are purely symbolic unities constituted upon the basis of the perceived things and the relations of those things. "Force," "energy," and "gravity" "themselves" can never be perceived as such. They cannot be perceived *in principle* because they are ideal relations, and ideas, or categorial unities, cannot be perceived; they are *of* and *about* the things, but not themselves "things."

Husserl evidently misconceived the eidetic essence of an "atom" because it has proved perceivable, at least in principle. It is not *just* an intentionally constituted categorial unity. An "atom" can be ascribed the ontological status of a "reality" even though it is currently unobservable *in fact*.

Interestingly, however, Husserl's statement that "if an unknown cause exists at all, it must be perceivable in principle, if not for us, at least for Egos who see better and farther than us," suggests that he would have avoided the denial of ontological status to atoms if he had understood them to be entities *perceivable in principle* or even if he had understood them to be entities intentionally implicated by that which is perceivable. That they ever were not perceived *in fact*, or even not intentionally implicated *in fact*, is an historical contingency to which Husserl was victim.

Husserl's statement concerning the "vision of egos" also suggests his response to the problems surrounding the development of new instruments such as telescopes, microscopes, and cloud chambers that allow the once-unobservable to become observed. If "egos" can perceive the correlate of some intentional unity, or even if that correlate is intentionally implicated as something perceivable in principle, it "exists," in principle at least, and can be ascribed ontological status until factual evidence accumulates suggesting "it" not to exist, or, what is more likely, until it is shown to be unneeded to explain that which clearly exists. And all of this might well occur through the mediation of instruments—what Don Ihde calls "instrumental intentionality."[40] On the other hand, if a word-signification is indicative of beings unperceivable in principle, if its intentional, eidetic essence does not implicate any possibility of perception, then its would-be referent does not exist and cannot be ascribed ontological status. Of course these distinctions are deceptive because it is not always clear what hypothetical posits will prove perceivable, as Husserl's comments about "atoms" amply show. To some extent only further constitutional analyses and further "perceptions of egos" can determine which "unobservables" are ontologically real and which are ideas. Husserl's later thoughts on the historical contingencies of the natural scientific enterprise made space for such phenomenological-historical investigations to complement his more extensive and earlier eidetic investigations.[41]

Determining the sense in which different kinds of objects can be said to "be" is the process of dissolving the brackets. With the determination of the objects of consciousness as things of the world or as idealities, the problems of ontological status (of the particular objects and object-types under consideration) are resolved, though only in piecemeal fashion. And, with the resolution of the problems of ontological status, via the understanding of constitutional processes and eidetic essences, a significant part of the *work* of phenomenology is done.

NOTES

1. Descartes, *Meditations on First Philosophy*, trans. Laurence J. Lafleur (Bobbs-Merrill, 1977), p. 29. *Philosophical Works*, p. 154.

2. Descartes, *Meditations*, p. 29; *Philosophical Works*, p. 154.

3. Descartes, *Meditations*, p. 30; *Philosophical Works*, p. 155.

4. Descartes, *Meditations*, p. 30; *Philosophical Works*, p. 155.

5. Descartes, *Meditations*, p. 30; *Philosophical Works*, p. 155.

6. Descartes, *Meditations*, pp. 27, 29-30, 69-74; *Philosophical Works*, pp. 152-53, 154-55, 190. The locution "descending abstractive hierarchy" is borrowed from Eugene Kaelin.

7. Descartes, *Meditations*, p. 30; *Philosophical Works*, p. 154.

8. Descartes, *Meditations*, p. 30; *Philosophical Works*, p. 155.

9. J. J. C. Smart, "Descartes and the Wax," *Philosophical Quarterly* 1 (1950): 50-57.

10. Descartes, *Meditations*, pp. 60-63. *Philosophical Works*, pp. 179-81.

11. For a similar reading of the wax experiment, see Bernard Williams, *Descartes: The Project of Pure Inquiry* (Pelican Books, 1978), pp. 213-24.

12. On this see Robert Sokolowski, *The Formation of Husserl's Concept of Constitution* (The Hague: Martinus Nijhoff, 1964). Sokolowski's entire work is relevant to this issue but see especially pp. 185, 189-90.

13. Ludwig Landgrebe, *The Phenomenology of Edmund Husserl*, ed. by Donn Welton (Cornell University Press, 1981), p. 97.

14. Mss. BI 13I, p. 8. Quoted by Sokolowski, *The Formation of Husserl's Concept of Constitution*, pp. 179-80.

15. For a highly successful attempt to salvage the sense of Husserl's thought on the "immanent domain," see Shaun Gallagher's essay "Hyletic Experience and the Lived Body," *Husserl Studies* 3 (1987): 131-66.

16. But see *C* §71, p.249, where Husserl still makes statements such as ". . . [one] makes the psychic accessible for the first time . . . *only* if one penetrates from the externalized intentionalities to the internal ones which constitute the others intentionally."

17. Sokolowski, *The Formation of Husserl's Concept of Constitution*, pp. 4-5.

18. Suzanne Cunningham, *Language and the Phenomenological Reductions of Edmund Husserl* (The Hague: Martinus Nijhoff, 1976).

For another formulation of this problem, see Ross Harrison, "The Concept of Prepredicative Experience," in *Phenomenology and Philosophical Understanding*, ed. by Edo Pivćević (London: Cambridge University Press, 1975): 93-107. For a Derridian formulation, see Harvey and Hintikka, "Modalization and Modalities," forthcoming.

19. On the issue of "exploding perceptions," see David Smith, "The Case of the Exploding Perception," *Synthese* 41 (1979): 239-69.

20. Maurice Merleau-Ponty, *Phenomenology of Perception*, trans. by Colin Smith (New Jersey: Routledge & Kegan Paul, Humanities Press, 1962), p. 58.

21. Jean-Paul Sartre, *L'Imaginaire* (Paris: Gallimard, 1940), pp. 240-41. Maurice Merleau-Ponty, *Phenomenology of Perception*, pp. 4-5.

22. Martin Heidegger, *Being and Time*, trans. by John Macquarrie and Edward Robinson (Harper & Row, 1962), §§15-16.

23. For a consideration of these distinctions in Husserl, see Ulrich Claesges, "Intentionality and Transcendence: On the Constitution of Material Nature," in *Analecta Husserliana* II, ed. by Anna Teresa Tymieniecka (Dordrecht: D. Reidel, 1972), pp. 283-91.

24. Bertrand Russell, "Knowledge by Acquaintance and Knowledge by Description," *Proceedings of the Aristotelian Society* XI (1910/11): 108-28. Reprinted in *Mysticism and Logic and Other Essays* (New York: Doubleday, 1957).

25. Descartes, *Philosophical Works*, p. 443. This is a classic example of the *petitio principii* inveterate to naturalistic epistemologies. See above §3.4.

26. J. N. Findlay, "An Ontology of Senses," *The Journal of Philosophy* 79 (1982): 551.

27. Alain, pseud. Emile Chartier, *Quatre-vingt-un chapitre es sur L'Espirit et les Passions* (Paris: Gallimard, 1941), p. 19.

28. For a more extended analysis of the processes of idealization in relation to geometry, see John J. Drummond, "The Perceptual Roots of Geometric Idealizations," *Review of Metaphysics* 37 (June 1984): 785-810.

29. I thank James Garrison for help in understanding the method transformation from geometry to algebra and for a number of other points that follow. For Garrison's work on the development of geometry as a form of "theory-ladenness" in natural science, see James Garrison, *Geometry as a Source of Theory-Ladenness in Early Modern Physics* (unpublished dissertation) Florida State University, 1981; for his reading of Husserl's theory of idealization,

see his article "Husserl, Galileo and the Processes of Idealization," *Synthese* 66 (1986): 329-38.

30. Descartes, *The Geometry of René Descartes*, trans. by David Eugene Smith and Marcia L. Latham (Chicago: Open Court, 1925), p. 2.

31. Descartes, *The Geometry of René Descartes*, pp. 5-6.

32. The following analysis of experimentation as a form of idealization is developed from accounts given by James Garrison and from Steven Gaukroger's accounts of the same in *Explanatory Structures*, (Harvester Press, 1978), Ch. 6.

33. Galileo Galilei, *Two New Sciences*, trans. by Stillman Drake (Madison: The University of Wisconsin Press, 1974), p. 72.

34. Galileo Galilei, *Two New Sciences*, p. 75.

35. This graphical representation is offered by James Garrison in "Galileo, Husserl, and the Processes of Idealization," *Synthese* 66 (1986): 329-38.

36. The "effects" were noted by Galileo; the terms, I believe, were coined by Stephen Gaukroger, *Explanatory Structures*, pp. 214-18.

37. Husserl would not always seem to agree with this claim. For instance, in the essay "Phenomenology and Anthropology" he writes that "the epoche is permanent" (*SW* 319), and in the *Crisis* he writes that the phenomenological attitude is taken up "once and for all" (§40, p.150). We will address this difficulty more fully below and then again in §6.2b.

38. This seems to be the recurring point made in Henry Pietersma's series of fascinating papers on Husserl's phenomenology and "epistemic appraisal." See his essays "The Phenomenological Reduction," *American Philosophical Quarterly* 16 (1979): 37-44; "Husserl's Concept of Existence," *Synthese* 66 (1986): 311-28; "Intentionality and Epistemic Appraisal," *The Southern Journal of Philosophy* 25 (1987): 381-94; and "Contextual Objects and the Problem of Knowledge" (unpublished essay).

39. A number of the points to be made here, with others, appear in my essay "Husserl and the Problem of Theoretical Entities," *Synthese* 66 (1986): 291-309.

40. Donn Ihde, *Technics and Praxis* (Dordrecht: D. Reidel, 1979), Ch. 1-4, esp. pp. 33-39.

41. For the development of this thesis, see my essay in *Synthese* 66 (1986): esp. p. 305.

6
HUSSERL'S REVALUATION OF EPISTEMIC VALUES

THE PERPETUAL BEGINNER in Husserl may never have allowed him to see the architectonic of his phenomenological method as if it were completed. If we have succeeded in depicting the motivating forces and projected completion of this architectonic more clearly than did Husserl, it is because only the large problems loom large for merely good philosophers, whereas the small ones, as well, loom in their importance for truly great philosophers. Husserl never ceased to acknowledge even the smallest problems and slightest implications of his thought, and he never ceased to start again when these new problems and implications emerged. This was Husserl's great virtue and, perhaps, his great vice.

If phenomenology has lost its way in recent times, it is, at least in part, owing to the lack of a map that is both detailed and rigorous without being infinitely complex, as is the phenomenological landscape that it attempts to depict. But neither can such a map be so general that its markings tell us nothing in depth about the land that it charts. Often investigations in phenomenology, for good reasons of their own, lean in one of these two directions. Consequently, a stiff glimpse at pure phenomenology writ large has been needed of late, especially if particular phenomenological investigations are to carry on, and if we are to understand their position within the Husserlian project as a whole. I have attempted to provide such a perspective. If I have succeeded, it should now be possible to draw a number of conclusions concerning the relations of the Husserlian topography to the traditional and contemporary philosophical landscapes that surround it.

Let us begin with the case that has guided our reading of Husserl's work: the case of the natural reductive sciences.

6.1
NATURAL SCIENCE, PHENOMENOLOGY, AND THE RESTORATION OF MEANING

The problems that grew from the philosophy of physicalistic rationalism have proven, since the seventeenth century, to be the most troublesome problems for philosophy. It is not too great an exaggeration to say that the history of philosophy since that time has been a response to and a commentary on these problems. The would-be metaphysical foundations of natural science generated the great split between body and spirit, experience and world. A. O. Lovejoy has captured the spirit of much early twentieth-century philosophy as a response to these problems by reading it under the banner of a "revolt against dualism."[1] If our interpretation of Husserl's phenomenology has been cogent, then Husserl's work, too, and phenomenology in general, can be seen as part of this "revolt."[2]

When the ideal meaning structures of natural science became reified in the first primitive attempts to articulate the conditions for the possibility of natural scientific knowledge, these reified idealities usurped the "being" from the ordinary beings of the world. Thought to be the most real of all realities, the purely corporeal "things in themselves" were estranged, a priori, from all possible intuitive experience. The "world" beyond experience came to be conceived of as the real world, while the epistemically vague world of experience was conceived to be merely subjective.

When the empiricist philosophers attempted to provide a complementary science, a science of the subjective, they found that insofar as the natural scientific world was concerned—from the position of the science of subjectivity—"we cannot get there from here." The world of experience, the world of life, seemed hopelessly estranged from the world of natural science, yet the world of natural science was presumably the cause of the world of experience.

The riddle of cognition thus arose. It had been implicit in philosophy since Descartes' *Meditations* and burst into the limelight with Hume's skeptical arguments: not only the transcendence of Nature (transcendence$_2$), but also the transcendence of nature and world (transcendence$_1$), seemed incomprehensible. Starting from either the world of experience or the world of natural science, it seemed impossible to reach one from the other. Because of this epistemic-ontological hiatus, the depletion of the meaning of natural scientific formulae and life-world experience began, and because of the reversal of ontological priorities that motivated and accompanied this depletion, the perversion of meaning threatened the very sense of those formulae and the experience from which they grew. For these reasons the crisis of the European sciences was, for Husserl, the crisis of European humanity; it was a crisis of rationality itself. The loss of the sense of natural scientific formulae motivated the loss of European humanity's belief in itself because it motivated the loss of the sense of its connection with the world. If one of these conjuncts were to lose its sense, so too would the other. And such was the condition in which Husserl found himself. Husserl's phenomenology can, then, be read as an elaborate and systematic attempt to provide a corrective to these problems.

The act of phenomenological epoche is an attempt to suspend all judgment based upon the *source* of these problems. If no appeal to the natural scientific "world," as a causally efficacious world of real things *in* themselves, is made, and if we can then reattain this world from the experience left over, that is, from "reduced" experience, then we *can* "get there from here," and for the first time understand what that "there"—the "Nature" of natural science—really amounts to. Constitutional analyses are nothing more than an attempt to describe the formative processes of the human consciousness and the conscious body that allows us, the human animal, to constitute the world in the ways we do. If, instead of presupposing our knowledge achievements, we observe and describe the processes by which they are achieved, then we do phenomenology. That is, we *connect* the often estranged results of these achievements with the cognitive acts from which they arise.

Epoche and reduction allow us to carry out these descriptions by giving us an enhanced perspective on the processes of constitution. That is, if successful, they allow us to view and describe *knowledge in the making*. By the carrying out of well-connected descriptions of these processes, the actual foundations of knowledge are revealed while simultaneously any would-be metaphysical postulates once thought to be needed for explaining our knowledge are dissolved. If constitutional analyses are carried out correctly (and repeatedly), then meaning will be restored to the formulae of natural science as well as to the world in which we live.

If this method and project of Husserl's phenomenology has been successfully demonstrated, then at least some of the depleted meaning should have been restored to some natural scientific formulae; and, if Husserl's project as a whole is a possibility, then the threat of a negation of meaning is seen as absurd. The negation of the meaning of our formulae and our experience could only occur if there really were a world in itself that we could never experience. If there is not, then *nothing* cannot usurp the meaning from something—and that something is our world of experience, part of which is the domain made articulate through natural scientific knowledge.

6.2
THE CRISIS OF HUSSERL'S PROJECT FOR TRANSCENDENTAL PHENOMENOLOGY AND A REPLY TO HIS CRITICS

In light of the foregoing analyses of Husserl's project for transcendental phenomenology, we can conclude by attempt ing to respond to a number of the problems that have come to haunt the Husserlian project.

(a) Idealism and Realism

In Husserl's phenomenology there is no question of idealism *versus* realism. There is, however, a very definite sense in which the traditional notions of "idealism" and "realism" are related to pure phenomenology.

Husserl's phenomenology, broadly defined, is the attempt to *apply a methodological* idealism in order to gain an understanding of the realism inherent to the natural and the natural scientific attitudes. An understanding of such everyday realism is the chief aim of phenomenology, and this understanding is striven for by analyzing one's empirically real experiences in terms of a methodological idealism, that is, in terms of phenomenological descriptions of experiences purified of their naturalistic components.

When Husserl brackets reality and suspends judgments based upon the belief in transcendencies, he does not reject or negate the "real"; he simply suspends or epistemically nullifies all appeal to it as an explanatory hypothesis. When he claims that "nothing is lost to the epoche" (*PL* 7, 12; *C* §41, p.152, §52, p.176), that beyond consciousness "there is nothing" (*I* §49, p.139), and finally that, "*The proof of this idealism is . . . phenomenology itself*" (*CM* §41, p.86), he can be understood to be referring to the regulative ideal of a completed phenomenology where constitutional analyses would have regained all that was suspended by epoche, and regained it strictly in its ontic, everyday mode of being for consciousness. After bracketing reality and reducing back to the pure experience of objects (reduction$_1$), or to pure transcendental subjectivity (reduction $_2$), constitutional analyses of these purified experiences will reestablish the truth, validity, and especially the sense, of the empirically real—as well as the *reasons* for our belief in it *as* real.

To say that "phenomenology is the proof of transcendental idealism" is just to say that an understanding of the empirically real is tantamount to a well-connected description of the conscious processes that occur as transcendentally constitutive of empirical reality; and, simultaneously, that transcendental phenomenology is the proof for the truth of our beliefs in the world as empirically real. Together, these doxic certainties establish the "proof" of the world itself as empirically real. Thus Husserl writes, "There can be no stronger realism than this, if by this word ["realism"] nothing more is meant than 'I am certain of being a human being who lives in this world, etc., and I doubt it not in the least' " (*C* §55, p.187). However, Husserl adds, "The problem is to understand what is here so 'obvious'." This "obviousness" of realism *is* the problem for phenomenology. And Husserl's statement in the *Crisis* that "the point is not to secure objectivity, but to understand it" (*C* §55, p.189) remakes this point.

Husserl was always aware that "objectivity" is always already given and given *as* real. In fact, Husserl's use of epoche and reduction does not imply an embracing of subjective idealism; quite the contrary, the very *need* for these methodological devices is the lasting proof of his belief in "realism" as a truth of ordinary natural experience. *Epoche and reduction are needed precisely because of the factual truth of realism.* But the *fact* of realism is not the *sense* of realism; and an understanding of its sense requires a transcendental idealism. The transcendental idealism is achieved via epoche and reduction, and demonstrated as the case through constitutional analyses that regain the real. The "zig-zag" procedure of phenomenology is thus the movement *from* the empirically real or ideal (epoche), *to* the transcendentally "ideal" (reduction), and then back again to the empirically real or ideal (constitutional analyses). Upon this return realities and idealities will be understood as one or the other in terms of their constitutive origins, and hence, understood aright.

Insofar as Husserl's phenomenology is an idealism, then, it is one that presupposes a realism. But such naturalistic realism is not presupposed as a premise. Rather, it is acceptable to phenomenology only insofar as it has functioned as the initial subject matter to be suspended, reduced from, and then reconstituted; that is, made comprehensible through concrete work in transcendental phenomenological idealism, which means through actual descriptions in the constitutional sense-analytic.

The reason the debate over Husserl as "realist" or "idealist" has been such a raging one is that he is both.[3] Husserl is a "realist" prior to epoche and reduction, indeed, realism promotes the need for these devices; and he is a (no longer naïve) realist after the act of will that dissolves the epoche or the completion of constitutional analyses that regain the world within the scope of the interpretative achievements of those constitutional analyses. But while at work performing constitutional analyses within reduction and with epoche in effect, Husserl is a *methodological* idealist.

Consequently, Husserl's phenomenology is necessarily *both* an idealism and a realism because (to abuse, once more, Kant's well-worn phrase) without naturalistic realism, transcendental phenomenology is empty and without initial subject matter, while without a transcendental phenomenological idealism, naturalistic realism is blind, absurd, and depleted of meaning. Phenomenology needs naturalistic realism for its subject matter, and naturalistic realism needs phenomenology for an understanding of its own sense. But while a phenomenology at work is both "realistic" and "idealistic," a zig-zag between two kinds of consciousness, phenomenology "completed" is *neither* "realistic" nor "idealistic" because the dichotomy vanishes before a finished phenomenology.

(b) The Dissolution and Permanence of the Epoche

If constitutional analyses are successful, that which was suspended is regained. And insofar as reattainment occurs, so, conversely, should the brackets dissolve, the act of suspension cease.

In the previous chapter we denied that the completed effect of Husserl's phenomenology would be like that of the Wittgensteinian ladder trick, where the steps via which a position was reached were destroyed once it was reached. Such a comparison would hold only under two conditions: (1) if the epoche were simply canceled at will, in toto, and then the world appeared aright; (2) if, upon cancellation of epoche, the constitutional analyses that regained the world were seen as nonsense. However, the constitutional analyses that regain the world are precisely the sense of the world and, though the epoche can be canceled with one act of will (*C* §35, p.137), its constructive effects only reach so far as actual constitutional analysis has proceeded while it was in effect. For these reasons it is preferable to speak of the "dissolution of the epoche," rather than of "breaking the brackets," or even "removing" them. Done correctly, phenomenology changes our interpretative understanding of the world only gradually. The transformation of a way of understanding the world and the dissolution of the brackets are one.[4]

Husserl suggested more than once that phenomenology done correctly is the *least profound* of sciences (*PRS* 144). Profundity is an affective response to disconnected truths and insight; it is truth disconnected from its foundations. But constitutive phenomenology, as a series of *well-connected descriptions*, desires no such disconnected statements precisely because it desires to reveal systematically the transcendental ground of all life-worldly truths, and the life-worldly ground of all natural scientific truth (which, in the end, is life-world truth as well). Hence, "profound phenomenology" is phenomenology done poorly.[5]

The ultimate "change of signature" effected by the methods of epoche, reduction, and constitutional analysis would be a completed, interpretative, "inversion of the meaning of being." And a complete inversion of the meaning of being would be a *revaluation of the ontological signature on epistemic values*. The "inversion" and the "revaluation" occur each time a transcendent reality and its physicalistic causal powers have undergone suspension, have been experienced in reduction, and have been constitutionally analyzed for what they actually are—things, ideas or relations intentionally constituted as unities of significant reference-relations. Indeed, as Hume suspected long ago, though he lacked the radicalism to exploit his suspicion, "causality" is not only constituting, it is also constituted; and with each particular revelation of this transcendental fact, the meaning of being is inverted, it undergoes a permanent "change of signature."

The dissolution of epoche is also, simultaneously, the dissolution of speculative metaphysics. Epoche$_1$ originally suspended all "meta-realities"—from the "pure corporeality" of natural science to the "pure spirits" of theology. With the performance of constitutional analyses *of* the constituting consciousness that relates to such meta-entities, those meta-entities are recognized as *Ideae*. They are interpretative, purely signitive hypotheses for understanding the world, and perhaps for constituting it further—as "Nature," for instance. But the phenomena encountered at this level of reattainment (constitutional analyses$_2$) are not realities, they are, one and all, idealities. This is true by phenomenologically attained definition because if such "entities" prove perceivable, then they are not meta-entities, not simply *Ideae*, but things of the world, albeit, not ordinary-sized or commonly encountered things.

Husserl's phenomenological technique of metaphysical dissolution proves more respectful, more convincing, more subtle, and more efficient, than any such *program* of the purely positivistic philosophers. In this area, Husserl, like Nietzsche, does philosophy with a hammer, that is, with a tuning fork,[6] rather than with the programmatic "sledge-hammer" used by the positivists of the same era. In pure phenomenology speculative metaphysics simply dissolves along with the epoche in inverse proportion to the success of constitutional analyses.

But many of these statements sound foreign to what is normally called "pure phenomenology." Aren't these bold types of conclusions precisely the kind from which pure phenomenology must abstain? And doesn't Husserl himself suggest more than once that the "epoche is permanent" and that it is taken up "once and for all" (*SW* 319; *C* §40, p.150)?

The strangeness of the previous statements in pure phenomenology is owing to the fact that because constitutional analyses can never be completed in fact, Husserl, and most pure phenomenologists after him, have abstained from making or projecting judgments on the initial *results*, actual or implied, of phenomenological investigations. But if phenomenology is to remain a vital philosophy, it must, at some point, make judgments about ontology; it *can* do this, and was, if our interpretations are correct, *designed* to do this—albeit through an epistemological route that dissolves classical ontological dualisms. Its judgments about such matters, however, are not profound judgments disconnected from well-connected descriptions; they are simply the results of descriptive constitutional investigations. Hence, the fundamental significance of Husserl's statement that ". . . phenomenology . . . will supply the final determination of the sense in which . . . objects can be said to 'be' " (*I* §62, p.166).

Husserl's comments about the "permanence of the epoche" can be given two different interpretations. The first, and more common, is that since phenomenology is never complete, since it is an infinite task, it must refrain from all ontological commitment until complete — which is never; and hence, it must refrain from all ontological commitment, forever. But this would make phenomenology existentially sterile, of no interest or importance to philosophy, to science, or to the world in general. The other interpretation, if less faithful to Husserl's temperament, is at least more fruitful as a consequence of his project, which, like everything else, occurs within a life-world that demands results — even if somewhat hasty and imperfect ones.

Husserl's statements about the "permanence of the epoche" and the adoption of the phenomenological attitude "once and for all" may also be interpreted as projections towards a "completed" phenomenology.[7] Insofar as constitutional analyses have been successful, the natural attitude and the natural scientific attitude have, to some extent, become tainted with the phenomenological attitude because their objects have, *even in the natural attitude*, been recognized *as* intentionally constituted unities of meaning. If this revaluative-revisionary moment did not occur then the significance of phenomenological activity would vanish at the moment the suspension clause was dropped. But owing to this revisionary factor, in a fully complete phenomenology the "permanence of the epoche" would be synonymous with its complete dissolution. Since epoche dissolves only insofar as the "objects" suspended by it have been regained, its complete dissolution would equal total reattainment, and total reattainment would equal a world experienced as phenomenologically sense-constituted wherein naturalistic and physicalistic causality are understood *from a phenomenologically laced "natural" perspective* to play their own kind of constituting roles.

The permanence of the epoche is consciousness within the interpretative scope of the constitutional analyses performed while epoche was in effect. When Husserl writes that "outside of consciousness there is *nothing*" (*I* §49, p.139), he is making an *assertion* that projects to the final *proofs* of phenomenological constitutional analysis—which is, of course, a regulative ideal. When constitutional analyses were "complete," Husserl believed, all talk of an "outside of consciousness" would be recognized as, literally, analytically, and necessarily, *incomprehensible*.

As he wrote in the *Cartesian Meditations*, "If transcendental subjectivity is the universe of possible sense, then an outside is precisely—nonsense" (§41, p.84). Even that which is projected *as* "outside" must be "inside," if it has sense—and all experience is inherently senseful—even that type we call "absurd." If the transcendent refers to a thing, then the thing *can* appear within consciousness—directly, only in part, but "fully," as an intentional sense. Similarly, if the transcendent refers to a concept, it too can and must appear within consciousness, for therein it has its meaning and its being. Hence, Husserl is correct when he writes, "... *even the higher transcendence of the [purely] physical thing does not imply any reaching out beyond the world of consciousness*" (*I* §52, p.146). If it does then the "riddle of cognition" makes its appearance once more, and the problems of physicalistic rationalism reappear.

The reattainment of the world is synonymous with the phenomenological comprehension of consciousness as the supreme constituter of the sense of the world. Hence, in the projected completion of this phenomenological project, the permanence of the epoche would signify its total dissolution, and its total dissolution would signify its permanence. Either would signify the (ideal) "end" of phenomenology. There would no longer be anything that could be, should be, or need be "bracketed-out," because all entities would be phenomenologically grounded and understood *as* intentional unities of constitutive consciousness, personal and communal; they would be understood as beings and meanings *of and for* consciousness.

In this sense a completed phenomenology is neither realistic nor idealistic because, in finished phenomenology, consciousness and world are understood as an inseparable unity — an "outside" of which is a surd if that "outside" refers to something outside *in principle*. Hence, Husserl writes:

> Neither a world nor any other existent of any conceivable sort comes "from outdoors" into my ego, my life of consciousness. Everything outside is what it is in this inside, and gets its *true being* from the givings of itself, and from the verifications, within this inside — its true being, which for that very reason is something that itself belongs to this inside . . . . (*FTL* §99, p.250)

"Finished" phenomenology refers to the maximal proof of the universal a priori of correlation — the correlation between world and consciousness. Where there is no outside, there is no inside; in the projected and forever ideal completion of constitutional analyses, consciousness and the world and even "Nature" become the universal noetic-noematic relation; each is irreducible to the other; yet each, without the other, is *incomprehensible*.

(c) Constant Constitution and the Problem of Reduction

One criticism of Husserl's phenomenological method has arisen time and again throughout this investigation. In its most famous form it is expressed by Merleau-Ponty when he writes that ". . . the most important lesson which the phenomenological reduction teaches us is the impossibility of a complete reduction."[8] Here, and throughout the *Phenomenology of Perception*, Merleau-Ponty is referring, in particular, to the impossibility of the transcendental-phenomenological reduction, the reduction to the transcendental constituting ego. This criticism, we will argue, aims only at the deepest reduction, and is the criticism normally held by Husserl's continental successors such as Heidegger, Sartre, and Gadamer, along with Merleau-Ponty.

These critics of the reduction have been replied to at different places throughout the text. They all criticize the reduction with their own axes to grind, and each criticism is a variation on a common theme: each of these critics offers and applies, or at least simply applies, perhaps without knowing it, a different sort of reduction that is believed to represent the deepest point of possible reduction. They thereby believe that they have disqualified Husserl's radical series of methodological reductions that claim to penetrate deeper into consciousness than the nadir of reduction that the critics themselves believe they have established. Indeed, in one form or another, all of these critics—Heidegger, Sartre, Merleau-Ponty, and Wittgenstein—*perform* some form of reduction; they *need* it for their own particular positive investigations and could not perform their investigations without reduction—yet they deny its possibility.

In concluding this work, we will attempt to show, first, how the "crisis" of Husserl's transcendental phenomenology—which is the constant struggle to achieve and maintain reduction—is a constant crisis only because of the deep truth it exposes concerning the constancy of constitution and its resultant sedimented layers of meaning; and, second, how Husserl's critics, and philosophers in general, nearly always strive to perform reduction when doing philosophy. After all, philosophy is necessarily reflective, and Husserl's procedural techniques of epoche and reduction are methods for the achievement of reflection of the most radical sort, namely, unprejudiced reflection upon our typical processes of understanding.

When Husserl was "taken aback" in *The Idea of Phenomenology* because of the hidden implications ("transcendencies") that he discovered to be packed into even the most reduced phenomena, he recognized for the first time, and hence only inchoately, the indefinite depth of constituted meanings that inhere in every conscious experience whatsoever. This was *his* first clue that the reductions could never be complete, that even they could not provide adequate knowledge of their objects, and that phenomenology was thereby, necessarily, an infinite project. It is not an exaggeration to say that the rest of Husserl's career was spent struggling with the implications of this realization, and this struggle occurred as the struggle between "static" and "genetic" phenomenology.[9]

The indefinitely deep strata of sedimented meanings that have always already forged a world forced Husserl into genetic phenomenology and likewise forced him to recognize the extraordinary *strain* inherent in performing and maintaining reduced perspective.[10] Maintaining reduced perspective, maintaining the suspension of what we normally believe, is like fighting gravity when one leaps into the air. The natural attitude, like the earth, always pulls us back. And here lies the great *irony* inherent to Husserl's discoveries: *Reduction is so difficult to achieve and maintain because constitution is so difficult to negate and to stop. The strain of maintaining reduction is the pull of the natural attitude, and the pull of the natural attitude is the pull of a history of constitutive acts.* These acts have been solidified in and as "the world."

Once written into the world, our cognitive and manipulative intentional achievements do not easily erase. The constant possibility of always "seeing more" is natural to consciousness because consciousness "constantly constitutes"; but the attempt to "see less," as in reduction, is unnatural to it. That is why Husserl could say that phenomenology itself is both "unnatural" and "unworldly" (*P* 123).[11] Like the mythical "perpetual motion machine," consciousness, as a "perpetual meaning 'machine'," has difficulty retrieving its creations once set aloft. Nevertheless, reduction through these meanings can and does occur, and at first in ways that we all understand.

In the case of epoche and reduction, as was so often the case in Husserl's work, the deed preceded the word. As we have noted, Husserl applied epoche and reduction before he announced them as method. But in their case something more may have occurred: Husserl *experienced* reduction before he made it a method either in deed or in word.

When introducing the transcendental epoche in the *Crisis*, Husserl writes, "Perhaps it will even become manifest that the total phenomenological attitude and the epoche belonging to it are destined in essence to effect, at first, a complete personal transformation, comparable in the beginning to a religious conversion. . . ." (*C* §35, p.137). And slightly after this he claims that the epoche is destined to effect ". . . a new way of experiencing, of thinking, of theorizing . . ." (*C* §41, p.152) for the philosopher. This new way of experiencing is experience within reduction, and this radically unbiased experience is a "total change of the natural attitude of life" (*C* §39). But *why* does Husserl refer to the effects of epoche as similar to a religious experience?

In the beginning, we suggest, the *reduction happens to us*. Only afterwards, perhaps, can the "shift of standpoint" (the "change of attitude") be performed at will. Husserl's procedural techniques for inducing the "shift" are an attempt to articulate a certain strange experience that has happened to philosophers, to artists and poets, and perhaps to everyone save the hopelessly sane, now and again throughout their personal history. This strange experience is the experience of the strangeness of experience, and of the world.[12] And this strangeness is nothing more (nor less) than the act of *seeing through* the sedimented meanings that one inherits and develops, and that structure one's world.

This reduction to the strangeness of the world usually occurs when our beliefs about the world become undone. In Heideggerian language, it occurs when the "care-structure" of our existence is shattered, for example, by radical boredom or the death of an Other. Or, for Nietzsche, reduction first seemed to occur with the "death of God" — "he" who constituted transcendent values, which our ancestors then allowed to constitute their world. With God's death the *Übermensch* had to become the constituting agent *par excellence*. Or again, Sartre's "Roquentin," who simply awoke one day "feeling a little strange" to finally realize that "something has happened to me."[13] "Things are somehow different."[14] Or, finally, even Wittgenstein's thoughts on "astonishment" and on the tendency to run up against the limits of language,[15] points to a reduction — a distancing from everyday acceptances. All these experiences are experiences of the breakdown, or the nullification, of transcendently posited world-structuring beliefs. And such nullification, of course, is the effect of epoche.

Husserl, unlike these other philosophers, attempted to devise a philosophical method for the achievement of this privileged perspective. Reduced experience as a privileged perspective on the constitutional processes that make sense of the world would provide the basis for philosophy as rigorous science. Through this experience of reduction, Husserl was the first to explicitly recognize the constitutional achievements of intentionality when such reduction occurred — though Hume and Nietzsche, in particular, seemed to have had sustained glimpses of these achievements. Perhaps this hidden history of reduced experience — the history of reduction as an "emotive" experience — accounts for Husserl's otherwise cryptic statement in the *Crisis* that ". . . our aim is to turn all romanticism into responsible work . . ." (*C* §56, p.197). This "responsible work" is the "extremely subtle and differentiated work" referred to later (*C* §71, p.257), namely, the constitutional analyses that become a possibility with reduced experience. This work would be "romantic" because its results place the human subject *back home* in the world and back in the nature from which Nature derives. And the achievement of this "rigorous romanticism," through the constitutional descriptions of reduced experience, need not rely on dying Gods, radical boredom, existential *Angst*, or even philosophical astonishment; epoche alone should bring it about. And perhaps it is only when brought about in such a methodical manner that reduction can be transformed into "responsible work."

Let us now conclude by noting how some of Husserl's most famous critics have put the reductions to "responsible work" and consistently *used* some level of epoche and reduction, while simultaneously denying that such levels of reduction were possible.

(d) The Reductions of Husserl's Critics

When the critics of the reduction assert that some given level or type of reduction is not possible, they almost always unite this claim with concrete phenomenological analyses of the region of experience that they claim depicts the *actual nadir* of possible reduction.

Heidegger, for example, rejects the radical transcendental reduction (what we have called the second level of reduction) and argues that "Dasein" as involved Being-in-the-world is the ultimate foundation for sense.[16] He then proceeds to provide the concrete phenomenological analyses of that meaning foundation.

Sartre also rejects the radical transcendental reduction, by arguing that the very possibility of reduction *to* a "transcendental ego" would make consciousness "thingly"; it would place a "plenitude" at the heart of consciousness that could not transcend itself, and hence the most essential facet of consciousness would prove unamenable to phenomenological consideration.[17] That is, it could not be dealt with as a constituted (noematic) object pole. Hence, Sartre analyzes the ego as a transcendent pole (transcendent to a radically empty consciousness), which is in-the-midst-of-the-world undergoing pressures in the Heraclitean flux of too much meaning and too many things.

Merleau-Ponty argues that the body is basis; all reduction stops at the body; its kinaesthetic manipulative intentionality is the source of all would-be purely cognitive intentionality; and all would-be reduction to a transcendental ego finds that ego bound to the organism as a "bodily ego."[18] Hence, Merleau-Ponty analyzes the body as the vital intentional and constitutive being, which *is* a being-*at*-the world (*Être-au-Monde*).

The radical hermeneuts also offer reason for abandoning belief in what they understand to be transcendental reduction. Some of them, for example, Derrida, claim that the wash of time and history are so strong that all belief in a radically reduced present perspective is just another form of the old "metaphysics of presence."[19] There is no privileged perspective on things, knowledge, or meanings because things, knowledge, and meanings are irreducible to their current historical-temporal milieu, and this milieu-of-meaning is what it is only once, and that "once" is spurious as soon as we acknowledge it, and gone as soon as we notice it. Consequently, Derrida would have us "play" with inherited meanings, rather than reduce to their primal founding; we should perhaps attempt to "follow the trace," though without hope of recovering its meaning in original presence.

Finally, Wittgenstein, *apud* Susan Cunningham or Ross Harrison, would claim that the meanings of "public language" are the final arbiters of significance and all reduction carries these meanings with it; thereby, reduction has no possibility of reducing below such communal significance.[20] As such, Wittgenstein performs constitutional analyses on the language games constitutive of public language, which games are contextually correlated with different "forms of life."

Although an extended particular analysis of each of these philosophers and their use or variation of reduction is both warranted and deserved, we cannot, at this point, develop these analyses in full; that would require another book. Let us, however, conclude by developing a perspective on their positions that has been suggested in a number of instances already.

In each of the above cases, the concrete analyses these philosophers offer (in lieu of a reduction to purified experience) occur from one reflective level lower, one level deeper, than the subject matter they analyze. And they *necessarily* do this, else their subject matter could not become an *object* of phenomenological consideration. To continue using Husserl's infelicitous jargon, each and all reduce "to" the phenomenological *regulative idea sine qua non*: the guiding *methodological function* of a "pure ego"; and it is this "ego," this reflective consciousness, which is just the permanent possibility of reflecting again, that carries out the constitutional analyses of the domains or objects under consideration.

Although Husserl himself tended (verbally) to reify the pure ego, in many instances it *functioned* for him as an Idea in the Kantian sense, an intuited *act* allowing for the possibility of further reflecting.[21] For instance, in *Ideas* he writes that ". . . no disconnecting can remove the form of the *cogito* and cancel the 'pure' subject of the act. . . . this Ego is the *pure* Ego, and no reduction can get any grip on it" (*I* §80, p.214). The "pure ego" cannot be grasped even in reduction because the "shaft of attention is not separate from the Ego . . ." (*I* §92, p.249), and consequently each time the ego chooses an object, even from the vantage point of reduction, the ego that chooses remains anonymous, while that which is chosen becomes the object (*EP* I, pp.262-63). Hence, the ". . . 'I' that I attain in the epoche . . . is actually called 'I' only by equivocation . . ." (*C* §54, p.184). The equivocation is "essential" because there is something that intuits wherever an object appears, and this "something" is more than a mere logical necessity in the Kantian sense. It is a phenomenological *datum* of all reflective experience, yet a datum that is known only as pure act, and never seen objectwise. Insofar as an object appears, it appears *for* a consciousness.

Let us, like Husserl at his least problematic, call this consciousness which flees before every gaze (because it *is* the gaze), the primal consciousness, or the "pure ego," and note how Husserl's critics rely upon "it" in reduction while denying it in fact.

Consider again Figure 9. The "existential" philosophers *en groupe*, viz., Heidegger, Sartre, and Merleau-Ponty, can be said to have pulled the phenomenological facets of reduction$_2$, the pure temporal stream and the appearing manifestation of the world, "up" into the world of life and then considered that world in its bracketed form, that is, without appeal to the truth claims of natural science that had been suspended by epoche$_1$. They asserted the primordiality of the life-world, and carried out their investigations in terms of that world. "Dasein," as being-there-in-the-world, "Nothingness," as a consciousness that is just the actualization of itself as a possibility, and the Body, as being-*at*-the-world, all upsurge (to use Sartre's term) in the midst-of-the-world—a "world" that is always already there.

But notice that the first level of epoche and its effect of reduction$_1$ is *not* rejected by the existential philosophers. Rather, it is so thoroughly accepted and taken for granted that it is rarely even mentioned as an issue.[22] Instead, the existential philosophers simply *start* their analyses from the world that epoche$_1$ and reduction$_1$ give us — without bothering to explicitly bracket the "world in itself." Husserl had shown the idea of such a world to be unneeded to explain the phenomenon of knowledge, and to be absurd insofar as it was postulated as existing in itself.

The "world" of natural science or the world of idealities is dealt with as a constitutional achievement by the existential philosophers (we have called this Objectification$_2$/Idealization$_1$), but it is never explicitly bracketed[23] because the world as given (and metaphysical "meta-reality" as *not* given) is simply a phenomenological given, taken for granted by the existential phenomenologists. Because they had inherited the work of Husserl, they could afford to start from the world; not because Husserl had clarified the concept of world, it may well have been Heidegger who finally did this, but because Husserl pointed the way back to the things themselves. His existential successors simply started from those "things" without as explicitly bracketing or battling with the great usurper of the world, the metaphysics of early modern science.

It is true of course that both Heidegger and Merleau-Ponty did go on to contribute to the constitutional analyses of the natural scientific world — adding, in the process, to the analyses Husserl had inaugurated.[24] But if "existence," as being-in-the-world, is to function as the meaning fundament, how do we manage to *see* this fundament of meaning in order to provide phenomenological analyses of it?

It seems obvious, in answer, that *we reduce below it*, and only then can we provide a phenomenological description *of* it. Husserl has no debate with the claim that the world-of-life is the *natural* meaning fundament; but, if *involved* being-in-the-world were the *final* level of significant understanding, then we could not provide phenomenological analyses of *involved* being-in-the-world. Involvement would be complete; authenticity (ownness) and inauthenticity (not-being-one's-own) would not even be possibilities; existence would be a plentitude like other inanimate things.

An existential analytic, like Heidegger's, can occur only because reduction below everyday existence is possible. As noted earlier, reduction below everydayness is even *forced* by certain aspects of existence such as death, nausea, boredom, and other such phenomena. Hence, even existence can be "objectified" in a purely phenomenological fashion by transcendental reduction — the actual *work* of the existential phenomenologists is the *proof* of the possibility of this reduction.

With consciousness as No-thing, and ego as "thing," something similar is the case. The great irony of Sartre's criticisms of Husserl's concept of the ego is that Husserl's pure ego is so much like Sartre's Nothingness. As a regulative ideal for the permanent possibility of reflection, the pure ego is precisely no-thing because as soon as it objectifies even "itself," "it" is gone; "it" is below the object, which is then called the "empirical ego" (*EP* 262-63).

The analysis of the ego as "thing," as a magical pole for the guidance of behavior, is possible only because we can reduce below that "magical unity" by carrying out transcendental reduction. Husserl did this when he analyzed the ego as an empirical phenomenon (*LI* 541, 544) and as a substrate of habitualities (*CM* §§30-32). Even consciousness can become objectified as "ego," though it is still always a deeper consciousness that objectifies. Again the very analysis of the ego as a transcendent pole is *proof* of the possibility of transcendental reduction.

Finally, to consider the case of Merleau-Ponty, even the body can be existentially analyzed only if it can become an object for the reflecting consciousness. The body may well be the source of mundane consciousness and being-at-the-world, and even transcendental reflection is oriented from a living body; but, insofar as reflection reflects on the body's modes of constituting world and "Nature," then the body, too, has become "object" and this again *for* the pure ego that has achieved radical reduction. If the body were the deepest part of reduction, this body, even *as* body-consciousness, could not become an object for phenomenological or existential reflective investigation.

An existential constitutional body-analytic can occur only because reflective consciousness can reduce below the body as body-consciousness. The body as the intuitional source and zero-point of constitution is an object at the level of reduction$_1$, and can be seen as such only by engaging in reduction$_2$. Again, then, the phenomenological constitutional analyses of the body as an intentional and constitutive power is a *concrete demonstration* of the possibility of transcendental reduction.

Throughout the existential tradition there has been a tendency to believe that the *subject matter* of investigation is indicative of the lowest level of reduction, when in fact one must always reduce one level deeper than the subject matter at issue in order to perform constitutional analysis on that subject matter. It is ironic that even Husserl's immediate followers were so fascinated by the objects of their concern that they failed to appreciate the reduction that made their concern with these objects an investigative possibility. It was the *explicit* use of epoche, Husserl believed, that was constantly needed to remain free from the blinding fascination of the object pole; and it was, perhaps, precisely their lack of explicit epoche that led the existential phenomenologists to a misunderstanding of their own use of reduction.

So, what about history and what about language?

Derrida's charge that belief in reduction is adherence to a "metaphysics of presence" would have an element of truth to it if phenomenology were only static phenomenology. After the 1905 lectures on the *Phenomenology of Internal Time-Consciousness*, however, phenomenology would never again be just static phenomenology, because static phenomenology and the belief in a nontemporal, nonimplicative "given" was recognized as an abstraction from phenomena as they truly gave themselves even within reduction. Husserl realized this even in *Ideas*, where he still engaged, "for simplicity's sake" (*I* §81, pp.216-17), in statically oriented analyses.

With his instauration of genetic phenomenology Husserl realized that the dream of *adequate* knowledge was over because the past and future inhered in even the radically reduced present objects of pure conscious experience. And with this recognition Husserl himself was the first to realize the problem of the "trace." There is no doubt that Husserl maintained his emphasis on the "primal now"; but this zero-point, it seems, is inevitable even for the most radical hermeneuts. If the "trace" is to appear at all, it must appear in the present; and even if the present constantly dis-appears, the trace of an object or meaning can be "traced" only from the focal point of the present appearance: even its dis-appearance, its absence, is significant only from the perspectival present. Robert Sokolowski's work with the roles of presence and absence in Husserlian phenomenological analysis makes this point *in concreto*.[25]

Hence, to consider the case of hermeneutics generally, historical reflection is not just a mode of blind and fascinated inherited engagement. If we can even realize that meanings are historical-temporal-social phenomena, then we have reduced below historistic experience (though, of course, our reduction occurs *in* history). To struggle with the problem of the trace, to play with the meanings we have inherited, or to try to reconstruct them rationally, as the more moderate hermeneuts would do, is to *distance* ourselves from our historical inheritance. Through reduced, reflecting consciousness, we can and do achieve this distance. If we were *merely* inheritors of the meanings from the past, even if we changed these meanings by our very inheritance of them, by *their* entrance into *our* world, we could never consciously "play" with them and never consciously attempt to "reconstruct" them in terms of a past-present, if in the present-present we could not reduce, at least partially, below the grip of historical inheritance.

The purely hermeneutical activity of meaning-reconstruction, of hermeneutical-postmodernist meaning-variation, can occur only because even the historical meanings of past-presents and their entrance into the present-present can become "objects." And they become objects through transcendental phenomenological reduction. The conscious activities of meaning-reconstitution of the "old" hermeneuts and meaning-variation of the "new" hermeneuts is demonstration again of the possibility of transcendental reduction, this time reduction below our inherited history. But as always, of course, such reduction is never complete.

In all these cases the *possibility* of transcendental reduction is established by the *actuality* of concretely developed constitutional analyses, which are a possibility only from the vantage point of such a reduction.

Finally, the problem of language.

There is no denying that the problem of ordinary language is one of the stiffest problems faced by Husserl's theory of reductions. And this problem, in part, is again the problem of hermeneutics — though with its historical aspects played down. Here too, however, transcendental reduction can and does occur, though more than with any other issue, the impossibility of complete reduction must be admitted. While Husserl does make some rather cryptic suggestions to the effect that words have a different meaning when spoken under phenomenological constraints (*I* §89, p.240), these claims are incomprehensible and fantastic without further clarification.

The "different meaning" that ordinary language has when used in reduction is just the different meaning that "things" have when noematically modified. The inverted commas around an object-word, which "object" is in suspense, modifies the significance of the word just as the sense of the "thing" signified by the word is modified. The "change of signature" undergone by the bracketed object is the change of signature *signified* by the inverted commas around the noun referring to the noematically modified object. This modification may occur *while* operating within the methodological idealism of phenomenological description, or it may be the *result* of these analyses once completed. When Husserl claims that with reduction, "the meaning of being is precisely inverted" (*I* §50, p.139), so, too, presumably, are the meanings of the words that refer to beings (or Being, in general) inverted. The change of signature, once established, is a change of significance, and a change of significance is a change of meaning, and in most cases it involves a revaluation of meaning from naturalistic-causal significance to phenomenological-constitutive significance. It is in this sense that words take on different meanings in phenomenological reduction, and these new meanings may then become concretized through constitutional descriptions. Insofar as the world is phenomenologically modified by epoche and reduction, so too is the language that normally refers to that world. And just as constitutional analyses allow for the gradual dissolution of the epoche, so, too, do they allow for the dissolution of the scare-quotes around our phenomenologically modified referential language.

Of course, when Husserl suggests that words and language can portray the world just as it is (*I* §66), and that words and language are not constitutively productive (*I* §124, p.321), he is adhering to a "realistic" (and perhaps naïve) view of language. This realistic view of language, however, is just the counterpart to his realistic view of the world *prior to epoche and reduction*. Just as the realistic understanding of the world is the necessary background and subject matter for phenomenological transcendental idealism, so, too, does the naturalism inherent in ordinary language usage become the background and *subject matter* when epoche and reduction are performed in relation to the natural language that it normally uses to articulate the world. And even if it is the case that language is the "universal medium" for understanding,[26] this should cause Husserl's theory of reduction no more problem than his own claim that ". . . consciousness is the universal medium . . ." (*I* §85, p.226). If consciousness is the universal medium and has the permanent possibility of reflecting again, then so too should language, if it is the universal medium, have the same possibility (perhaps call it "articulating again"). In fact, "ordinary language philosophies," and indeed any linguistic philosophy that uses language as a "calculus," seem to realize this; and, insofar as they are successful in the attempt to "objectify" language, they, too, have demonstrated the possibility of transcendental reduction—here, in relation to language.

In order to analyze ordinary language one must reduce from it. If not from all of it (which is probably impossible), at least from part of it. "Language," as a universal medium, does not mean that language cannot also be a "calculus." It implies this no more than the claim that "consciousness is the universal medium" implies that consciousness cannot reflect on its constitutional activities as one consciousness reflecting upon another. Language analysis, too, becomes a possibility because reduction is possible, and indeed language modification is an essential part of reduction. In ordinary language analysis, that is, in the analysis of "public language," the natural meanings and beliefs inherent in the words are suspended in order to reduce below that language and thereby gain perspective on its ordinary, naturalistic, and realistic use.[27]

It is probably true, however, that the development of a hierarchy of languages in the Russellian sense[28] is more similar to carrying out a series of reductions than is ordinary language philosophy or linguistic hermeneutics. The reason is that in the language hierarchy, just as in the reduction series, each new level (of language or consciousness) refers to the level before it, though it cannot refer to itself. Nevertheless, it is still true that even the possibility of using a language-game to understand a language-game, that is, of taking one position in the hermeneutical circle to refer to another position in it, is grounded in the possibility of transcendental-phenomenological reduction. The hermeneutical circle or the circle of meanings, *and* the "circle games" within that life-world circle, are observable, in the first instance, only because they are seen, as they have been expressed in the life-world, from reduced perspective.

The transcendent-transcendental circle underlies the circle of transcendent meanings, the circle of objectified, life-world meanings. The hermeneutical-linguistic circle can only be recognized from the transcendental perspective, and a position within that circle can be taken up and *recognized* as such and such a position within it, only because one *can* and does reduce below it. In this way the sense-bestowing consciousness bestows sense upon the hermeneutical language-games that claim to reveal the actual sense of the language inherent in different "forms of life."

Language and language-games can become objects for constitutional analysis, that is, for ordinary language philosophy, only because transcendental-phenomenological reduction allows us to reduce below them. And it is chiefly because the "change of signature," the restoration of meaning, can become a lasting change even in ordinary language, that Husserl's methods of epoche, reduction, and constitutional analysis can, in theory at least, effect the "final" revaluation of the ontological index placed on epistemic values. This revaluation is the restoration of meaning to a meaning-depleted world and a meaning-depleted science, and it is the revisionary force of Husserl's "pure" phenomenology.

Philosophers have been struggling for the "inversion of the meaning of being" more than they have realized. And even more often, they have used phenomenological reduction without realizing it. Many have simply called the attempt at "inversion" the "dissolution of philosophical problems." What they have not realized is that those philosophical problems grow directly from the "world of life" and the "attitude" that makes that world what it is. These problems then enter back into the life-world to determine it further. Consequently, for the dissolution of philosophical problems, this world of life must itself be "dissolved" — albeit, not forever — if we are truly to dissolve the problems of philosophy. Epoche, reduction, and constitutional analysis are the means for achieving this. They are the first phases of a truly radical "humanism."

The "inversion of the meaning of being" is naught but the death of an untenable metaphysics and its replacement by well-connected descriptions of the manner in which we "constitute" our worlds — *one* of which we call "Nature." To show this, as we have tried to show, was Husserl's intent throughout his career and especially in writing the *Crisis of European Sciences and Transcendental Phenomenology*.

NOTES

1. Arthur O. Lovejoy, *The Revolt Against Dualism* (London: George Allen & Unwin, LTD, 1930).

2. This feature of Husserl's phenomenology is actually worked out more explicitly by J. N. Mohanty than it is by Husserl himself. For instance, see his essay "Intentionality and the Mind/Body Problem" in *The Possibility of Transcendental Philosophy* (Dordrecht: Martinus Nijhoff, 1985), pp. 121-38.

3. This does not reduce to Harrison Hall's argument that "Husserl is neither." Hall's arguments depict Husserl as neither realist nor idealist even when Husserl is *at work* doing phenomenology. See Harrison Hall, "Was Husserl a Realist or an Idealist?," contained in *Husserl, Intentionality and Cognitive Science*, ed. by Hubert Dreyfus (Cambridge, MA: MIT Press, 1982), pp. 169-90. As we have seen, while doing phenomenology Husserl is a methodological idealist working the "zig-zag" procedure between a constitutive idealism and the "real" world that consciousness constitutes. It is only true to say Husserl is neither a realist nor an idealist *after* the ideal completion of constitutional analyses, after the dissolution of the epoche.

4. For a more developed reading of the critical method inherent to the use of epoche and reduction, see Richard Zaner's essay "On the Sense of Method in Phenomenology," in *Phenomenology and Philosophical Understanding*, ed. by Edo Pivcević (Cambridge University Press, 1975), pp. 125-41. Also see my essay "Husserl's Phenomenology as Critique of Epistemic Ideology," *International Philosophical Quarterly* (forthcoming).

5. This is Husserl's criticism of Heidegger's type of phenomenology. In the margin of p. 13 of his copy of *Sein und Zeit*, for example, Husserl wrote, "Heidegger transposes or transforms the constitutive clarification of all realms of entities and universals, the total region of World into the anthropological. The whole problematic is translation, to the ego corresponds Dasein etc. Thereby everything becomes deep-soundingly unclear, and philosophically it loses its value." Quoted by Dagfinn Føllesdal, "Husserl and Heidegger on the Role of Action in the Constitution of the World," contained in *Essays in Honor of Jakko Hintikka*, ed. by Esa Saarinen *et al*. (Dordrecht, Holland: Reidel, 1979), p. 369.

6. Friedrich Nietzsche, *Twilight of the Idols*, trans. by Walter Kaufmann, contained in *The Portable Nietzsche* (New York: The Viking Press, 1967), pp. 465-66.

7. A thesis similar to the one we will develop here is developed by William McKenna in *Husserl's "Introductions to Phenomenology"* (The Hague: Martinus Nijhoff, 1982), where McKenna distinguishes between Husserl's general *argument* for the thesis that consciousness constitutes the world and the *demonstration* of that general argument. The argument, McKenna claims, points to the projected proofs of transcendental phenomenological idealism, whereas the demonstration is the proof via concrete constitutional descriptions of object constitution. The proof, however, unlike the argument, can never be completed *in fact*. See "Husserl's argument" in McKenna's index.

8. Maurice Merleau-Ponty, *Phenomenology of Perception*, trans. by Colin Smith (New Jersey: Routledge & Kegan Paul, LTD, Humanities Press, 1962), p. xiv.

9. On this reading of Husserl's phenomenology, see Robert Sokolowski, *The Formation of Husserl's Concept of Constitution* (The Hague: Martinus Nijhoff, 1964).

10. The points that follow have been made in my discussion on "The Existential Foundations of Phenomenological Reduction," *Journal of the British Society for Phenomenology* 17 (May 1986): 193-97.

11. Though, as we have argued in the previous section, if phenomenology is successful and if done for a long enough time, the phenomenological attitude might infiltrate the "natural," i.e., "normal," attitude. This is probably why, towards the end of his life, Husserl could quite sincerely write that the phenomenological attitude is "permanent" (*SW* 319), and the epoche, a "habitual accomplishment" (*C* §35, p.137). For Husserl this had probably become the case!

12. On the phenomenon of "strangeness" inherent to phenomenological reduction, see Maurice Natanson, *Edmund Husserl: Philosopher of Infinite Tasks*, pp. 81, 83, 127, 134ff, 142, 159.

13. Jean-Paul Sartre, *Nausea* (New York: New Directions Pub. Co., 1964), p. 4.

14. Jean-Paul Sartre, *Nausea*, pp. 1-4.

15. Ludwig Wittgenstein, "On Heidegger on Being and Dread," contained in *Heidegger and Modern Philosophy*, ed. by Michael Murray, (New Haven & London: Yale University Press, 1978), pp. 80-81.

16. Martin Heidegger, *Being and Time*, trans. by John Macquarrie and Edward Robinson (New York: Harper & Row, 1962), §12.

17. Jean-Paul Sartre, *The Transcendence of the Ego*, trans. by Forest Williams and Robert Kirkpatrick (New York: The Noonday Press, 1966), pp. 37-42.

18. Maurice Merleau-Ponty, *Phenomenology of Perception*, trans. by Colin Smith (New Jersey: Routledge & Kegan Paul, LTD, Humanities Press, 1962), pp. 370ff.

19. Jacques Derrida, *Speech and Phenomena*, trans. by David B. Allison (Evanston: Northwestern University Press, 1973), pp. 3-16.

20. Suzanne Cunningham, *Language and the Phenomenological Reductions of Edmund Husserl* (The Hague: Martinus Nijhoff, 1976). Also see Ross Harrison's nicely argued essay "The Concept of Prepredicative Experience," in *Phenomenology and Philosophical Understanding*, ed. by Edo Pivcević (London: Cambridge University Press, 1975), pp. 93-107.

21. Douglas Heinsen correctly argues that the "transcendental ego" must be distinguished from the "pure ego." The transcendental ego, Heinsen argues, does have content and can become an object of phenomenological reflection; while the "pure ego" does not have content, it is pure act, and is that which reflects on the ego as transcendentally self-constituting. See Douglas Heinsen, "Husserl's Theory of the Pure Ego," contained in *Husserl, Intentionality and Cognitive Science*, ed. by Hubert L. Dreyfus (Cambridge, MA: MIT Press, 1982), pp. 147-67. For a developmental reading of Husserl's thoughts about the self, see Joseph J. Kockelmans, "Husserl and Kant on the Pure Ego," in *Husserl: Expositions and Appraisals*, ed. by Frederick A. Elliston and Peter C. McCormick (University of Notre Dame Press, 1977), pp. 269-85.

22. Merleau-Ponty is an exception to this claim. His explicit suspension of the "constancy hypothesis" of the natural sciences (i.e., the hypothesis of a real world of being, existing steadfastly in itself) throughout the *Phenomenology of Perception* has much the form and effect of Husserl's first epoche.

23. Again, the exception is Merleau-Ponty.

24. For work done on these philosophers along these lines, see, e.g., Theodore Kisiel, "On the Dimensions of a Phenomenology of Science in Husserl and the Young Dr. Heidegger," *Journal of the British Society for Phenomenology* 4 (1973): 217-34; also, "Heidegger and the New Image of Science," *Research in Phenomenology* 7 (1977): 162-181. Joseph J. Kockelmans, *Heidegger and Science* (Lanham, MD: University Press of America, 1985). Kockelmans and Kisiel, *Phenomenology and the Natural Sciences* (Evanston, IL: Northwestern

University Press, 1970). Joseph Rouse, "Kuhn, Heidegger, and Scientific Realism," *Man and World* 14 (1981): 269-90; also, "Merleau-Ponty and the Existential Conception of Science," *Synthese* 66 (1986): 249-72. Hans Seigfried, "Scientific Realism and Phenomenology," *Zeit f. Philosophische Forschung* 24 (1980): 395-404; also, "Heidegger's Longest Day: *Being and Time* and the Sciences," *Philosophy Today* 22 (1978): 319-31.

25. Robert Sokolowski, *Presence and Absence* (Bloomington: Indiana University Press, 1978).

26. The not completely happy distinction between "language as a universal medium" and "language as a calculus" is offered by Jaakko Hintikka as important for an understanding of the *modus operandi* of such philosophers as Frege, Wittgenstein, Russell, and Quine, not to mention Hintikka himself. Hintikka's distinction is an extension of one suggested by Van Heijenoort between "logic as language" and "logic as calculus." See *Synthese* 17 (1967): 324-330. For Hintikka's version of the distinction, see Jaakko Hintikka, "Wittgenstein's Semantical Kantianism," contained in *Ethics: Proceedings of the 5th International Wittgenstein Symposium*, ed. by E. Morschen and R. Stranzinger (Vienna: Holder-Pichler-Tempsky, 1981), pp. 375-90; see esp. §8. Likewise: "Semantics: A revolt against Frege," *Contemporary Philosophy: A New Survey* (The Hague: Martinus Nijhoff, 1981), v. 1, esp., pp. 58-61.

27. J. N. Mohanty develops arguments along these lines when he suggests that thinking, despite its linguisticality, constantly exceeds language, and when he argues that: "Not only is the consciousness of speaking not itself a speaking consciousness, what is still more: the grasp of meanings continually exceeds the bounds of language insofar as one searches for the appropriate expression for a thought one has his grips on, or experiences the inadequacy of an available expression to express a given thought." In *The Possibility of Transcendental Philosophy* (Dordrecht: Martinus Nijhoff, 1985), p. 215.

28. See Russell's suggestion along these lines in his introduction to Wittgenstein's *Tractatus Logico-Philosophicus*, trans. by D. F. Pears and B. F. McGuinness (London: Routledge & Kegan Paul, 1961), p. xxii. Also see his *Inquiry into Meaning and Truth* (London: George Allen & Unwin LTD, 1940), esp. Ch. IV.

BIBLIOGRAPHY

References to Husserl's works are internal to the text. Those works and the abbreviations for them are given on pp. v-vi.

Alain, pseud. Emile Chartier, *Quatre-vingt-un chapitre es sur L'Espirit et les Passions*. Paris. Gallimard, 1941.

Berkeley, George, *A Treatise Concerning the Principles of Human Knowledge*. La Salle, IL. Open Court, 1963.

Boehm, Rudolf, *Vom Gesichtspunkt der Phänomenologie*. The Hague. Martinus Nijhoff, 1968.

Bossert, Philip, "The Sense of 'Epoche' and 'Reduction' in Husserl's Philosophy," *Journal of the British Society for Phenomenology* 5 (1974): 243-55.

————, "Plato's Cave, *Flatland* and Phenomenology," contained in William S. Hamrick, ed.

————, *The Origins and Early Development of Edmund Husserl's Method of Phenomenological Reduction*. Unpublished dissertation. St. Louis. Washington University, 1973.

Brentano, Franz, *Psychology from an Empirical Standpoint*. Trans. by Antos C. Rancurello, D. B. Terrell, and Linda L. McAlister. New York. Humanities Press, 1973.

Burtt, E. A., *The Metaphysical Foundations of Modern Physical Science*. Garden City, NY. Doubleday Anchor Books, 1954.

Carr, David, *Phenomenology and the Problem of History*. Evanston, IL. Northwestern University Press, 1974.

————, "Husserl's *Crisis* and the Problem of History," *Journal of Southwestern Philosophy* 5 (1974): 127-48.

————, "Husserl's Problematic Concept of the Life-World," *Philosophical Quarterly* 7 (1970): 331-39. Also contained in Elliston and McCormick, ed., pp. 202-12.

————, "Phenomenology and Relativism," contained in William S. Hamrick, ed.

Cassirer, Ernst, *Substance and Function*. La Salle, IL. Open Court, 1923.

————, *Das Erkenntnis-problem in der Philosophie und Wissenschaft der neueren Zeit*. 3 volumes. Berlin, 1906-20.

————, *The Philosophy of Symbolic Forms*. "The Phenomenology of Knowledge." New Haven and London. Yale University Press, 1957.

Cho, Kah Kyung, ed. *Philosophy and Science in Phenomenological Perspective*. Dordrecht. Martinus Nijhoff, 1984.

Compton, John, "Phenomenology and the Philosophy of Nature," paper delivered as the "Gurwitsch Memorial Lecture" at the 1985 meetings for the Society for Phenomenology and Existential Philosophy.

————, "Natural Science and the Experience of Nature," in *Phenomenology in America*. Ed. by James Edie. Chicago, IL. Quadrangle Books, 1969.

Cunningham, Suzanne, *Language and the Phenomenological Reductions of Edmund Husserl*. The Hague. Martinus Nijhoff, 1976.

De Boer, Theodore, *The Development of Husserl's Thought*. The Hague. Martinus Nijhoff, 1978.

Derrida, Jacques, *Of Grammatology*. Trans. by Gayatri Chakrvorty Spivak. Baltimore and London. The Johns Hopkins University Press, 1976.

————, *Speech and Phenomena*. Trans. by David B. Allison. Evanston, IL. Northwestern University Press, 1973.

————, *Edmund Husserl's Origin of Geometry: An Introduction*. Trans. by John P. Leavey, Jr. Stony Brook, New York. Nicholas Hays, LTD, 1978.

Descartes, René, *The Philosophical Works of Descartes*. Trans. by Elizabeth S. Haldane and G. R. T. Ross. Cambridge University Press, 1969.

————, *The Geometry of René Descartes*. Trans. by D. E. Smith and M. L. Latham. Chicago, IL. Open Court, 1925.

Drake, Stillman, *Discoveries and Opinions of Galileo*. Garden City, NY. Doubleday & Co., 1967.

Dreyfus, Hubert L., ed., *Husserl, Intentionality and Cognitive Science*. Cambridge, MA. The MIT Press, 1982.

Drummond, John J., "The Perceptual Roots of Geometric Idealizations," *Review of Metaphysics* 37 (June 1984): 785-810.

————, "The Phenomenology of Perceptual Sense," *The Southwestern Journal of Philosophy* 10 (1979): 139-46.

Elliston, Frederick A. and McCormick, Peter, eds. *Husserl: Exposi-tions and Appraisals*. Notre Dame. University of Notre Dame Press, 1977.

Evans, J. C., *The Metaphysics of Transcendental Subjectivity*. Amster-dam. Verlag B. R. Grüener, 1984.

Findlay, J. N., "An Ontology of Senses," *The Journal of Philosophy* 79 (1982): 545-51.

Føllesdal, Dagfinn, "Husserl's Notion of *Noema*," contained in Hubert L. Dreyfus, ed.

————, "Husserl and Heidegger on the Role of Action in the Con-stitution of the World," contained in *Essays in Honor of Jaakko Hintikka*. Ed. by Esa Saarinen *et al*. Dordrecht, Holland. Reidel, 1979.

Freud, Sigmund, *Introductory Lectures on Psychoanalysis*. New York. W. W. Norton & Co. Inc., 1977.

————, *An Outline of Psycho-analysis*. New York. W. W. Norton & Co. Inc., 1969.

————, *The Standard Edition of the Complete Psychological Works of Sig-mund Freud*. Ed. by James Strachey. London. The Hogarth Press, 24 vols., 1953-74.

————, *A General Selection of the Works of Sigmund Freud*. Ed. by John Rickman, M.D. Garden City, NY. Doubleday Anchor, 1957.

Gadamer, Hans-Georg, *Wahrheit und Methode*. 2nd ed. Tubingen. Mohr, 1965.

Galilei, Galileo, *Two New Sciences*. Trans. by Stillman Drake. Madison, WI. The University of Wisconsin Press, 1974.

Gallagher, Shaun, "Hyletic Experience and the Lived Body,"*Hus-serl Studies* 3 (1986): 131-66.

Garrison, James, *Geometry as a Source of Theory-Ladenness in Early Modern Physics*. Unpublished dissertation. Tallahassee. Florida State University, 1981.

————, "Husserl, Galileo and the Processes of Idealization," *Syn-these* 66 (1986): 329-38.

Gaukroger, Steven, *Explanatory Structures*. Harvester Press, 1978.

Gurwitsch, Aron, *Phenomenology and the Theory of Science*. Ed. by Lester Embree. Evanston, IL. Northwestern University Press, 1974.

Gutting, Gary, "Husserl and Scientific Realism," *Philosophy and Phenomenological Research* 39 (1979): 42-56.

————, "Phenomenology and Scientific Realism," *New Scholas-ticism* 48 (1976): 253-66.

Hall, Harrison, "Was Husserl a Realist or an Idealist?," contained in Hubert L. Dreyfus, ed.

Hamrick, William S., *Phenomenology in Practice and Theory*. Dordrecht, Holland. Martinus Nijhoff, 1985.

Harrison, Ross, "The Concept of Prepredicative Experience," contained in Edo Pivcević, ed.

Harvey, Charles, "Husserl and the Problem of Theoretical Entities," *Synthese* 66 (1986): 291-309.

———, "A Note on the Existential Foundations of Phenomenological Reduction," *Journal of the British Society for Phenomenology* 17 (May 1986): 193-97.

———, "Husserl's Phenomenology and Possible World's Semantics: A Reexamination," *Husserl Studies* 3 (1986): 191-207.

———, "Husserl's Phenomenology as Critique of Epistemic Ideology," *International Philosophical Quarterly* (forthcoming).

Harvey, Charles and Hintikka, Jaakko, "Modalization and Modalities," (forthcoming).

Heelan, Patrick A., *Space Perception and the Philosophy of Science*. Berkeley, CA. The University of California Press, 1983.

———, "Natural Science as a Hermeneutic of Instrumentation," *The Philosophy of Science* 50 (1983): 181-204.

———, "Husserl's Later Philosophy of Science," (forthcoming).

Heidegger, Martin, *Being and Time*. Trans. by John Macquarrie and Edward Robinson. New York. Harper & Row, 1962.

Heinsen, Douglas, "Husserl's Theory of the Pure Ego," contained in Hubert L. Dreyfus, ed.

Hintikka, Jaakko, "Wittgenstein's Semantical Kantianism," contained in *Ethics: Proceedings of the 5th International Wittgenstein Symposium*. Ed. by E. Morschen and R. Stranzinger. Vienna. Holder-Pichler-Tempsky, 1981.

———, "Semantics: A Revolt against Frege," *Contemporary Philosophy: A New Survey*. The Hague. Martinus Nijhoff, 1981.

——— and Harvey, Charles, "Review of D. W. Smith and R. McIntyre, *Husserl and Intentionality: A Study of Mind, Meaning, and Language*," in *Husserl Studies* 1 (1984): 201-212.

Hume, David, *A Treatise Concerning the Human Understanding*. Oxford. Clarendon Press, 1975.

———, *An Enquiry Concerning Human Understanding*. Indianapolis, IN. Hackett, 1977.

Ihde, Donn, *Technics and Praxis*. Dordrecht. D. Reidel, 1979.

James, William, *Principles of Psychology*. New York. Dover Pub., 1950.

Kern, Iso, *Husserl und Kant*. Den Haag. Martinus Nijhoff, 1964.

Kisiel, Theodore, "On the Dimensions of a Phenomenology of Science in Husserl and the Young Dr. Heidegger," *Journal of the British Society for Phenomenology*, 4 (1973): 217-34.

————, "Heidegger and the New Image of Science," *Research in Phenomenology* 7 (1977): 162-81.

Kockelmans, Joseph J., *Heidegger and Science*. Lanham, MD. University Press of America, Inc., 1985.

————, *Phenomenology and Physical Science*. Pittsburgh, PA. Duquesne University Press, 1966.

———— and Kisiel, Theodore J., *Phenomenology and the Natural Sciences*. Evanston, IL. Northwestern University Press, 1970.

Kohak, Erazim, *Idea & Experience*. Chicago and London. University of Chicago Press, 1978.

Köhler, Wolfgang, *Gestalt Psychology*. New York. Mentor Books, 1975.

Koyré, Alexander, *Etudes Galiléennes*. Paris. Herman, 1966.

Kuhn, Thomas, *The Structure of Scientific Revolutions*. Chicago and London. University of Chicago Press, 1970.

Küng, Guido, "The Phenomenological Reduction as Epoche and as Explication," *The Monist* 59 (1975): 63-80.

————, "The World as Noema and as Referent," *Journal of the British Society for Phenomenology* 3 (1972): 15-26.

Landgrebe, Ludwig, *The Phenomenology of Edmund Husserl*. Ed. by Donn Welton. New York. Cornell University Press, 1981.

Locke, John, *An Essay Concerning the Human Understanding*. New York. Dover Publications, Inc., 1959.

Lovejoy, Arthur O., *The Revolt Against Dualism*. London. George Allen and Unwin, LTD, 1930.

Mall, R. A., *Experience and Reason*. The Hague. Martinus Nijhoff, 1973.

McKenna, William, *Husserl's "Introductions to Phenomenology."* The Hague. Martinus Nijhoff, 1982.

————, Harlan, R. M. and Winters, L. E., ed. and trans., *A Priori and World: European Contributions to Husserlian Phenomenology*. The Hague. Martinus Nijhoff, 1981.

Mensch, James R., *The Question of Being in Husserl's Logical Investigations*. The Hague. Martinjus Nijhoff, 1981.

Merleau-Ponty, Maurice, *Phenomenology of Perception*. Trans. by Colin Smith. New Jersey. The Humanities Press, 1962.

Miller, Izchak, "Husserl's Account of our Temporal Awareness," contained in Hubert L. Dreyfus, ed.

————, *Husserl, Perception and Temporal Awareness*. Cambridge, MA. MIT Press, 1984.

Mohanty, J. N., *Edmund Husserl's Theory of Meaning*. The Hague. Martinus Nijhoff, 1969.

————, *The Possibility of Transcendental Philosophy*. Dordrecht. Martinus Nijhoff, 1985.

Molesworth, W., ed. *The English Works of Thomas Hobbes*. London. 1 (1839).

Murphy, Richard T., *Hume and Husserl: Towards Radical Subjectivism*. The Hague. Martinus Nijhoff, 1980.

Natanson, Maurice, *Edmund Husserl: Philosopher of Infinite Tasks*. Evanston, IL. Northwestern University Press, 1973.

Needleman, Jacob, *Selected Papers of Ludwig Binswange: Being-in-the-World*. New York. Harper Torchbooks, 1967.

Nietzsche, Friedrich, *Twilight of the Idols*. Trans. by Walter Kaufmann. Contained in *The Portable Nietzsche*. New York. The Viking Press, 1967.

Null, Gilbert, *Noetic Processes of Identification Experienced in Carrying Out the Method of Physical Science*. Unpublished dissertation. New York. New School for Social Research, 1974.

_____, "The Role of the Perceptual World in the Husserlian Theory of Science," *Journal of the British Society for Phenomenology* 7 (1976): 56-59.

Pietersma, Henry, "The Phenomenological Reduction," *American Philosophical Quarterly* 16 (1979): 37-44.

_____, "Husserl's Concept of Existence," *Synthese* 66 (1986): 311-28.

_____, "Intentionality and Epistemic Appraisal," *The Southern Journal of Philosophy* 25 (1987): 381-94.

_____, "Contextual Objects and the Problem of Knowledge," unpublished essay.

Pivcević, Edo, ed. *Phenomenology and Philosophical Understanding*. Cambridge University Press, 1975.

Polanyi, Michael, *Personal Knowledge: Towards a Post-Critical Philosophy*. Harper Torchbooks, 1964.

Popper, Sir Karl, *Conjectures and Refutations*. London. Routledge & Kegan Paul, 1962.

Ricoeur, Paul, *Husserl: An Analysis of His Phenomenology*. Evanston, IL. Northwestern University Press, 1967.

Rouse, Joseph, "Merleau-Ponty and the Existential Conception of Science," *Synthese* 66 (1986): 249-72.

_____, "Kuhn, Heidegger, and Scientific Realism," *Man and World* 14 (1981): 269-90.

Russell, Bertrand. *An Inquiry into Meaning and Truth*. London. George Allen and Unwin, LTD, 1940.

_____, "Knowledge by Acquaintance and Knowledge by Description," *Proceedings of the Aristotelian Society* XI (1910/11): 108-28. Reprinted in *Mysticism and Logic and Other Essays*. New York. Doubleday, 1957.

Ryle, Gilbert. *The Concept of Mind*. New York. Barnes & Noble, 1949.

Sallis, John, ed. *Husserl and Contemporary Thought*. New Jersey. Atlantic Highlands, 1983.

Sartre, Jean-Paul, *L'Imaginaire*. Paris. Gallimard, 1940.

———, *The Transcendence of the Ego*. Trans. by Forest Williams and Robert Kirkpatrick. New York. The Noonday Press, 1966.

———, *Nausea*. New York. New Directions Pub. Co., 1964.

———, *Being and Nothingness*. Trans. by Hazel Barnes. New York. Washington Square Press, 1975.

Seigfried, Hans V., "Scientific Realism and Phenomenology," *Zeit f. Philosophische Forschung* 24 (1980): 395-404.

———, "Heidegger's Longest Day: *Being and Time* and the Sciences," *Philosophy Today* 22 (1978): 319-31.

Smart, J. J. C., "Descartes and the Wax," *Philosophical Quarterly* 1 (1950).

Smith, David, "The Case of the Exploding Perception," *Synthese* 41 (1979).

Smith, David Woodruff and McIntyre, Ronald, *Husserl and Intentionality*. Dordrecht, Holland. Reidel Pub. Co., 1982.

Sokolowski, Robert, *The Formation of Husserl's Concept of Constitution*. The Hague. Martinus Nijhoff, 1964.

———, *Husserlian Meditations*. Evanston, IL. Northwestern University Press, 1974.

———, *Presence and Absence*. Bloomington, IN. Indiana University Press, 1978.

Solomon, Robert C., "Husserl's Concept of the Noema," *The Journal of Philosophy* 66 (1969): 680-87. Also contained in Elliston and McCormick, ed., pp. 168-181.

Spanos, William V., *Martin Heidegger and the Question of Literature*. Bloomington. Indiana University Press, 1979.

Spiegelberg, Herbert, "Is the Reduction Necessary for Phenomenology? Husserl's and Pfänder's Replies," *Journal of the British Society for Phenomenology* 4 (1973): 3-15.

Tieszen, Richard, "Mathematical Intuition and Husserl's Phenomenology," *Nous* 18 (1984): 395-421.

Tymieniecka, Anna-Teresa, Ed. *Analecta Husserliana*, II. Dordrecht. D. Reidel Publishing Co., 1972.

Wagner, Hans, "Husserl's Ambiguous Philosophy of Science," *Southwestern Journal of Philosophy* 5 (1974): 169-85.

Watson, John B., *Behaviorism*. New York. W. W. Norton & Co. Inc., 1970.

Welton, Donn, "Husserl's Genetic Phenomenology of Perception," contained in John Sallis, ed.

————, "Structure and Genesis in Husserl's Phenomenology," contained in Elliston and McCormick, ed.

————, *The Origins of Meaning*. The Hague. Martinus Nijhoff, 1983.

Wittgenstein, Ludwig, *Tractatus Logico-Philosophicus*. Trans. by D. F. Pears and B. F. McGuinness. London. Routledge & Kegan Paul, 1961.

————, *Remarks on Color*. Trans. by Linda L. McAlister and Margarete Schättle. Berkeley and Los Angeles. University of California Press, 1978.

————, "On Heidegger on Being and Dread," contained in *Heidegger and Modern Philosophy*. Ed. by Michael Murray. New Haven and London. Yale University Press, 1978.

Zaner, Richard M., *The Way of Phenomenology*. New York. Pegasus Books, 1970.

————, "On the Sense of Method in Phenomenology," contained in E. Pivcević, ed.

A Note about the Author

Charles W. Harvey is Associate Professor of Philosophy at the University of Central Arkansas. He is the author of numerous articles on phenomenology.